THE QUEST FOR HOLINESS

By Adolf Köberle

(2)

Dr. Adolf Köberle, professor of theology in the University of Basel, is one of the outstanding theological scholars of the world, and a leading thinker among confessional Christians in Germany.

His, *The Quest for Holiness*, is a significant contribution to world religious literature, a work of abiding value. As such it well deserves translation into the English language and widespread distribution among English language readers. The first printing in America by Harpers and Brothers is entirely sold out. Assuming publishing rights with this second printing, Augsburg Publishing House is pleased to make this excellent translation from the third German edition by the Rev. John C. Mattes, D.D., available to the English reading world. A valuable feature of this second printing is the inclusion of a classified index.

Although written by a profound scholar, this book is not merely for theologians but for all who desire a sound, Scriptural setting forth of the truths and the implications for each individual embodied in the all-important steps in the way of salvation known as *justification and sanctification*. For simplicity, clarity and completeness on this subject this book is unsurpassed. "It is written not merely with ink but with the lifeblood of the true believer striving daily for greater ss and God-pleasing

D1272008

THE QUEST FOR HOLINESS

THE
QUEST FOR HOLINESS

A BIBLICAL, HISTORICAL AND
SYSTEMATIC INVESTIGATION

By ADOLF KÖBERLE, D.D.

Professor at the University of Basel

Translated from the Third German Edition

By JOHN C. MATTES, D.D.

AUGSBURG PUBLISHING HOUSE
MINNEAPOLIS, MINNESOTA

THE QUEST FOR HOLINESS

Manufactured in the United States of America

2750

CONTENTS

Preface to the English Edition

THE theological development of the last century has corrupted the Gospel in three different ways. Under the influence of Kant and Ritschl it was diverted more and more into a moralism. We inquired eagerly about man's activities but we no longer concentrated our attention on the heart of the Gospel, what God has done *for us* in Christ. The overwhelming influence of Schleiermacher caused it to be transmuted more and more into a psychological account of the conditions of pious experience. We industriously examined the inner processes of the soul and in doing so forgot what God had spoken to us in His Word and how He had there given us an objective basis of truth. As an aftermath of the idealistic philosophy it was frequently changed into a sort of rational knowledge. What was not agreeable to reason, criticism rejected as useless.

The opening chapter of this book seeks to show how far such ideas of self-salvation have spread in the Christian Church and in theology. The second chapter battles against moralism and the various psychological and idealistic misunderstandings of the Gospel. This is followed by an unfolding of the essential character of the Gospel. The Gospel is the self-disclosure and self-impartation of God in Jesus Christ. This coming of God to us is a purely miraculous gift of divine love and this love, which has been disclosed in its fullness in the delivery of Jesus to death on the Cross, is the only basis for peace with God and for our fellowship with God and our neighbor. Justification through faith alone brings with it the certainty that I may be God's dear child. But that also implies that henceforth I do not belong to myself but to Another, Who has established His kingly rule over my life. So the ability to live a new life and the desire to render a new obedience grow out of the gift of the forgiveness of sins. The new life of faith is fully conscious of that fact and consequently there is no place in it for self-admiration, nor does it cherish delusions of perfection, but yet, in spite of all its weaknesses and failures, it is a real deliverance from the bondage and dominion of sin.

The New Testament speaks of sanctification both in the imperative and indicative moods. It is described as a divine gift and at the same time as a result of our obedient choice. "For we are his workmanship, created in Christ Jesus unto good works, which God hath before ordained that we should walk in them" (Eph. 2:10). This antithesis must be maintained in Christian ethics with the utmost care. Man must be denied all credit but dare never be relieved of his full responsibility.

The way in which we discuss the gift of sanctification bestowed on us by God seeks to avoid a double danger. On the one side is the peril of fanaticism. Here man knows no bounds. He becomes constantly more exalted in his estimation of himself and talks more loudly, confidently, enthusiastically of the stage of sanctification that he has attained. He no longer is conscious of the presence of the old man and regards the daily prayer for forgiveness as something rather superfluous. But in contrast to this danger there is another that makes so little of the testimony of the Holy Ghost, Who quickeneth us, that we might think Christ had never risen and Pentecost had never happened. Here the new life appears as a purely transcendental thing, as a mere object of hope and as something quite beyond the possibility of attainment in our present historical situation. As opposed to such views, we seek here, in the manner of the New Testament, to unite possession and expectation, having and hoping for, present sanctification and eschatological fulfillment on the basis of justifying faith.

In the criticisms of the book by German theologians the question has been raised whether it is right to place justification and santification thus side by side like two distinct magnitudes. In this connection there has been frequent objection to the *"and"*[1] of the title. Now it is undoubtedly true that faith always embraces the whole Christ, Whom God has made for us righteousness, sanctification, and redemption. The fullness of grace that forgives my sins and heals my infirmities is always present to faith. Nevertheless theological reflection has the right and the duty to distinguish clearly, as concepts, matters that are never separated nor would dare to be separated from each other in actual experience.

[1] The German title is Justification and Sanctification.

The Lutheran Fathers were certainly correct when they stated in the Formula of Concord (Sol. Decl. III): "Though regeneration and sanctification is also a work of the Holy Ghost it does not belong to the article concerning justification." We cannot sufficiently admire the theological wisdom of such a statement. In the first place justification always remains the moral basis that makes sanctification possible. Only "where there is remission of sins, there are also life and salvation." And in the second place, the grace that is above us always remains greater than the grace that is within us. The pardon which faith receives is something entire, perfect, rounded out, complete, which neither requires nor is capable of enlargement. On the other hand, the new creation which faith experiences through its communion with Christ always remains a fragmentary and progressive work. In a theological treatment the complete and incomplete should not be confused, though their inseparableness in connection with the one Christ Who bestows both, still remains. Only the correct inner succession and the inner superiority of the one gift over the other must be clearly preserved.

The author of this book is a child of the Lutheran Church. Luther's faith, Paul Gerhardt's piety and the ideas of Vilmar, Löhe and Hermann Bezzel will therefore greet the Lutheran reader with their familiar expressions on every hand. We Lutherans in Germany feel that in the present battle for the maintenance of the Gospel we are bound by many ties to Karl Barth. Karl Barth has once more quickened the conscience of Christendom to a realization of the fact that the Gospel is not to be confused with pragmatic moralism, with psychology or with the conceptions of idealistic philosophy. Long before him other theologians of our own Church spoke their warnings against the secularizing of the Gospel, only their admonitions did not meet with the same far-reaching results as those which followed the efforts of Karl Barth. More than ever we need such stalwart watchmen's voices at the present time to recall the Church of Christ to a renewed appreciation of the foundations of the Gospel and of the Confessions.

Nevertheless, as Lutheran theologians of the homeland of the Reformation, we feel that the powerful influence of the Barthian theology is also a danger to our Church. Karl Barth's message breathes the spirit of the Reformed Church and its theology. His influence in many cases threatens to destroy the specifically Lutheran understanding of the nature of the Church, the Sacraments and the nature of the gift of the Spirit. In view of this situation our book proceeds from this basic position: we Lutherans will gladly learn from Barth whenever he has something valuable to tell us, but we will also be careful that we do not become estranged from the rich and glorious heritage of our Lutheran Church and from her theology and piety by a theological achievement which is undoubtedly outstanding but which has certainly not developed out of the spirit of our Church.

On the basis of the German edition of his book the author has already received many cordial assurances of fraternal agreement in the faith from American Lutherans. May this edition then contribute something towards a still closer and more intimate union of Lutheran theologians in all lands. To the esteemed translator and to the official groups that suggested this edition and made its publication possible I would express my sincerest thanks for their confidence in me and their understanding of my purposes.

ADOLF KÖBERLE,
Professor and Doctor of Theology

Translator's Preface

THIS brilliant theological study, that attracted so much attention in Germany that within a few years it passed through three editions, is here offered to the English-speaking world in the hope that its influence may be as blessed here as it has been in German lands. The translator is painfully aware of the fact that much of its original beauty of style must inevitably be lost in a translation but the attempt has been made to preserve the often unusual manner of presentation as nearly as possible. The text followed has been that of the third edition with the exception of certain omissions that have been indicated by Prof. Köberle himself. These have been almost altogether of two classes. Small portions of the text that dealt with purely local religious movements, limited to certain Continental territories and practically unknown in America, have been omitted. So have a number of footnotes that referred chiefly to German periodicals and books that would not be available to the average English reader, nor would be particularly useful to any one restricted to the English language. Those who may be stimulated by the reading of this volume to further research concerning the vital questions of theology and practical life that are here discussed are referred to the third German edition for the supplementary matter and the more elaborate literary references.

J.C.M.

THE QUEST FOR HOLINESS

CHAPTER I

Man's Attempts to Sanctify Himself in God's Sight

THE desire for sanctification is always first aroused in man when he has become conscious, in some painful way, of his lack of peace and the erring restlessness of his life. So the experiences of age and suffering, of sickness and death that surround us may completely destroy the boundless, worldly, sensuous pleasures that have caused us to devote ourselves, perhaps in a coarser, perhaps in a more refined way, to the enjoyment of life and they awaken within us the hunger for a more enduring and deeper meaning to life. The recognition of the transitoriness of all things temporal raises the question of eternity. The realization of our moral weakness and uncleanliness, the continually repeated neglect of our duties toward our neighbor awakens a desire for supernatural strength and purity. The limitations of all scientific investigation, the short span of all human activity drive us to seek some avenue to a final, more comprehensive understanding and explanation of the universe. A feeling of defectiveness, a longing to overcome human limitations, a desire for communion with God, and a true social intercourse with our brethren—these are the powerful motives from which the striving after holiness has always arisen in men. These are the momentous hours when we have come to the point that secular values can no longer satisfy us; when the need of aspiring to God is recognized and we unite in the longing cry that is the hidden theme of all human history: "Dona nobis pacem." Then the decisive hour has come when the question confronts us whether we will honestly recognize what makes for peace in our peaceless extremity or prefer to go on, as eternal wanderers, on ways that never lead to any goal.

A glance at the history of the religious and spiritual aspirations of mankind shows us that the attempt to attain to communion with God

I

has always been made in three ways, that at the end come very close to each other. Whenever and wherever the question concerning God has arisen among a people or in the life of an individual we meet with a grandiose attempt to possess God and to become sure of Him by means of increased spiritual power. A mighty development of all natural talents and abilities begins. The will, the spirit, the understanding, by a conscious course of training are to draw continually nearer and nearer to the infinite and finally reach absolute perfection. "The one who ever striving, struggles on, we can redeem", becomes the watch-word that, with countless variations, is repeated everywhere. The sanctification of conduct by the strengthening of the will; the sanctification of the emotions by a strenuous training of the soul; the sanctification of thought by a deepening of the understanding; moralism, mysticism, speculation, these are the three ladders on which men continually seek to climb up to God, with a persistent purpose that it seems nothing can check; a storming of Heaven that is just as pathetic in its unceasing efforts as in its final futility.

We know from modern psychology how impossible it is to separate from each other these three factors of consciousness, the will, the understanding and the spirit. In fact they never manifest themselves separately, but mutually dependent, they remain mysteriously united. The relative strength of these three faculties varies in each individual according to sex, temperament or circumstance. Now one is so highly developed that it almost seems to exclude the others, now all three are so mingled that it is almost impossible to distinguish between them. This psychological fact, which is universally true, we shall have to keep in mind in this connection. In the self-sanctification of men, whether by way of the intellect, will or spiritual emotions, no one of these three is ever the sole factor. Moral energy always unites itself as readily with the cultivation of subjective mysticism, as with the rule of autonomous reason. Speculation can be bound up with a contemplative attitude of the soul as well as with ethical activity. So the separate description of these three ways may easily seem artificial, nevertheless, aside from the clarity thus gained in a systematic presentation the difference in emphasis that enables us to distinguish clearly between them justifies such a separate treatment.

The will has always been reckoned as a mighty factor, and in the opinion of many, as the real center and predominant function of the entire personality. With uncanny energy, driven on by the goadings of the laws of this or that religion, it has been developed to the point of virtuosity. No matter what confusing abundance and diversity of images immediately arises before our eyes, the one who looks more deeply recognizes behind all the different efforts the common idea that through the spurring on, the increase and multiplication of the natural powers of the will it becomes possible for man to grow holier and finally through sheer moral aspiration to bring himself into union with God. In the moral discipline of the teachings of Confucius, in the self-discipline of Stoic morals, in the desperate efforts of the Buddhist monk to destroy all enjoyment of sin, in the Pharisee, "the pious churchmen", who conscientiously torments himself about the keeping of fasts and tithing, in the ethical humanist and idealist, who is proudly conscious of his autonomous personality that "takes up divinity into his will", in the lodge brother who by moral effort out of the raw material of his nature makes himself free—masoned, all alike are sure that the communion with God may be attained by the fulfilment of ethical duties. In the history of German thought Kant and Fichte exercised the greatest and most lasting influence in encouraging these ideas. The categorical imperative with its exclusion of all foreign or eudemonistic motives from moral actions (even though it operated only in a formal way) and its insistence on faithfulness and stability in the performance of duty gave a certain exalted tone to Protestant culture. It supported the Ritschlian ethics of vocation, which in its strongly developed optimism believed that in the complete fulfilment of the duties of each one's calling it would possess the Kingdom of God. Fichte who through the "self affirmation of the moral ego" arrived "at last at the affirmation of God," which in its moral dealings and its experience of an unconditioned obligation felt a union with a divine power, impressed on his times the stamp of moral firmness of character. His moralistic adaptation of Romans 8:28, "All things work together for good to them that love God," became the cue for an exalted ethical service of the state. We still stand beside the same stream, no matter how the scenery may have been changed outwardly, when we find Tolstoi and Fr. W. Foerster, treating the Sermon on the Mount as a world code of morals. The same idea glows behind the ideal of a league of nations and a world peace, the dream of progress, the hope of a redemption of the world through the efforts of men. And all the reform movements from total abstinence to vegetarianism, from the breathing exercises of the "Mazdaznan" movement on to the exclusion of interest from money transactions are equally permeated with the hope that by such exemplary labors they will bring about a new day of the Lord both for themselves and for the whole world.

Besides the purely legal moralism, which poses as the "direct expression of the relation to God" there are mixed forms where human activity and divine assistance cooperate in reaching the goal. Most of the religions of redemption must be included here and above all the Roman Catholic type of Christianity. Here there is a consciousness of the wretched weakness of human volition. There is an understanding of the fact that in spite of all honest, zealous efforts at improvement, the support of divine grace is necessary, a grace that is regarded either as preceding or at least as accompanying man's efforts. The main stress, however, still lies throughout on man's own work. Man is to do all that he can and then God supplies what is lacking by grace,[1] as if it were possible to determine the exact maximum that each one was able to supply. Everything in Romanism indicates that it must be included in this classification. It is the "devotions of large figures" (H. Preuss). The religion of quantitative accomplishments, that surge up from below to heights approaching Heaven; the idea of the monk who brings the "great obedience" as a sacrifice to God and therefore progresses toward perfection more rapidly and more surely than the one who is engaged in some secular vocation; the distinction between mortal and venial sins that constitute a greater or lesser

---

[1] *Si homo facit, quod in se est, deus dat gratiam.* Or Jerome: *Nostrum offerre, quod possumus, illius (scil dei) implere, quod non possumus. Dialog. contra pelag.* The same conception of salvation governs the Jewish teaching of grace. Cf. The treatise of Felix Aber: "Merit and Unmerited Grace" in the bi-monthly, Der Morgen (IV, 5, p. 423, Berlin 1928, Philo-Verlag), which might be regarded as the "Zeitwende," as the "Hochland" of cultivated modern believing Judaism; "When man's efforts have finally reached the point that marks the limits of his natural powers, grace completes the work.—Only our own efforts and works make us worthy of divine grace."

hindrance on the "way" to God; the opinion, bordering on blasphemy, of the supererogatory works of the saints that gathered like a gigantic treasure are placed at the disposal of the Church; the teaching of the veneration of the saints that has been so evilly distorted through the idea of merits and rewards; the purpose of the mass where the gift of the redemptive work of Christ is turned into a human work that man offers God, all these opinions, that have even influenced the Protestant Church in a weakened form and have produced a certain neo-pietistic, vulgar Protestantism, can only receive such great significance in those quarters where self-sanctification by human works is positively affirmed as a presupposition, taken for granted.[2]

Both among Christians and among non-Christians these varied efforts to gain holiness have entailed much discipline, labor and devotion. Half yearningly, half defiantly the attempt is made to compel God's favor by moral fervor. It is a struggle to gain personal righteousness by way of the law, which can hardly be gainsaid by our enervated, irresolute times. All these attempts have one trait in common, they do not regard the human will as evil, as something that absolutely separates us from God, that is a deadly offense against His holiness, but only as something that is weak and imperfect, whose defects must continually be overcome. The extent and character of this weakness is variously estimated. The teaching of the Council of Trent is certainly severer than the Socratic optimism about the possibilities of educating the young, than Kant's cheerful "you shall and therefore you can," than Goethe's "believe in the nobility and native goodness of man," or than Schiller's confident affirmation that "man has been created free, though he be born in chains." Quite in agreement with this attitude are the two types we most frequently meet; the one is the figure of the ascetic and penitent, filled with anxious introspection, subjecting himself to painful discipline and despondently tormenting himself with the thought of the unattained goal; the other figure is that of the confident, untroubled man who in the proud con-

[2] We have not forgotten that in the consideration of Roman Catholic dogmatics and the theology of the orders a distinction must be made between a grosser (Jesuitic-Molonistic) teaching concerning works and a more temperate synergism (Dominican-Thomistic) and a critical consideration (Franciscan-Scotist) of the question of good works.

sciousness of his good fortune and with unshaken confidence in himself continues to carry on his previous achievements. But whether the feeling of depression or that of confident victory is the dominant one, in either case the fundamental thought that permeates the whole life is the idea that by the aid of renewed, rigorous self-interest and discipline man will finally be able to liberate his spirit from the prison of a base sensuality and, thanks to his personal efforts to gain holiness, he will be able to last to appear just before God.

Besides the attempt to construct a bridge across to God by the power of the human will the effort is often made to draw near to God by an intensification and stimulation of the powers of character and soul. Humanity has always tried this second method as eagerly and as enthusiastically as the first. The emotions are regarded (not only since the days of Schleiermacher) as being, even more than the will, the special province of religion, the central point where God's contacts are made. Yes, we are safe in saying, that in no other domain, has the attempt been made as thoroughly as here to break through the limitations of the visible world and to realize the highest aspirations of the soul. We continually find examples (often united with a clear aversion towards everything that involves the intelligence and will) of men who devote the most intense love and every imaginable care to the cultivation, nurture and strengthening of their inner emotions and spiritual powers. But here again it is necessary to distinguish between two forms, a romantic-aesthetic naturalism and a delicate, purer form of mystical religiosity, though both of them, as we shall presently see, are often enough intermingled.

Bold as such immediateness may seem, man has always ventured to embellish his natural erotic animal passions with religion and to sanctify them when they have been stimulated to a white heat, as a means of direct union with God. The names given it vary but behind them there is always the unrestrained cult of a profound excitement of the emotions and senses. Once it is called orgasm and temple prostitution, then it is the "strong and beautiful man," the *homo naturalis* of the Renaissance, about whom Nietzsche raved like a drunkard, where each one, like an artist, develops out of himself all the creative faculties in harmonious perfection. Now its commendation appears as a complete naturalism and conformity to the rhythm of a vegetative existence as it is found in Rousseau's extravagant "retour à la nature," now as in romanticism, in a song of the "primitive and immediate character of emotions," now, as we find it in Stefan George, in the cult of youth, whose developing beauty is accounted the sublimest incarnation and revelation of divinity on earth. In this connection art and especially music must be included, for again and again the attempt has been made to exalt them to the status of a world philosophy. So, even in our own times, Richard Wagner's work is regarded in wide circles with positively religious veneration, not so much because of the occasionally ascetic tendency of his productions, but rather because of the glowing, sense-intoxicating, sensuous Bacchanalians of the tone colors. The drunken splendor of this heavy, saccharine music has been correctly interpreted as a great confession of salvation through Eros.[3]

To many it will seem offensive if we place mysticism, that men have been fond of calling a "delicate, noble flower on the tree of religion," immediately beside this materialistic intoxication with life. It is true that mysticism has none of the robust, vigorous, impelling power of the tendencies we have just described. It is quieter, flabbier, more inward, often broken by pessimism, ennobled and purified by suffering. But keen observers have always correctly noted that "all mysticism arises out of intensified sensation," that there is no qualitative difference but only a subtle, sentimental transformation of the other tendency.

Mysticism lives on the assurance that in the depths of our souls

[3] For this reason there should be an end to the attempts to use Wagner as a witness for the Christian view of the world. The master, who himself called music "a woman" (a term quite appropriate for his handiwork), whose voluptuous, cloying sensualism and the ascetic-mystic teaching of salvation that is always associated with it, point alike clearly to India, has always mutilated and degraded evangelical Christianity even when cooperation was attempted, and has never furthered it. Adolf von Harless, whose highly developed artistic nature was exceedingly susceptible to poetry and music, and whose grand piano always accompanied him, even to the universities, especially disliked Wagner among the moderns. He declared that an attack of the gout had been induced by a nephew who played Wagner for him for one whole evening. In marked contrast is the extravagant regard that is given Richard Wagner as the forerunner of a renewed, spirit-filled cultus, in the circles of the "Christengemeinschaft" and those surrounding Rudolf Steiner. One single instance of this sort often tells much more clearly than a long theological demonstration the completely different foundations and spiritual attitudes of Lutheranism and "Anthroposophism."

flow hidden springs of divinity. Though in contrast to the glorification of natural life it may regard the surface of our spiritual consciousness as ever so unclean and corrupt, yet, if we only penetrate deeply enough into the innermost being of the soul[4] we will come at last to a "secret, blissful sphere," into a holy temple inclosure, untouched by sin, where the "hidden, inner, pure essence of the soul" rests in God, where the inner principle recognizes itself as a part, as a breath of the divine nature. Much of the refuse and ashes of sin may have been deposited on the soul in the course of human life but whosoever attacks the task of removing it with sufficient zeal will find at last the "little spark" that can never be extinguished because it is a part of God Himself. The most complete development of the teaching of the essential unity of the human soul with its divine source has undoubtedly taken place in India. There we are told that the distinction between the universal ego and the single ego is a delusion, that fundamentally there is no duality. According to the teaching of the Upanishads salvation consists in the mere recognition of the unity of Atman, the basis of the soul, with Brahma, the basis of the world. "As the spider draws the thread out of herself, as the sparks fly out of the fire," so all beings spring from the primal source and return to it again. Even where the idea of an equality has been weakened to one of a similarity, as in the Chinese Tao-mystic, in Persian Sufism, among the Orphic or Dionysian cults, the basic idea is that of a divine nucleus in which the divinity dwells. Whether it be the enthusiastic cry "Θεός εἰμι" at the taurobolium, or the Neoplatonic conception of the soul that regards the soul as an outflowing of the ocean of divine reason, or the belief of the fanatic in an inner life, where the conscience is regarded as the place where emanations "from the flowing light of divinity" are received; whether it be the presumptuous identification of God and man in Angelus Silesius' *Cherubic Pilgrim*,[5] or in the modern mysticism of the *Stundenbuch*, where

---

[4] St. Theresa speaks of seven chambers of the soul which we must pass through, and Johannes Klimakus tells of thirty rungs in the ladder that leads to our union with God.

[5] "Nothing exists save Thou and I, and if we two were not
God would be God no more, the heavens would fall.
I am God's other self, in me alone He finds
What in eternity will be both like and similar to Him."

God, Who cannot live without humanity, first reaches perfection by developing in us—all these, regardless of all differences of time and place, are united by their pantheistic basis, by their belief in the infra-worldly divine nature of the essence of the soul.

The great mystics of the Christian Church deserve special consideration. How are we to consider the religious leaders of medieval Catholicism, a Tauler, Seuse, Bernhard and Ruysbroeck, or how the "Friends of God" of early Protestantism, Seb. Franck, Schwenkfeld and Val. Weigel? It is not possible to class them without qualification with the mysticism of the infinite that we have just been considering. Just as moralism could only develop within Christianity in a partial and restricted way, so the mysticism that is found in Christianity, in contrast to all other forms with their timeless and unhistorical tendencies, has always been restrained and limited by the historic fact of the revelation in Christ. Mysticism was once correctly defined as "the form of piety that finds its highest satisfaction in the *immediate* union of the soul's essence with the divine essence." This "immediate union" the Christian mystic no longer ventures to seek so directly. He is too firmly bound by his dependence on the historic facts of revelation, too much restrained by "the great interpolation; the word concerning Jesus Christ." So here there is a continual and often desperate conflict between the unhistorical, immediate enjoyment of God and the union with God that is conditioned by an historic revelation. So, for example, the Neoplatonic mysticism of the infinite cultivated by the Victorines is much more unrestricted and unhistorical than the *devotio erga carnem Christi* of the mysticism of Bernhard or of the Brothers of the Common Life. So Tauler, whose meditations on the Passion often reach an almost evangelical loftiness and strength, seems to me to be unjustly claimed for modern mysticism on the basis of his supposed "immediate" pantheism. In spite of all such historical limitations, at the end Christian mysticism finds itself in the company of the unempirical, immediate contact of Platonic ideas. The connection with a Biblical faith exists only at the beginning. The Word and Sacraments are means for the furtherance of contemplative rapture but are never the abiding and only permanent foundations of faith; in the end the history of salvation is left far behind, for its value was only to make that visible, in particular cases, which is universally valid and which exists by itself. The soul may kindle the fire of the love of God through the example of Christ but only so far as afterwards to realize it *independently* by virtue of the qualitative, natural unity of being, by the ascent to ecstatic deification.

That this is no exaggeration is evident from the language and the similes that Christian mysticism everywhere appropriated, without question, from purely pantheistic mysticism. Here too are the same naturalistic symbols that we regularly find in India, Persia and Greece, whose ascetic charm and beauty dare not blind us to the fact that the personal and voluntary relationship between God and man that is taught in the Bible has been utterly betrayed and forgotten. The sickly, sentimental, erotic bridal metaphors of the syncretistic Hellenistic cults, the passionately sensuous language of Persian Sufis that are all too closely related to Wagner's burning strains in the Venusberg, have been permitted to cross the threshold of Christian devotional literature unhindered in the allegorizings of the Song of Solomon by Bernhard, Mechthild, Theresa and Zinzendorf.[6] While the Old Testament, with unmistakable clearness, uses the frequently recurring metaphor of "betrothal" as a picture of fidelity, but uses it in a strictly legal, moral sense, Christian mysticism revels in the most turgid, questionable pictures of sexual impulses as the expression of the loss of personal consciousness in the ecstatic union. Besides the erotic sensations all sorts of comparisons have been drawn from natural relationships to express the thought of absorption, intermingling, dissolution and submersion. The stupefying intoxication of mysticism that overtakes every youth who is susceptible to artistic impressions, at least once in his life is doubtless and chiefly due to the poetic force and beauty of the imagery that meditative contemplation has always been creating anew in inexhaustible profusion. The single drop of water that is absorbed in the infinite ocean, the little flame that loses itself in the original fire, the wandering summer cloud that dissolves into the azure sky, the diminishing sound that dies into silence, the shadow that fades in the light, all become for the mystical suppliant a parable

---

[6] Seuse, "the one who drinks at Mary's breast together with the divine Child." The nuns who become pregnant through Christ.

of the submersion, absorption and disappearance, the dissolution and fusion into the divine "onliness."

Still more clearly than in its forms of speech we can see the final unity of all mysticism, whether naturalistic, religious or Christian, in the common way which, with only small and trivial differences, is everywhere prescribed for the attainment of the divine goal. Starting with the presumption that man possesses qualification for exultation in himself, a clever ladder is devised by which, if we use sufficient persistence we must at last reach the vision of God. In this process the mystagogue, who has a certain technique to teach the novice, plays an important role. Through contemplative exercises, by an ascetic liberation from created things and by the greatest possible intensification of the strength gained by spiritual experiences, the ego, liberated from the burden of the earth, is continually to raise itself upward to an ultimate penetration of the universal ego. Here we encounter heavily scented flowers, fire and storm, intoxicating music and cult dances, the use of alcohol, ritual lustrations, fastings and flagellations, mystic consecrations; there is no gross or subtle narcotic, no disciplinary rigors that this spiritual gymnastics has not pressed into service. A tremendous expenditure of energy is demanded in the completion of such a course of training and consequently neither weariness nor despair are lacking. But the hope of finally being able to attain to God and compel His presence through such self-discipline ceaselessly drives men on to fresh attempts to storm heaven in this way. We might truthfully apply to all forms of mysticism the words of a modern poem (Klein, *Die Erlösung des Pilatus*):

> "If peace were to be found by wandering through the world,
> All those who seek would find it here concealed."

The two *viae eminentiae* of the will and soul which we have been considering have been the two most commonly used by men, in all ages, as a means of attaining to union with God. But besides them there is a third way, the *via sapientiae*. Because of its rigid, objective method of procedure it has been used by only a comparatively few, aristocratic spirits, who however have displayed a no less titanic and passionate zeal than those who travel the broader road. "The devotion of thought," this form of piety has been fittingly called. Compared with the ecstatic, sentimental and emotional beatitude of other forms of mysticism we here breathe a clearer, keener atmosphere. The mood has become more sober and academic. But all the clear-cut, dialectic propositions which we meet here must not deceive us, for the fundamental idea is still the same. Here too God must be attained by the mystical, monistic way of immanence and identity. Just as in the common opinion of mysticism God finds Himself in the essence of the soul, so here God, the Absolute, the Infinite Spirit finds Himself in the finite spirit. The autonomous reason that sprang from the divine Logos is able to evolve out of itself the ultimate metaphysical truths (Descartes' *lumen naturale*, Spinoza's *amor intellectualis*). Even the mere process of thinking, the mere act of intellectual contemplation gives the *ratio* a share in the world reason. In the process of thought the existing unity with the eternal spirit is realized anew each time. The same assured feeling of a self-contained power that the moralism of the will possessed is here shared by the self-creating reason in connection with the possibilities of knowledge that lie open to it.

Just as the "Jew" is the type of those who seek salvation by a legalistic morality, so the Greek is the prototype of those who "seek wisdom" and by it would reach God. Greek thought subsists on the belief in an ultimate, religious *a priori*, which, like the soul spark of the mystic, lies hidden in the spirit of man and which is regarded as having been pre-existent. The original bond with the world above may always be restored by virtue of the gift of memory. The teacher, in the Socratic sense, can hasten the enkindling of divine truth in the scholar by means of dialectic conversation. But he never *produces*; he only stimulates what was already a hidden possession. When, however, the ultimate explanation of all things can be discovered independently in the depths of man's spirit, history necessarily loses its significance. When what is eternally valid can be recognized in this immediate way, prophets and mediators as the heralds of divine ideas and commands naturally no longer have any essential significance. The concrete facts of history become mere accidents and side issues; the universal and eternally unchangeable alone become essential. Then for pure thought, strictly speaking, there is only an unhistoric rationalism, like that which Lessing in the eighteenth century logically developed out of his classic traditions. Thanks to innate ideas it is possible for reason to deduce for itself the *verités de raison*, that is the absolutely valid fundamental ideas of metaphysics. The *verités de fait* have only a passing significance in illustrating that which is already established for the κοινὸς λόγος, the universal source of reason within us. Hellenism came into the West through Augustine, who never really overcame his Neoplatonic past, and it there was developed with great clearness and conclusiveness in the ontological realism of medieval philosophy. According to the opinion of the older Franciscan school (Alexander of Hales, Bonaventura), in the act of thinking a direct contact is established between the human and the divine spirit. The *esse in intellectu* corresponds to the *esse in re*: the light of natural reason by self-illumination can establish eternal truth for itself.

But just as the influence of Christianity broke both moralism and mysticism in its immediate form, so the unrestrained stream of "monistic" thought has again and again been checked in its progress by the Biblical mountain masses of historic facts. The Thomist school, that had originated under strong Aristotelian influence, showed itself rather more critical towards the evidence involved in the ontological establishment of certainty in a naive realism. According to its view the transcendent cannot be known by means of direct speculation; there is no immediate insight into the essence of things divine; all spiritual contents are first mediated by the impressions received by the senses. From these the universal conceptions, whose prototypes are eternally present in God, are first formed. This weakened realism tried to do justice to both sides, to the natural, autonomous reason, which was to be allowed to retain the possibility of conceiving of a transcendent reality, and to the grace revealed in Scripture, which was guarded by the teaching authority of the Church and which was to establish and enlarge the natural knowledge of God. Within the doctrinal structure of the Church the Aristotelian-Thomistic consideration of the particular then led on to the erection of that harmonious superstructure of nature and grace, whose clear, definite beauty still delights all those who seek a pleasant reconciliation of reason and revelation. Later on, in circles that were not restricted by churchly authority, the dome of the structure, the supernatural revelation, was lacking and the attempt was made to understand the supernatural solely through the perceptions of the senses. Nature becomes the great portal to the divine world; *per visibilia ad invisibilia!* Before us rises the procession of Spinoza, Goethe and Schelling. The heart beats of the universe are to be found in every flower. Everywhere nature becomes transparent and reveals the realities behind it. A mystical sympathy with nature and a monistic theory of knowledge have always been most intimately united.[7]

German Idealism in its beginnings is not pure "Greek" thought. Even those philosophers, like Schleiermacher or Fichte, who at first stood nearest to the Platonic view were restrained by Christian ties or by Kantian influences. The "conflict between ought and is," between the finite and infinite, between good and evil in its inherent dualism was not overlooked but was everywhere clearly recognized. It is true that the intrusion and influence of the Greek spirit became evident in the attempts to solve these antitheses. No matter how deep and contradictory the antinomies of our thinking may be, man's spirit overcomes them in creative synthesis by means of logical postulates. It is even possible in a final connecting, living unity to survey the contradictions that have arisen in human development and view the opposites in an intelligible union. Of course God and the world are not placed on an equality. The spirit has first to work its way through a "field of hindrance" (Brunner), but finally, through its own independent reflection, arrives at the *coincidentia oppositorum*. Even the most difficult of all human questions, the solution of the misery of sin, has been dragged into this speculative movement. All the dark shadows of sin, all the dissonances of life are the necessary, indispensable background against which light and euphonious harmony alone can come into existence. The negative pole as a creative power is just as important in the production of the current as the positive. The powerful contradictions, the tension of opposites, first produce the

---

[7] The entire symbolism of the Roman cultus rests ultimately on this view, which, as we have shown, found a place in the epistemology of Aquinas.

fullness and richness of life. So sinning becomes the "necessary inner disruption of man" who only finds his way home by erring and only by falling can rise upwards.

The movement of the human spirit pressing upwards to God can be associated with three characteristic names: Plato, Goethe, Hegel. For Platonism the immediate knowledge of the absolute is not bound to any special viewpoint. For Goethe nature serves to illustrate the universal. For Hegel history becomes a source of divine revelation. The lasting significance and real merit of German idealism is that it secured for history its proper place in the confines of spiritual thought. According to Hegel the eternal is not to be recognized through a purely intellectual, religious *a priori*, nor by a symbolism of nature after the fashion of Spinoza but only by what is actual and historical. Here deeds become parables of the unseen. It is in particular, concrete happenings that we discover the traces of the Divine Spirit. Only out of the particular events of history is it possible to understand the development of the totality. These general principles of the philosophy of history Schleiermacher in his *Reden* then applied specifically to religion and showed that the idea of a natural religion was an abstraction of the imagination, that every living religion possessed local color and always had a well-defined historical impress stamped upon it. These ideas, in contrast to that spiritual attitude that regards everything temporal as only a symbol, gave valuable assistance in furthering a comprehension of the historic uniqueness of Christianity. But the autonomous reason was not willing on that account to be bound to dependence on a certain date in history. As in the philosophy of Giordano Bruno the totality of nature becomes transparent and the revelation of divine activity, so here it is the totality of human history. Over the entire stream of time there lies the sunlight of divine transfiguration. At any place we choose, a cross section can be made that will disclose to the reflective spirit as it contemplates the totality what is universally valid. So in the end no period of time is unique as compared with the rest. Everywhere the reflective spirit recognizes the divine truth that is behind the particular temporal events and unites itself with that truth in an inclusive, clear act of perception. The equally universal validity of history, however, it again lowers to a mere natural phenomenon. There is no certain goal towards which history is progressing according to God's will; no sovereign divine bounds within which single historical events have a special pre-eminent value or unique effect. They are all only "images" of passing significance, only eternally changing individualizations for which at any time others might have been substituted. The value of history lies only in its eternal content, which the spirit, through the power of its own divine endowment, everywhere and at all times alike vividly perceives behind the historic and temporal forms. The place of dogma is taken by the myth, that personification of an idea taken from history or nature, for which history has only a passing significance as the materializing of something that is valid in itself. While Hegel's dialectic during his life time was restrained in its immediacy by the "philosophy of history" found in the fifth chapter of the Epistle to the Romans, Fichte carried the symbolic thinking of historic idealism to its logical conclusion. If the Gospel according to St. John was for Luther the "tender, real, chief Gospel" because of its paradoxical "God so loved the world," so for Fichte (as well as for Lessing, Herder, Schleiermacher and the later Schelling) it became the most beloved Gospel because of its spiritual, transcendent, eternal character. St. John is for him the only New Testament writer with whom "the philosopher can concur." The New Testament teaching of justification seems to him a deterioration of the Johannine conception, which unfolded itself in Paul out of the traditions of his Pharisaism. For "only the metaphysical and never the historical saves; the latter only makes it comprehensible." So history has come to be nothing more than the occasion by which the autonomous spirit kindles the fire of its self-recognition, soon to leave behind it everything that is historic and transient in the free, unmediated union with the eternal Spirit.

And so we have surveyed the restless search of men into which their homesickness for the long-lost Paradise has ever and again driven them. It is intensely moving to see the fervor, the passionate tenacity with which men try to swim across the wide stream that divides the two shores of time and eternity, that separates God from man. Every power of the soul that man possesses is exerted to produce a sanctification that shall result in a holiness worthy of God. Stoic morals and the ethics of Protestant culture, the erotic transformation of all nature, the sublime mystical trance, Platonic wisdom and idealistic speculation, all these and countless other manifestations of similar kind are all in the last analysis closely related. In all their variations the same great fundamental theme is constantly recurring; the idea of passing by an elevation, purification, deepening, on to a final apotheosis! Sometimes this constant development may be restricted to only one of the ways we have noted and may be united with a strongly critical attitude towards the other two. Frequently two or even all three of them may be combined in equal proportions. Hegel derided Schleiermacher's emotional definition of religion. He was simply unmoved by such an ardent mysticism of emotion. On the other hand, in spite of the earlier restraint in his theorizing, he fell into the danger of empty speculation. Kant was absolutely immune to the intoxication of romanticism: "That reason, which should think, turns instead to fancy is never pardonable." But in moral idealism he had the most unbounded confidence. It was the same with his follower Ritschl, who was delightfully sober and sound in his attitude towards pietistic raptures, Dionysian mysteries and Areopagitic visions, as well as towards Wagner's music, but he succumbed to the danger of moral perfectionism. On the other side Schleiermacher was an opponent of intellectualism and moralism, but in his strong emotional enthusiasm he was throughout a religious evolutionist. Combination forms are much more frequent. The spiritualism of the fanatics unites a strict moral sanctification with feelings of mystical immanence. The old and new gnosis combines with a resolute discipline of the will, while mysticism and speculation have always been most closely associated. Pantheistic mysticism and mystical pantheism cannot be distinguished. They are invariably mutual attendants in Laotse as well as in Plotinus, in Meister Eckhart as well as in Seb. Franck. Fichte and—no one need be indignant if, in spite of all other differences, these two names are joined in *this* connection—Fichte and Rudolf Steiner have been most alike in joining voluntaristic ethics, contemplative mysticism and speculative metaphysics in their respective systems.

Countless are the altars at which humanity has brought its offerings to the "unknown" God in the hope of reconciling Him and earning a claim to fellowship with Him. It believes that access must at last be gained because the separating interval is not of a qualitative but merely of a quantitative nature, and it seems only a part of transitory weakness and imperfection, as something preliminary but never as an absolute interruption in the personal voluntary relation of God and man. Such a "dynamic" deficiency must finally be overcome by a progressive increase of the energies of the will, by more extensive purification, by perfecting the spiritual endowments or by penetrating more deeply into the fields of knowledge. In its last analysis, that which always gives men renewed courage and strength to continue climbing these steep paths is the secret proud feeling of satisfaction in being able to develop and grow by a self-achieved or at least a co-operative process of sanctification. No matter how hard and difficult the requirements may be it does not matter if only we can come to God with *full* hands and not with those that are quite empty, if only *we may give something ourselves* out of the abundance of our own willing and knowing and being.

CHAPTER II

God's Judgment on Man's Self-sanctification

W E HAVE learned to know the yearning, struggling development of the man with religious aspirations in all its variations of character, time and place, as well as in its final common conception of a way that leads with certainty to its goal. Now we must try to enter the world of Biblical ideas and listen to its original messages, unmixed with other conceptions. First we must see what traits the Bible has in common with other religious confessions that claim to be sacrosanct and canonical testimonies. Here too we find the same idea of suffering that springs from the death pangs and the transitoriness of our unclean lives, from the confusion and helplessness of this sick world; there is the same sighing, thirsting, crying out for some way of overcoming the remoteness of God, "to come where we may see God's face." But when we come to the question as to the method of overcoming this grievous antagonism the ways part completely. Even in Israel the thought came up repeatedly that God could be reached by way of a moral self-perfecting, by a naturalistic, fanatical Baal mysticism or through a speculative cosmogony and theodicy.[1] Paul particularly understood the three human ways of salvation that we discussed in the preceding chapter. In all his missionary journeys he continually came into closest contact with pharisaic moralism, with the exalted deifying mysticism of Asiatic religious cults and with Greek wisdom. But though prophets and apostles were very familiar with these enthusiastic forces they never attempted to overcome the painful separation from God through the aid of any such human devices. Whence is this peculiar restraint that

---

[1] We have only to recall the Chokmah literature of post-exilic times that was so strongly influenced by the cosmic-universalistic speculations of Alexandrine Hellenism. That these writings were not taken up in the canon was no mere accident.

we always find in the Biblical characters and how is it to be understood?

Without doubt the pleasant hope of gaining God's favor by determined energetic action lay closest to the Jewish way of thinking. They possessed the Law that freed them from the helpless, restless quest that accompanies an ethical relativism and which most exactly regulated their relations towards God and their neighbors. They had the promise in connection with the Law: "Which if a man do he shall live thereby." In this way the proper aim and attitude were given to every really devout person with unmistakable clearness. But Deuteronomy also contained that other statement of sharpest moral severity: "Cursed be every one who does not keep all the words of this law to do them." "For if any man keep the whole law but sin in one point he is guilty of all"; this statement of the Epistle of St. James was also understood by the synagogue.[2] With this unconditional absolute demand, which Israel faced with austere courage, the ethical crisis had to burst out over them irresistibly. When "everything or nothing" was demanded by God unconditionally the man with a quickened conscience was crushed. All those who have taken unreservedly to heart the command to love God "with the whole soul and heart and mind" and to love their neighbor with a love equal to their love of themselves have likewise despaired of fulfilling it. Such was the experience of Job and the Psalmists, of Peter and Paul, of Anselm and Luther.

Just among the people who were the most fervent zealots in worshiping God according to the Law there was awakened, in the really devout, an overwhelming understanding of the radical evil of the human heart, that is sinful even when its sinfulness remains hidden from the consciousness. No one can say: "I have made my heart clean, I am pure from my sin" (Prov. 20:9), and we are reminded that "he putteth no trust in his saints." The touching penitential prayer in the ninth chapter of Daniel and the confessions of sin in the 51st and 130th Psalms contain in a prophetic, worldwide survey of conscience, a final judgment on all human dreams of moral proficiency. "O Lord righteousness belongeth unto thee, but unto us confusion

[2] Lev. 18:5; Deut. 27:26; St. James 2:10.

of faces." "We have sinned and committed iniquity, and have done wickedly, and have rebelled, even by departing from thy precepts and from thy judgments." Sin involves a guilt in God's sight that cannot be compensated for in any way. If He, the Holy One, should impute sin no one could stand before Him. As the One Who ordains right-eousness and goodness, God can only hate evil. He can only destroy the sinner who presumptuously assails His majesty. Thus all human claims, all ethical qualifications cease in God's presence. In its place comes "prostration before Him in prayer, not through our righteous-ness but because of His great mercy." For this reason we find in the literature of late Judaism, most movingly in the Fourth Book of Ezra, the oppressive, eerie, apocalyptic mood of a despairing anguish of sin and an anxious expectation of the Messiah, the reconciler and the bearer of the Law's burdens. It is really moving to see how here on the territory of Israel there was a readiness to go the way of hope-less despair rather than to surrender the unconditional, holy, moral relation of justice between God and man, or to seek to substitute for it a way of approximating, ascetic work-righteousness.

When He began His ministry Jesus neither weakened nor removed anything from this Old Testament conscientiousness, but rather strengthened and deepened it. Even the 31st chapter of Job, that con-tains some of the loftiest ethical conceptions of the old covenant, fails to reach the heights of the utterly uncompromising ethics of divine requirements that was taught by Jesus. The last assurance through which man might hope to have some standing before God is here removed, and man is driven out of the last secret, hidden recesses in which he might imagine himself hidden and secure. The impure, lustful look, the angry thought, the secret desire that evil might over-take his neighbor, the coquetting with the lusts and pleasures of the world are in God's sight just as much an absolute break, a separation, a destruction of the communion with Him as the boldest and wildest deed of sin. With merciless insight He "who knew what was in man" showed how just where man seeks to be pious there often lurks, in a most subtle and disguised form, the most terrific pride and the most self-satisfied enjoyment of his own holiness. He knows the evil thoughts that continually arise in the heart, even when engaged in prayer, while doing good works and in the very worship of God. The left hand always knows what the right hand is doing. The "man of the mirror," admiring himself, asks continually, what am I accomplishing? The good deeds of men are always accompanied by an all-defiling, all-destroying pride that whispers to itself, "My name be hallowed." The broad boast, "I thank thee God that I am not like other men" is always associated with a pious conceit that despises others. When we are told of the elder son that "he was angry and would not go in" when the lost brother had again found his way home and gained his father's forgiveness, we have a picture of the proud moral man that is true for all ages. The work-righteous perfectionist is always envious because God is so gracious towards others. By such hateful, envious thoughts every deed is poisoned and corrupted; its value is gone. Though in word and appearance the mantle of devotion be hung around good deeds; though the accomplishments of an honor-seeking zeal tower ever so high, yet in spite of their magnitude and number they are still hollow and empty, filled with a vain, self-satisfied complacency that says "God's" but means its own glory. No matter how high the limbs of a tree may grow even the fruits that hang the highest are eaten away by the disease that has attacked the root. So the only counsel Jesus can give to Nicodemus, one of the chief Pharisees and a master in Israel, is to tear down what he has and to realize the need of a spiritual rebirth from on high. The radical demand, "Be ye perfect even as your Father in heaven is perfect," which was not only made by the Lord but was realized by Him through a unique obedience, purity of purpose and unity of will with the Father, put an end to all naive attempts to achieve a hybrid union with God on the basis of moral aptitude. Peter, who in his easily aroused enthusiasm could offer himself for the task, for which he deemed himself so well qualified, of assisting in the establishment of His earthly kingdom, collapses before the sinless person of One Who perfectly fulfills *all* the will of God and with his honest Israelitic zeal stammers the confession of human helplessness and conscious shame: "Depart from me, for I am a sinful man, O Lord."

Still clearer than any of the instances in the Gospels is the example of St. Paul, that impressive figure of a man who while seeking God was wrecked on the rock of moralism. He indeed had possessed everything of which a true Israelite could boast, circumcision, descent from the noble tribe of Benjamin, a Pharisaic training, a fanatical zeal for the attainment of his own righteousness through the Law (Phil. 3:5 *seq.*). He could say, "We are Jews by nature and not sinners of the Gentiles" (Gal. 2:15), and he could say it rightly, for the morals of the Israelite then far surpassed those of any of the heathen. This Law, which as God's will is holy and just and good (Rom. 7:12 and 16), he desired to fulfill and to live thereby. Jesus' Messianic lowliness, His resolute "No" to all political-religious use of force as a devilish perversion of the divine idea of salvation, His call to repentance and forgiveness from which even the devout were not exempt—all these humiliations which the original congregation, faithful to its Lord's will, demanded of its members, must have been revolting to a Saul who was so zealous in his proud, legalistic, arbitrary striving after divine righteousness. So it was till finally God Himself vanquished him and he swooned at the vision of the glory of Christ. Then his eyes are opened so that he can see the base motives that were concealed behind his striving after holiness and he learns, with painful shame, his share in the guilt of his people in procuring the crucifixion of Jesus. The legalistic Pharisee, who had imagined that he could purely and completely fulfill God's will with his own natural powers, lays aside the proud legal name he bore. The alpine heights of human piety and virtue become very small in his eyes as he views Him Who dwelleth in the heavens. The relative difference existing on earth, from which the vanity and self-consciousness of man draws its support, are all levelled (Rom. 1-3). Because only that which is perfect and entire counts before God; no flesh can stand before Him. Even if we were not conscious of any sin that would not be a cause for complacency because the final judgment on life belongs to God alone as His light penetrates into the darkest corners of existence (Gal. 3:10-12; Rom. 2:13; I Cor. 4:4; Ps. 139). With a conscience that now sees clearly, that views all the world, the Apostle beholds all humanity in its guilty, God-alienated corruption, in its dead bondage, yea, enmity towards God (ἔχθρα ἐις θεόν, Rom. 8:7) and sees the wrathful judgment of God that includes all.

It is well known how soon after the Apostle's death a Hellenizing process set in that exercised a widespread and questionable influence in the development of dogma and in apologetics, as well as in philosophical thought, and that brought about a dubious mingling of diverse forms of expression. Far worse, however, were its results in the statement of the moral and practical questions of life. The stern Biblical judgment of sin as an infinite misery and a guilt separating the soul from God was soon weakened to conform to Neoplatonic and Pelagian ideas and was supplanted by the idea of "sin sickness," which the free will (the αὐτεξουσία of the Greek fathers) was to heal and overcome by meritorious and compensating good works, even though in doing so it might require the support of divine grace. Augustine again had a deeper understanding of the *peccatum radicale*, the corrupt source out of which each single deed developed. He had personally experienced the helplessness of good moral intentions in too overwhelming a way to find any consolation or freedom of conscience in synergistic formulas. But he too understood God's redemption only as a sanctifying infusion of grace, as a mystical-sacramental transformation and not as a simple word of forgiveness that has restored our communion with God. His speculative idea of God, that was influenced by Neoplatonism, always came close to a neutral abstraction and had no place for the personal, voluntary relationship of the Old Testament. The entire Middle Ages continued to be determined by this oriental, Alexandrine idea of salvation, even when it was deepened. In Anselm's *Cur deus homo*, in passing, the Pauline misery of conscience and anguish of sin again came to light with intense insistence, a fact that should be recognized instead of trying to analyze it psychologically as a formal, theological working-out of "Germanic judicial ideas and customs," and in that way explaining it away. As for the rest, however, Thomas Aquinas, and still more Duns Scotus, Occam and the German mystics sought justification before God through a progressive medicinal, moral infusion of grace by which the sinful defects in man's soul would gradually be obliterated.

The older, deeply flowing stream, that could be designated by the names of Job, Jeremiah, John the Baptist, Jesus and Paul (but not Plato) first welled up again from the depths in its original power in Luther and the reformers and congregations that gathered about him. The hard, primeval rock of Biblical candor in dealing with the facts of reality and of the conscience was again uncovered. There were four mighty intuitions that flashed out with irrefutable logic before the terrified conscience of the young Augustinian monk, who had been reared in the modern theology of nominalism with its powerful Pelagian tendencies.

1. Only that is truly good which is done with a glad and cheerful will, out of love to God. But "we have to torment our will, which is otherwise inclined, to do the good deed." Our good deeds do not come from a holy impulse of our own nature, but the indolence and unwillingness of evil desires must always first be overcome by arduous compulsion. If the will finally obeys, it marvels and admires its own obedience. The hope of eternal reward, the fear of the punishments of hell, those motives that the Church at all times has stressed and preached industriously are after all nothing but the religiously garnished egoism of man, who in his work-righteousness keeps in mind his own advantage, his own self-enrichment.

2. This godlessness of the will that is eternally seeking its own and loving itself above all things, is not a harmless weakness (the *attenuata, infirmata libertas* of the Semipelagians); it is not a slight defect and least of all a mere clouding and erring of the intellect, as Socratic moral philosophy maintained, but a conscious enmity towards God. Sin is not merely something negative, not only a *privatio et carentia boni*, as his Erfurt teachers who followed Gabriel Biel, Gerson and d'Ailly, had taught; it is rather a tremendously serious, positive reality, a *hostilis impugnatio*, not a weakness but an opposition, not the promising preliminary of a yet unattained goal, but an innermost perversion, a real corruption. As the sharply drawn definition of the Formula of Concord later put it, man is not only *aversus a deo*, but *adversus deum*.[3] But this evil unbroken will, out of which all single

---

[3] The much attacked expressions of *Lapis et truncus* (Sol. Decl. 593, 19) are by no means the severest similes as they do not express the thought of a conscious, willful and aggressive opposition to God. Cf. Fr. H. R. Frank: *Die Theologie der Concordienformel,* Erlangen, 1858, II, pp. 138 *seq.*

evil deeds spring, like venomous sores, is unable to free itself of its own burden. The end of all monasticism is the experience of utter moral helplessness about which the lectures on Romans, the expositions of the Psalms and the great controversial treatise against Erasmus all discourse with such intense and insistent reiteration.

3. In matters of sin no compensation can be offered God. He is "not a trader Who establishes a mart for the forgiveness of sins" so that by haggling and trading good and evil works may be balanced against each other. For this reason all the subtle distinctions of the Roman confessional between venial and mortal sins are impossible and useless. Every sin means a complete destruction of the personal communion with God. The attempt to relieve the situation by diminishing God's claims has to be rejected unconditionally by the conscience. "An approach to the condition of blessedness" does not constitute a claim on salvation. There is no more dangerous temptation than the thought, "Do you suppose God will reckon so exactly with you?" (W. Ed. 3, 447, 31). God wants us to belong to Him with all our heart and with all our time and with all our might. The spot that stains the past cannot be erased by some later work of supererogation because the devotion of our *entire* future to God is only a self-evident duty. There is always a remainder that is never balanced, that remains eternally unpaid.[4]

4. But when the conscience has once grasped the solemn thought of the "irrevocable nature of time" the distress becomes infinitely great. For if God makes no concessions to sin; if it is not possible by any later exertions, however sincere, to remove the earlier, dirty pages from the book of life, then the central concern of my life is no longer devoted to the increase of religious power and life, but only to finding out how the guilt resting on the past, for which reparation can no

---

[4] Compare the beautiful statement of Kierkegaard in the penitential address, *Pureness of the Heart* (Munich, 1924): "It is ever untrue that the guilt becomes changed [by time] even though a century should pass. To affirm anything of the sort is to exchange the eternal for what is least like the eternal, namely human forgetfulness" (p. 23). To understand the need of guilt we do not need to hold to that absolute pessimism that regards *all* our actions as equally corrupt in God's sight. It is enough to recognize the fact that a good deed is always accompanied by a withholding of something. But with this contradiction the judgment has already been sealed, because before God only what is perfect, entire and complete can stand in the final judgment.

longer be made, may be removed and revoked. Luther was not satisfied with the Church's teaching of a quality of grace that gradually
replaced the power of sin. Nor was he satisfied with legalistic pro-
posals for reform (*evangelica lex*), as they were continually set up
and attempted, from the times of Hildebrand and Peter Valdez to those
of John Wessel and Savonarola, now by the authorities of the Church
and now by the opposition, sometimes in a cold and rigorous, again in
a warm-hearted or fanatical zeal. That he was the first who again
began with the fundamental question of the relation to God and desired a word of forgiveness that would remove the *guilt* of sin, marks
him out as a genuine reformer. Step by step, with piercing consistency
he went his way, not even terrified by the hardest and most humiliating self-revelations. He recognized the defiant, hostile weakness of
the will, and when he discovered that the way of a bargaining morality
(whether through private actions or by means of the vicarious works
of the Church) was completely closed, he found himself face to face
with the inescapable reality of sin.

It might appear a questionable procedure to connect a systematic
presentation so closely with the experiences of certain historic characters as we have done, but we have ventured to do so because Paul
and Luther show with unsurpassed clearness the terrible crisis into
which all legalistic ethics that attempts to be an expression of our
justification before God, thrusts men. Where the Way of the Law is
followed with absolute sincerity to its final conclusion, in whatever
convent, Church or school it may be, it turns confidence and fearlessness into terror so that the conscience no longer hears God's approval and acknowledgment, but only His accusing demands. Before
Him, Who alone is good, all religious activity, no matter how energetic it may be, must become very small and man is forced to surrender the legal claim that he thought he could establish with God
through his own works and merits. In place of the bold, self-confident
assurance comes the anxious question of despair: "Who knows how
you have lived?" The saint who has sought to gain salvation through
his own self-sanctification must perceive how behind his desire to
effect it there lies concealed the pride of self-esteem, which Luther

has called the "queen of sins."[5] Where there has been courage to face the facts honestly man just because of his zeal for the Law perishes through the Law (Gal. 2:19); there self-glorification crumbles; there the confidence in self-salvation is utterly destroyed. Man has to "learn the greatest and most difficult art known on earth," namely, to gain the consciousness of being a sinner; he must learn to regard his riches, his dependence on the results of his own efforts as his poverty, and the poverty of a humble contrite heart as his true riches.[6] Torn from the heights of dominion and growth and life, and cast down into the lowliness of decline and submission and mortality, man can only stammer, "Forgive us our trespasses." Whether he will receive an answer to his prayer is a matter quite beyond his own control.

If the pathway of voluntary discipleship cannot lead on high because of our own weakness perhaps by a vital or a mystical unfolding the way to heaven can be opened. Why is it that here again the Bible, both in the Old and New Testaments, shows the same remarkable mistrust towards such attempts, whether it be towards the riotous, orgiastic nature worship of the Phoenician Baal and Astarte, of the Syrian-Phrygian *Magna Mater*, or towards the beauty-intoxicating, transcendental cult of the Greek Artemis, that female goddess of vegetable life who possessed such splendid temples in Athens, Corinth and Ephesus, or towards the mantic-visionary schools of the pre-exilic prophets or towards the theosophic mystics in Colossae? With the most sharply defined precision the Biblical course runs between the two possibilities of a nature cult and of mysticism, recognizing both as ungodly and deformed distortions of primitive truth and consequently rejecting both. We shall try to understand the considerations that move the Bible to such a rejection, in the light of the problem of nature.

A strange dualistic, spiritualistic conception of the relation of soul and body runs like a hidden stream through the history of human thought. Notable leaders of thought in ancient times and in the east are its spiritual fathers; great occidental thinkers have followed them.

---

[5] W. Ed. 31, II, 259, 14, "regina peccatorum. Arrogancia, quae in bono suo quaerit gloriam." *Lectures on Isaiah,* 1527-1530. Is. 39: 1-2.

[6] Cf. Augs. Conf. Arts. XII, XVI and XXVII, 49. Christian perfection consists in the perfection of repentance and of the fear of God.

Their line can briefly be indicated by a few names: Plato (Phaedon), Pythagoras, Philo, Plotinus, Proclus, Buddha, Zarathustra, Mani, Apollonius of Tyana, Basilides, Origen, Scotus Erigena (*de divisione naturae*), the Victorines, Jakob Böhme, John Mich, Hahn. Behind them as followers comes the measureless host of Buddhist and Parsee Yogis, the Mandaeans and Neopythagoreans, the Gnostics, Essenes, Ebionites, Nicolaitans, Cabalists, Therapeutae, Encratites, Bogomiles, Cathari and numerous Christian anchorites.

The fundamental idea that unites them all, irrespective of time or place, is their teaching of the soul which denies the cosmos, and according to which God, Who Himself is pure soul substance, has created other spiritual souls out of such essence. These purely spiritual, immaterial essences were originally the only realities. Material existence, the body, nature and the world originated only as a subsequent disturbance, whether, as the Gnostics taught, it was the result of the unlucky work of a Demiurge, or, according to the theosophic view came as a materializing and congealing of the psyche that resulted from the fall. In any case, the spiritual, as incorporeal, and the immaterial are considered holy and good, the natural, on the other hand, because it is earthly is regarded as essentially low, evil and devilish. The consequences that result from such an equation where the material equals sin and the spiritual equals the divine are tremendous: the attitude of man towards his own body becomes one of complete negation. It is the source of all suffering, the chain, the cage, prison, grave, in which the soul, exiled from the distant world of God, is held against its will in bondage and servitude, in the material creation. This antagonism is particularly directed against the sexual character of humanity which is regarded as a low, sinful disfigurement of the flesh that has resulted from the loss of man's original state of purity. The contempt for marriage shown in the harsh descriptions that portray it as an immoral and defiling element, has its counterpart in the glorification of virginity (the new heavy burden of oriental-syncretistic origin that burdens the Roman Church) which was advocated with unbounded enthusiasm, particularly by the western fathers, by Tertullian, Ambrose and Jerome and by medieval and modern Romanism. Though great numbers of hermits and saints complain in

their confessions of the bitter anguish they suffered through the wild
erotic phantasies and desires that tormented them; though the burning, passionate bridal language of mysticism only ill conceals the
lewdness that was banished to this sphere yet, in spite of all, this failed
to change the opinion which came as a logical result of the dualistic
viewpoint, that abstinence from marriage was a holy work and that
by such "freeing from the senses" morality would be furthered.

But when there is no longer any connection between nature and
grace, creation and redemption, or they are placed in actual opposition, the necessary result is a striving after complete renunciation in
its double aspect, a renunciation of nature and of culture. Its symbol
is the cloister cell with its quiet isolation far from the noise and confusion of every-day reality, with its "one window that discloses nothing of the earth but only a bit of heaven." The world, as something
useless and unessential, is to be forgotten. Above all there is no understanding of the moral tasks and responsibilities of society. The
objective, unselfish appreciation of labor is lacking; where it is prac-
tised it is justified as a means of defense against the temptations of
the flesh, as an aid towards purification or for the glory of the Church
that mediates the distant heaven. There is not even a real fellowship
among the brothers associated in the same convent. It is true they are
all together but in the isolation of their own cells, each one engaged
in the individually isolated, subjective care of the soul. It is a necessary consequence of every belief in immortality that knows only of
"God and the soul," that forgets the little word "our." It becomes
evident what absolute value such ideas, that fundamentally despise
nature, must assign to moralism and asceticism, because it is only
possible on the foundation of such a world view to erect the whole
ladderlike structure of monkish virtuosity, or to establish the distinction between *praecepta* and *consilia evangelica* (as weaker or stronger
instruments for loosening the hold of the world). But it also becomes
evident how in other quarters, starting from the same premises, men
could arrive at a wild, unbridled sexual libertinism because the body
being "only" material, unessential substance had no connection whatsoever with God; because here, at least, they were moving in a completely neutral sphere. In both cases the motive is the same; the

destruction or despising of the corporeal on the basis and in the interest of an extreme spiritualism.

Viewed from such a standpoint of world-renouncing dualism, what is the situation in which man finds himself here on earth in respect to his relation to God? In its last analysis it is an exceedingly consoling one. The body belongs to what is beneath, to the earthly, to the animal; the soul belongs to what is above, to God, to what is essentially good. The misery of sin arises only from its entanglement with matter. If we are released from that yoke, whether by ecstasy or by death, the ray of light, that had only been darkened or concealed by its earthly hull, must return again to the eternal light. Under such conditions it follows logically that the essence of man needs no real repentance, no sharply defined conversion, no break with itself, but only a triumphant breaking through; no painful descent into the hell of death, only a bold, sure and joyous departure and ascension to life.[7]

The Biblical teaching concerning man and creation is a direct contrast to this teaching and completely excludes such an attitude of world negation. God not only breathed forth soul monads but He likewise created the stars and the earth, the grass and the flowers and the grain, yea, the very body of man. Man's inseparable unity of body and soul has come from God. He stands before God as God's own creation that in its marvellous physical as well as spiritual existence reverently praises the Creator for His greatness and goodness. Πᾶν κτίσμα Θεοῦ καλόν (I Tim. 4:4). It is true that the Bible recognizes the dissonances and disseverances of this world. In the book of Job we hear cries of despairing grief concerning this deformed and sorrow-laden aspect of the world that are more vehement than anything that any modern atheist has been able to utter. The New Testament speaks of those who sit in darkness and in the shadow of death, and St. Paul hears the longing sigh that arises from creation yearning to be delivered from this transitoriness.

But how utterly different is the explanation this gloomy fact re-

---

[7] It would require a special treatise to show how differently the various ideas concerning the nature of the soul have influenced the idea of death. Here we can indicate one such result. The Stoa, as a logical result of its spiritualistic psychology, both approved and recommended deliberate suicide as a means of liberating the soul.

ceives! That I live on the earth is not the cause of this misery; that
I have a body is not the reason for this perplexity. This whole division into two principles, rational and sensual, material and spiritual,
is too easy, too comfortable a solution of the riddle. Here the situation
meets with a sterner judgment: We first, it says, disfigured God's
lovely creation by our guilt (Rom. 8:20), we separated ourselves completely from God by our bold disobedience and have corrupted ourselves utterly together with all that we have and all that we are
by that rash act. As the soul *and* body in their original purity can
bear witness to the living God and rejoice in Him (Ps. 84:2b), so
both, carried by their guilt to destruction, now witness to the curse
of godlessness. Now our bones are vexed (Ps. 6:2) and the heart is
full of terror when we stand before the living God. The dark shadows
that slant across all life do not come from a natural, physiological
antagonism but from one that is moral and voluntary. The body and
the senses could be quite pure in themselves. God did not create
them essentially sinful, wretched and evil "in the beginning," and
so we feel that their destruction by age, sickness and death is something that is simply irrational, something that ought not to be.

But when the animistic conception of the deliverance of the soul's
substance from the "lower" substance through death is stamped by
conscience as a great delusion, then death becomes a most bitter
calamity. If our spiritual ego has been the original cause that has
plunged us into this antagonism to God, then the mere fact of the
separation of body and soul does not help one particle, for death as
such no longer means the entrance into life. The soul that has always
lived only for itself is not admitted to union with God by the mere
laying aside of this earthly vesture; quite the contrary, it must be
afraid to come before God's throne. Here the significance of the Old
Testament in the history of the world once more becomes evident as
with incorruptible sincerity of conscience it has made men refuse to
yield to the temptation of a Platonic way of salvation, though the
temptation lay near enough in post-exilic days. They only clung more
resolutely to their longing expectation of a Messiah sent by God, Who
would create a new heaven and a new *earth*. The same feeling has
given a certain austere character to the hymns of our Church that

sing of death and eternity. "For the fathers the terror of death lay in the fear of conscience" (Paul Althaus). From the moving hymn of John Kempf (1625), "When in death's bitter pangs I lie, and find no help nor counsel" there is no bridge that leads over to the confidence before death of the Stoa or to Seneca's: *"patent undique ad libertatem viae multae, breves, faciles."*

The Biblical conception of nature can be most clearly recognized in the person of Jesus Himself. According to the opinion of D. Fr. Strauss He belongs, with Buddha, in the great company of those who have taught, *naturalia sunt turpia*. But such an accusation of hostility to nature contradicts the whole attitude of His life. Jesus did not live like one who believes that man consists only of a soul. He also took the body seriously as the domain both of guilty destruction and of miraculous divine activity. How he viewed nature and its beauty with the eyes of pure devotion is told by His parables. The spiritualistic attitude of the mystic knows only of an "eros," in the sense of the Platonic mythology, in antithesis to nature; empty, transitory creatures are only to be helpful symbols for meditation on eternal, supermundane ideas. Jesus places opposite to nature the ἀγάπη, that immediate love which recognizes even the earth and the cosmos as creatures that have come from the hand of the Father and that praise Him through His own creation. The disfigurement and corruption of the world that He saw better than anyone else never caused Him to question God's workings but only those of men. Momentous consequences have come from the impression that the New Testament's use of "flesh and spirit" shows some relationship to the ancient oriental dualism. The truth is that its conception of the σάρξ is never a contemptuous reference to what is merely material but always means the lusting will of man that deifies itself in the creation, that is submerged and absorbed in things earthly and that strives against the "Spirit of God."[8] With ceaseless emphasis the apostolic teaching demands that we fight against this will of the flesh, not against the ὕλη of a spiritualism that despises the body. Above all, Jesus' bodily resurrection is the strongest expression of "the posi-

---

[8] This is accompanied by a simple, natural use of the word σάρξ in the New Testament that involves no moral judgment, e.g. Rom. 9:3; Col. 2:5; I Cor. 15:39.

tive relation of God to nature."[9] In the same way the eschatological pictures that are drawn by Jesus and in the Apocalypse (in contrast to the figurative language of mysticism) point to a corporeal "termination of the ways of God."

This long-drawn-out approach to the subject was for the purpose of arriving at a clearer understanding of the peculiar tension that exists in Biblical thought between heaven and earth, between God and man as a result of the fall. Only in this way is it possible to understand fully why both the vitalistic and the mystical aspirations were so brusquely rejected.

The man of the Renaissance, of a Dionysian enjoyment of the senses, of erotic-artistic intoxication, who would like to give himself free rein in the development of his bodily gifts and powers, in spite of a thousand distortions and perversions, has a correct feeling that God will also meet us in our corporeal existence. It often happens (as was particularly the case at the end of the fifteenth and beginning of the sixteenth centuries in Italy) that such an aesthetic excess comes as an angry reaction, a furious vengeance on the repression of what is earthly in the interests of a spiritually diluted, intangible belief in heaven, like that cultivated by the medieval monasticism. But in their protest against this withdrawal from the works of God into a colorless, false spirituality, men forget that while we are indeed *God's* creation we are likewise the *fallen* creation of God. They forget that through the desires of the evil will the body that seeks enjoyment without accountability and enjoyment without responsibility has also been corrupted and has lost its purity. Not that it is corrupt in its essence! Every healthy child is still a hymn in praise of the divine miracle of creation. Yet it is just to the body and its activities that we find clinging those demoniac passions that rob it of its original likeness to the Creator. God's judgment on a vitalism that seeks to drift on absorbed in the music of a divine harmony of beauty and enjoyment finds its expression in the terrible fact that just where man thinks he can develop most splendidly into something godlike he turns most easily into the beast (Rom. 1:18-32). It is just this gratification, intensified to white heat, that, with every step, leads on, ever

[9] A. Schlatter, *Das Christliche Dogma*, p. 310, Stuttgart, 1923.

more rapidly, to death. Where we imagine we have risen to the highest point we have in fact come terribly close to collapse and destruction. The naive songs in praise of blooming beauty, as an immediate expression of the relationship to God, are illusions which are mercilessly destroyed by the hard reality that the body must die.

So it is not prudery that causes the Evangelical Church to give a clear "no" in answer to the aspirations of a youthful nature-eroticism. It is simply an expression in a new form of the ancient contrast between the Reformation and Romanticism, between the Reformation and the Renaissance. We may venture the assertion that the romances of Strindberg and Dostojewski, and the pictures of morals found in some of the great French authors (Maupassant, for example) that speak of the curse of sexuality with such appalling candor, are less dangerous than the aesthetic portrayals of modern nudism in which the charm and sunlight of corporeal life are one-sidedly glorified while the graveyard aspect, the curse of sin, the sickness and transitoriness that grasp the body are completely ignored and denied. For this hybrid, that results when the body strives to be what it is not and refuses to be what it is, the Bible has only the striking comment that is found in the Old and New Testaments alike: "All flesh is as grass, and all the glory of man as the flower of the grass. The grass withereth and the flower perisheth but the word of the Lord endureth forever." (Is. 40:6-8; I Peter 1:24 seq.)

If religious eroticism is diseased with a boundless intoxication of worldliness, so mysticism suffers from an erroneous world flight, that fails to mend the matter. If vitalism will not recognize physical wretchedness, so this refuses to see the wretchedness within the soul. The clear-cut difference between mystical piety and that of the Bible can be seen most clearly in the attitude towards prayer. All mystical prayer stands and falls with the spiritistic conception of the soul that we have described above. If the soul be indeed the pure remnant, the divine, exalted spark from the eternal sea of flame, then prayer, after a preliminary purification, becomes a blissful absorption into divinity, where the personal consciousness ceases, like the impassible, dreamy rest of Nirvana. The experience of all Biblical suppliants stands in direct contrast to this beatific transcendence. When anyone has really encountered God Himself and not merely a higher ego or an imaginary, fantastic portrayal of God, he is roused from dreaming to watchfulness, from an impure approach to a terrified retreat, from the familiar confidence of bombastic prayers to words that express a real feeling of awe towards the One Who is so far above the suppliant himself. Isaiah's "Woe is me! for I am undone; because I am a man of unclean lips, for mine eyes have seen the King, the Lord of Hosts"; Abraham's cry, "Behold now, I have taken upon me to speak unto the Lord, which am but dust and ashes" (Is. 6:5; Gen. 18:27) show clearly that it is not possible for a sinful creature to enter into communion with God without further ceremony. For this reason, even in the Old Testament there is a profusion of mediators and of offerings for mediation; the Kapporeth, the Torah, the sin offering, the great Day of Atonement, the prophets as a spiritual aristocracy, whom God by His own choosing designated as His workmen and messengers of His will.

This sacredly guarded reverence towards God is fully maintained in the New Testament. How humble and attentive Paul, the servant of Jesus Christ, stands before his Lord and how little he makes of his visions and revelations! He knows that even the "natural" man with his finest and most hidden powers (including the powers of occult mediation, as we would say today) perishes (I Cor. 2:14). What is "natural" can as little inherit the Kingdom of God as flesh and blood, unless God in a freely given act of love, bestows the gift of the Spirit, Who alone leads men into life. But if man always remains in such a state of dependence on God every thought of mystic union and all speculations concerning identity with God are excluded from prayer. Even the famous passage about "Christ liveth in me" (Gal. 2:20) has been secured from misunderstanding by the fact, often overlooked, that it means a complete removal of all separation or indicates some sort of an anticipatory vision, as is clear from the words that follow: "the life which I now live in the flesh I live by the faith of the Son of God, who loved me, and gave himself for me."

In this matter Luther was a true pupil of St. Paul, in spite of the fact that during the determinative years of his development he was continually being tempted to travel the road of a mystical way of salvation. On the one side were the writings of Bonaventura and Tauler, which were much read in the monastery and which, for a time, exercised quite an influence over him, and on the other side he was pressed hard by fanatics like Carlstadt and Münzer. What prevented him from allying himself with either was his own painful spiritual experience to which he remained faithful in maintaining that introspection does not reveal a "divine remnant" nor an inner light but only the corruption of an evil will. For this reason he was fully convinced that prophets who "talked to the high majesty of God like a shoemaker's apprentice," whose attitude was that of a comfortable, familiar "Thou" relationship, did not really know God else they would not be able to dispose of their accusing conscience so easily and so quickly with their unreal dreams and delusions. The seriousness and reverence that so impressed Veit Dietrich when once he overheard Luther praying, was missing in them.

So the hard fact remains that neither the natural fire of vitalism nor the fire of love in mysticism can really help man in his misery. The lie that is concealed in the deification of the creative forces of natural life reveals itself with terrifying clearness in the wild, helpless hatred of the one-sided aesthetic man towards the hard decrees of God that judge all living flesh in all the earth. Goethe who cannot bear to see his aging friends, the French king who orders that his carriage shall never be driven past a burial ground, Nietzsche's indignant scorn for the picture of the *"Ecce Homo"* are all examples of despairing assaults, of attempts to forget fallen mortality which never really succeed and which in their final failure openly proclaim God's judgment on themselves. The deception and error of mysticism again shows itself in an opposite way by its unhappy and limited outlook in the world. How labored, how anxious is its attitude towards the beauty of the earth, towards the joy of one's calling, towards the riches of the child.[10] What a contempt for the First Article of the Creed is shown by this negative, ascetic conception of the world! Such estrangement from the world that is supposed to bring salvation

[10] When the birth of his son was announced to prince Sidharta (Gotama Buddha), shortly before his departure from his father's palace, he is said to have exclaimed, "A fetter has been forged for me!" Compare with such a sentiment Ps. 127: "Lo, children are a heritage of the Lord: and the fruit of the womb is his reward."

with it is condemned by the lives of men like Martin Luther, Paul Gerhardt, Mathias Claudius, Wilhelm Löhe, who lived with a feeling that they were exiles, who felt themselves to be in the "evening of the world," but who served God in holy, joyous artlessness and in the consciousness that it was not the world itself that was responsible for its misery but the disobedience of man who refused God the service of the heart.

If it is hard for man to humble his defiant will before the judgment of God, it is still harder to surrender the illusions of his spiritual riches but hardest of all is to admit the inadequacy and helplessness of his own understanding and judgment. "We are accustomed to admit that God is more powerful than we but not that He is wiser."[11] That moral efforts end in helplessness, that spiritual aspirations collapse in weariness we are ready on occasion to admit. But just as besieged troops after having been compelled to surrender two outlying fortifications become so much the more tenacious in the defense of their last stronghold, so man called to account by God gathers together his remaining strength for the defense of his own powers of understanding. If the will and the emotions have been compelled to leave the field, reason still tries to defend its own capability. It shall not be surrendered to the universal impotence nor be allowed to fall under the judgment of God. Men flatter themselves that here, at least, man has remained uncorrupted, that here the immediate contact of earth with heaven has never been interrupted.

But we are reminded that the Bible in its attack on human presumption does not make the least exception on this point. What is the significance of that exclamation point, so sobering to all spiritual arrogance, that speaks of the fear of the Lord as the beginning of wisdom; what is the meaning of that clear-cut statement of transcendence that speaks of God dwelling in light unapproachable? (Prov. 1:7; 9:10; Ps. 111:10; I Tim. 6:16.) What is meant by those two chapters at the beginning of the First Epistle to the Corinthians in which the Apostle asks the question, "Who hath known the mind of the

---

[11] W. Ed. 36, 155, 31 *seq.*: *Nos alioqui solemus deo omnia dare, quod potentior, sed hoc non, quod prudentior. Sermons of the Year 1532,* No. 16, 8th of March.

Lord?" with its implications, so unbearably offensive to the natural man, that he cannot perceive the mind of the Spirit nor fathom the depths of the Godhead? How can the Bible venture to call in question the participation of human wisdom in the universal reason of the world about which Marcus Aurelius writes with such proud assurance in his diary? Why do we meet the same bitter antagonisms in the domain of speculation, that we encountered in moralism and mysticism, between Jerusalem and Athens, between Paul on the one hand and Plato and Plotinus on the other?

We shall try to answer the questions as we take up the ideas of two Biblical theologians, who in spite of their different viewpoints and the dissimilarity of their emphasis are united in their resolute rejection of Greek rationalism. They are Adolf Schlatter and Karl Heim.

There is a twofold reason for the opposition of Schlatter to the intellectual ideals of Hellas. He first of all attacks with all his might the Platonic dualism—we might have mentioned him before in this connection—which condemns nature as being evil in itself and which thinks it can approach to God by more and more completely spiritualizing the concrete, by avoiding and suppressing it because it is only accidental and unessential, "the veiling and masking of what is divine." He who is "the empirically observing theologian" and who always begins with the single observation and not with a general concept, quite in the modern empirical spirit, calls it "cursed thanklessness" if we do not recognize the giver in the concrete gift that has been received by the individual and instead try to establish our contact with the absolute in generalities arrived at by abstraction.

Stronger still is another of his antagonisms to the Greek spirit. He does not reject pure thought as an approach to God because the intellect lacks ability. Schlatter knows no "fear of thinking." Quite on the contrary, from the standpoint of his "naive realism," he has a very high regard for the capabilities of the human understanding. He rejects the way of pure thought because it "lacks love and practical activity." We cannot enjoy God as an inactive existence, like some assured possession, without, at the same time, serving Him with a self-sacrificing will. The aristocratic "mere intellectualism," that forgets purpose and action in its knowledge of God and its contemplative intuitions of divine things, is the preeminently great sin. It is a vain delusion to imagine that we can view the truth without surrendering ourselves to it; that it is possible to restrict life to processes of thought and omit action. The very exaltation of knowledge over the will, which Thomism teaches in agreement with Aristotelian intellectualism, seems to Schlatter a dangerous perversion that has worked serious injury in all the theology of the Christian Church, even far beyond the confines of Romanism. He knows that in his conflict with this theoretical "scholasticism," which is an ever-present temptation in theology, he is in full agreement with the Bible, which regards a knowledge that lacks love as worthless and which knows that such knowledge without love only puffs up without bringing amendment. The Apostles warn their congregations against that fanciful and visionary dreaming about heaven when an unpurified, unsanctified nature flourishes behind the multiplication of trifling ideas. Instead of boasting of his wisdom each one should bring "into captivity every thought, to the obedience of Christ." (I Cor. 13:2, 8:1 seq.; I Tim. 6:5; Titus 3:8 seq.; II Peter 1:9; II Cor. 10:5.) It is walking in the light, the communion with God put into action and expressed by love to our brother, that makes our thinking clear. John, James and the Pastoral Epistles all state this very emphatically.

Here the congregation also has its example in Christ, "the perfect anti-Gnostic," who preserved the purity of His thinking by the fact that "He was always led exclusively by love and existed for its service." Whoever tries to cultivate the processes of thought alone and refuses obedience to God not only destroys the will but actually restricts "the logical functions," because sin has a "darkening power." We are reminded of Luther's lectures on Genesis, where he says that the transgression of the Law has already begun when men engage in their curious, alluring debates concerning God, in the *disputare de deo*. With every theorizing, "Did God say?" we place ourselves outside the truth, which is always given to us as acknowledged knowledge. The guilt of men reveals itself here in a particularly tragic way as they separate themselves from love by their egoistic desire for knowledge and so obscure the truth, because God is not a thing but a living, personal spirit, Who only reveals Himself to those who serve Him in active, moral self-surrender. "When God is gone," says Luther, "the fairy tales arrive." When His word is no longer understood as a demand, a threat, a challenge, but is regarded as speculative truth, then man becomes a fool in his wisdom (Rom. 1:18) and his wisdom becomes foolishness to God.

In this attack Schlatter mercilessly uncovered the difficulties of this purely rational, "Greek" thinking. There is no immediate, aesthetic vision of God separated from daily existence, neither through a purely Platonic structure of ideas nor through abstractions derived from nature or from history. But what is the prospect of success on a road to knowledge that is united with ethical activity, where, as with Fichte, the ego disdains a "reflective intelligence, divorced from life" and in creative devotion regards the world as his task? Here is the point where we should listen to the critical reflections of K. Heim.

From the very beginning Heim has been more skeptical than Schlatter in his estimate of the metaphysical powers of the intellect. Here he proves himself a follower of Luther, Calvin, Kant and Kierkegaard, who were all filled with a fundamental distrust of all speculative efforts. Luther's dislike for Aristotle, for the humanistic-Greek attitude of Erasmus, was doubtless partly due to the skeptical terminism of the Erfurt philosophy, but it grew ultimately out of his experience and out of the practical difficulties of his conscience. Kant's opposition to all deductive metaphysics did not, however, spring from an evangelical feeling of penitence. Simply by means of an incisive criticism, that was carried mercilessly to its ultimate end, he arrived at the conclusion, which was afterwards to have such tremendous consequences in theology, that human reason is not able to press up to God, even by its most intense efforts. By the categories of our thinking we remain bound to this empirical world and end in irreconcilable, inescapable theoretical and practical contradictions, that indeed point to a domain beyond these limitations which, however, can never be grasped by actual experience. Now Heim attempts to unite Luther's religious and Kant's philosophical recognition of the transcendence of God. To this end he carries the contradictions in which pure thought becomes involved beyond Kant and shows how not only the limitations and limitlessness of time and space, not only the tension between causality and freedom, between the simplicity and complexity of the world entangle us in difficulties that become inexplicable, but also that in the entire "Thou" and "I" relationship there is hidden an unsolved tension between subjective solipsism and objective realism. This antithesis is especially marked in the mutual relationship of the ego and the world, the ego and God. Then the existence of God is no longer a necessary idea since the opposite can just as readily be supposed without involving us in contradictions. So it would seem that every attempt to attain to God by a self-induced mental aspiration, whether of Platonic, Thomistic or Hegelian sort, had been finally disposed of, as in this way the wings of all soaring speculations have been effectively clipped.

And yet there are still two possible ways of evading this conclusion: by way of a practical logical postulate or by way of one resulting from a creative synthesis. The one way was used by Kant, the other by the German high Idealism. But now Heim follows thought in its flight from repentance even to this point and attempts to block both roads of escape.

Kant had locked heaven against the speculative reason but left it open for the practical reason. The intelligible ego, that absolute, transcendent magnitude of the eternal world, is completely inaccessible and incomprehensible to reason that is bound by its limitations of space, time and causality. Nevertheless it is given us with immediate practical certainty in the ethical experience of the categorical imperative.

If Kant as a thinker really possessed something of that "Protestant manliness" that had the courage to discern the barriers between God and man and reverently let them remain, yet, as an ethical philosopher, he showed an outspoken, "unprotestant" optimism. Here he was entirely lacking in the "incorruptible watchman's fidelity" for which he has been so highly praised. But this very dependence on Kant's ethics has been so momentous for Protestant theology and has brought about such an impoverishing dissolution of the content of Christianity into mere judgments of value, that we can only hear the references to him as the "philosopher of Protestantism," which were so common in the eighteenth century, with dubious approval. He is much closer to Erasmus than to Luther. The feeling of self-confidence in his own moral power possessed by the Kantian man, must be utterly destroyed, even if this last practical-moral avenue into the beyond were closed by the operation, before it would be possible to say of a radically critical philosophy that it "expresses a penitent disposition in the language of philosophy."

Heim attempts to furnish the final critical purification as he shows that all the morality that has been gained from the ethical *a priori* of the natural man suffers from the defect of relativity. We are faced by an infinite variety of antithetical ideals of life. Pure reason leaves us utterly helpless when it comes to determining which of these ways we shall choose. The defect of the categorical imperative lies particularly in the fact that before we can make use of it we must first know what is morally good. The content must first have been given from eternity and must show with unmistakable clarity and authority what it is that must be used by this categorical fidelity in completing life. It is true this objection applies only to a purely philosophical ethics. The Ritschlian school by placing the person of Jesus into the center of its considerations possessed a pattern for the construction of a clearly defined ethics, in whose fulfillment the religious relationship to God was to be realized and established. But here again it is necessary to force men to take a further step. It is certain that we encounter the might of God in moral actions, in the consciousness of an unconditional obligation, and in the following of Jesus, but we encounter it as an "inescapable, omnipresent demand" by which we are broken. Yielding to a moral standard does not convince us of our union with God but rather of our antigodly attitude, and our inability to fulfill His law. So we again find ourselves confronted by the theology of Luther, which Heim has inserted into Kant's system at that point where the great sage of Königsberg had left open a way for attempting escape, within the bounds of this world. Thus a critical philosophy has been constructed that really breathes "the spirit of the Old Testament" and that can possess a real significance as an introduction to a theocentric theology.

In the German idealism the expedient of a practical decision was also used as a means of direct approach to God, but it was not satisfied with such a solution. Reason wanted to penetrate to God in its own special domain. The speculative philosopher resolved the acknowledged separation between thinking and being into a monistic principle, and saw in the idea of the totality of the categories, which Kant had only required as a field in which experience would make its discoveries, the *ens realissimum* to which he is led by logical evidence. In Fichte's doctrine of science it appears as the identity of the relative and absolute ego; in Hegel as the infinite spirit arriving at a consciousness of itself in the finite spirit; in Schleiermacher as the common meeting point of the emotions in which the antitheses of reason and nature are surmounted. However, the further development of critical philosophy down to Vaihinger's illusionary pragmatism and the skeptical positivism of the Neo-Kantians shows that such a common point of union cannot be apodictically proved by philosophic deduction, that this twofold, separated development actually makes impossible the postulation of an absolute unity by a speculative solution, that rests on such an obvious logical leap. To make it clear Heim uses this comparison: Because Hagar is thirsty we cannot predict the existence of nearby wells; because trapped miners anxiously tap on the fallen rocks that separate them from the outside world it does not follow that they are being sought. In every assumed certainty of this sort the wish may be father to the thought. It by no means follows that there is an actual reality behind the pressing necessity of our thoughts. We have only to apply this self-manufactured solution of dialectics to such a central, practical question as the explanation of the wretchedness of sin and at once every awakened conscience, that understands its accountability for its own guiltiness, feels that every soothing, rational explanation of sin is an unjustified, presumptuous extravagance, a dangerous self-delusion, that has simply been spun out of some brain that was seeking a pleasant excuse. Such a reversal of dialectics could only come from God and could never be in some reconciling point of union devised by man.

In the same way the journeyings on the road to wisdom fail to reach the goal. As in the intoxicated prayer of mysticism, so here the spirit of man in its mental chase after an all-embracing unity meets the cherubim at God's threshold, who recalls to us our separation from God. God remains the hidden God and so our thoughts about Him and the world remain in darkness. Human reason and wisdom can only be aided as and when God gives Himself, when God of His own accord illuminates us with the brightness of His Spirit. So even the apotheosis of Promethean philosophy forces men to the recognition of the necessity of an objective revelation of God in history.

In the religious address of Kierkegaard on the theme: "The edifying aspects of the thought that we are always unjust before God," he remarks: "Is it not apparent that men will endure anything rather than admit their fault?" Nothing is harder in fact for man than to travel the *via negationis,* the road of the "removal of religious and moral false work" (Karl Barth). In the stubborn pride of his "I will do it all myself," he prefers to think that there is an ascending development, through innumerable reincarnations, rather than to turn from such aspirations to self-abasement. He would rather enlighten the darkness of his understanding with the feeble light that comes from the most intense introspection, than to accept the light of God as a gift. He would rather benumb his faculties with the ceaseless, feverish intoxication of erotic or mystical excitement so as not to have to see the death sentence that hangs over him. At any cost he wants to pay the price himself, to attain justification through sanctification, reconciliation through merits, salvation through soaring aspirations, the knowledge of God through the removal of limitations "by his own reason and strength!" And yet on each of these roads the honest man comes at last to those final limitations that turn the pride of the heart into despair. Infra-worldly as well as super-mundane mystical aspirations have never met with lasting success but have always terminated in insipid, barren emptiness; the will continually desires new bondage when it ought to be free and happy in its service; the titanic efforts of the intellect only plunge it into new contradictions.

Because a feeling of self-importance, that transforms its distress, always remains in the penitence of our own self-condemnation, God has disclosed His judgment on the world in the Cross of Jesus so as to crush us utterly and completely by the judgment it reveals. Here He shows the world what it would never have fully realized by itself, the end of its own wisdom and willfulness and the judgment of God on both. Legalistic Pharisees who boasted of their place with God, zealous scribes who desired to be a light to those walking in darkness (Rom. 2:17-20), intellectual Sadducees, politically clever rulers who possessed a quite up-to-date wisdom, enthusiastic disciples, eager crowds of pilgrims who riot in the pious emotions of the rich ritual of the great holy days, they all—this truly imposing multitude of the representatives of zealous seekers after holiness—they all despise, hate and put to death the Servant of God, because He did not bring them clever ideas, flattering praise or intoxicating power, but in its place condemning, redeeming, divine love. By their actions they all reveal the bankruptcy of humanity whose most intensified piety accomplishes nothing more than the derision and rejection of God in God's name. Here indeed, to use the language of the Formula of Concord, that is such a terrific blow in the face of all Thomistic and Tridentine weakenings of the bitter fact, is displayed "intima corruptio totius naturae et omnium virium imprimis vero superiorum et principalium animae facultatum in mente, intellectu, corde et voluntate."[12] Here in the execution of Jesus all the destructive corruption of the egotistic will comes to light in its unadorned nakedness as it reveals itself as a coarse or refined, as an individual or collective egoism, but always nicely adorned by itself or by others with plausible insignia to cover its nakedness. Now it is the priest at Bethel, Zion, Rome or elsewhere who speaks of the honor of God and the salvation of men, when he means the influence of his personality and the power of his Church. Now it is the party leader or the head of some sect who talks about the good of the whole nation and with ill-concealed vanity would offer his light for its illumination. How often in these quarters when the talk is of "practical Christianity" and of "work for the Kingdom of God," the motives

[12] *Sol. Decl.*, p. 576, 11, Müller ed., 1890.

turn out to be impure, the root diseased and the reputation undeserved.

So in the shadows of Good Friday the roads of salvation lead to
the final station of that mountain they seek to surmount, where there
is written: *perfecta cognitio sui ipsius*—the recognition of the sinfulness of all our ways. The Cross of Christ forces us to turn about.
It is true that we can still defy even this crucifixion sermon of God,
which speaks so much more convincingly than any personal message
of conscience; we can continue in our previous course, trying to bring
an imaginary satisfaction to God and a false quietness to our restless
heart. Even here we can again try to escape the accusing reality of
hard facts by submerging ourselves in some last mysterious unity. But
in this way we only pile up new guilt, become more and more involved in rebellion against God, Who, in the death of Jesus Christ,
has spoken His final judgment on every human attempt at self-salvation. We must abandon the intoxication of an apotheosis. The twenty-
fifth chapter of Job has spoken the final word: "How then can man be
justified with God? or how can he be clean that is born of a woman?
Behold even to the moon and it shineth not; yea the stars are not pure
in His sight. How much less man . . ." On the ruins of a perished
glory humbled man learns to seek the word of the Gospel.

CHAPTER III

Man's Justification before God through the Word of Forgiveness

EVERY magnitude, whether of spiritual or of heroic sort is worn down to one level by the ceaselessly flowing stream of time, and its importance becomes only relative. Great leaders who have sprung from the productive soil of their own race and culture may be able to interpret and disclose the soul of their homeland in living speech but to other races and times their achievements seem alien and are readily misunderstood. If we are ready to follow Otto Spengler in this particular, even the greatest creations of the western spirit will in time become unintelligible; they will be regarded with wonder by subsequent generations as the expression of an incomprehensible, utterly different spiritual outlook. When, under the terrifying influence of this πάντα ῥεῖ we come upon the person of Jesus we are involuntarily compelled to pause. Time that elsewhere "devours, as the rust consumes the iron" has no effect on Him. It seems that He is raised above the stream of time. Ever new, ever manifesting the same power and life, He draws the thoughts of men to Himself with a mysterious mighty power. No one is able to ignore Him. Even those who relentlessly persecuted Him are a proof that He was the cause for the hidden restlessness of their hearts. But far greater than the antagonism He aroused was the reverence and admiration He received as men tried to include Him in their own systems of power and wisdom. It is true that this gain was dearly paid for, because in these adaptations of Him to their own standards men distorted and dishonored the image of Christ. Any one who is familiar with the historical research on the Life of Jesus, or any one who has examined the almost illimitable number of old and new pictures of Jesus (whether in art or in literature) must be overwhelmed with pain and displeasure when he sees how greatly the New Testament account has continually been changed and disregarded by the intrusion of the author's or painter's own personality.

We will leave out of consideration the coarsest and crudest views that have been fully refuted by calm, objective science; the popular glorification of His Aryan racial purity; the accusation of epileptic hysteria and pathological conditions, which fit in so badly with Jesus' physical and mental soundness. But besides these there are the widely recognized and accepted attempts to interpret Him and glorify Him as the outstanding leader of His own movement of religious uplift. In the classification of the three inner-dynamic ways of salvation, He is regarded, because of His religious genius, as the hero and the classic example of religion, Who towers above all other *homines religiosi* like the highest peak of a mountain chain. The man who refuses to give up his virtuosity in the spheres of moralism, mysticism and esoteric gnosticism has turned Jesus into an image "like unto himself."

As the rigorous, exalted "teacher" in the Socratic sense, in the role of a *novus legislator*, He gives the individual a catechism of ethical precepts by whose fulfillment we can attain to the sphere of divinity. In this sense the Enlightenment, English moral philosophy, Deism, Free Masonry, Tolstoy's principles for the reformation of life, even Islamism have always recognized Him and have sung His praise. In connection with the conditions existing among the masses Kalthoff and Kautsky (under the influence of D. F. Strauss and Renan) have carried on propaganda for the morality of Jesus as a revolutionary social program and as a movement for a proletarian redemption of the world. Above all the "mystical" natures, artists and ascetics have tried to claim Jesus for themselves. The poets have admired the plastic power of His speech, the artistic construction of the parables. Others have glorified Him as a gifted master of the art of life, as the possessor of occult spiritual powers, as the "first scientist who has demonstrated the power of spirit over matter." World-weary dualists, satiated with the earth and what it has to offer, laud Him, a supposed member of the Essenian party, as their confederate. To meditating suppliants He appears as "a man distinguished by the absolute power of His religious consciousness." Spiritualistic sectarians appeal to Him as the prototype of fanatical enthusiasm. Closely connected with this is the conception of Jesus as the herald of speculative wisdom. Like the dying and reviving gods of Babylon, Phoenicia, Phrygia and Egypt (Tammuz, Marduk, Adonis, Attis, Osiris) His life illustrates the ancient Mandaic-Iranian nature myths of the conflict between light and darkness, between matter and spirit: the Asiatic mystery and redemption teaching which was united in Paul with Hellenistic thought in an exalted syncretism. Men are still repeating the procedure of Alexander Severus. They place the image of Christ along side of that of Apollonius of Tyana, beside Socrates, the divine seer Orpheus, and the whole multitude of ancient demigods. In the historic development of the Church the spiritistic Kyrios and sacramental mysteries find a place in Eastern theology, which in its dogma and cultus teaches and adores the λόγος τῆς ἐνσαρκέσεως, Who permeates mortal nature with divine power.

The attempt has even been made to prove the unique greatness of Jesus through this assumed manifoldness of His revelation. The unbounded facility for absorption and adaptation is supposed to prove the universality and the "complete and exalted value" of Christianity. But such talk is only the betrayal of Jesus with a kiss. Whosoever has nothing more than that to say must finally surrender His absoluteness because when it comes to the attributes that have been mentioned other religions of the less degraded sort can rival them. The ethics of an Epictetus and Marcus Aurelius, of Julian the Apostate and particularly the rabbinical ethics of later Judaism as it is found in the Talmud have high standards that are quite worthy of being ideals for the most earnest striving after moral perfection. The heart of the mystic beats as fervently in India and Persia as it did in the charming saints of the Middle Ages. Zoroaster and Laotse offer the Gnostic seeking after wisdom more completely developed cosmogonies than those of the evangelists. So it is quite in line with the various views we have been discussing when the explanation is given that though Jesus may be a particularly bright medium for transmitting the light of the divine Logos, though He may be particularly adapted to be a purifying guide of souls, the contact with God and the communion with God is by no means restricted to Him on that account. The divine

Light is indeed manifested at all times and in all places, and only the various degrees of sanctity make it permissible to establish various grades in the history of religions, as has been attempted time and again, from their various viewpoints, by Herder, Hegel, Max Müller, Siebeck, von Pfleiderer, Troeltsch, Rudolf Otto and Heiler.

All these explanations of the Gospel as the result of an inner evolution forget one thing, namely, that Jesus grew up within Judaism and so on a "sharply anti-mystical soil," where no one had the audacity to attempt to find God or to enjoy Him in the depths of his own soul, or to unite himself with the Cosmos through reflection. Prophets and psalmists, those "servitors in the service of God," whose words the growing Child heard and learned in the synagogue of Nazareth, were no mystics, no teachers of a secret *sapientia* whose taste (*sapere*) should bring the soul to God.[1] In its services the congregation was always reminded of Moses who, because of the divine wisdom that had been forced on him, in faith forsook the riches of Egypt and chose to share the reproach of his fathers and brethren. (Heb. 11:23-27.) The prophetic messages of Isaiah and Amos attacked all efforts to reach God through some sort of religious technique, through ecstasy or magic. Even the belief in ethical merits, the expectation of salvation through the keeping of the Law, had been largely shattered among the devout by the teachings of the penitential psalms and through God's judgments as they had been manifested in the history of the nation. In place of the crisis in other religions, that caused men to turn to mysticism and Gnosticism, we have the Messianic eschatology of Judaism; we find incarnation not apotheosis; the hope of God's appearance on the earth and the consequent removal of enmity and the establishment of a real communion with Him.

How then does Jesus differ fundamentally from all others who have been founders of some form of religion? He does not give directions for the purification of the soul like those which in all mystery religions are accounted the indispensable condition for any communion with divinity; He does not point men to the creative springs within His own soul that through them he might find the satisfaction of devo-

[1] It is no mere accident that in all ages the Old Testament has always been violently attacked or else allegorically interpreted by the Gnostics.

tion; He does not make wisdom and virtue conditions of His fellowship. Just the opposite is true. Without regard to any moral attainments, spiritual fervor or intellectual wisdom He "receives sinners and eats with them." His attitude towards the fallen world and towards those still in the bondage and servitude of sin is one of unconditional compassion and to them He preaches the word of pardon that He offers to the world with the power of a divine omnipotence.

Outside of Judaism such a message was largely incomprehensible. Where sin is regarded only as weakness or as a relative defect that could always be overcome and atoned for by an active exercise of self-discipline and by the merit of good deeds, the word of forgiveness can only mean the declaration of the rational truth of God's graciousness, which is evident even to pure reason, or else the pleasant and comforting assurance that God was not so very particular about the required exertions—a pleasant mitigation that necessarily ends in moral laxity.[2] In the Old Testament piety, the attitude is a different one. Here men are sure that if every sin is an affront to God's majesty and a mocking of His holy will, then forgiveness can neither be taken for granted nor be acquired. Only a single way of salvation still lies open, a way that man himself does not control, namely, when God Himself through a paradoxical, free εὐδοκία which cannot be forced nor set in motion by any human means, decides to overlook and pardon sin, and so, by His act, makes communion possible! The statement to a palsied Israelite, "Son be of good cheer, thy sins are forgiven thee," could only be the words of a blasphemer—or the words of God Himself. In Israel the proclamation of the remission of guilt could never mean that the fear of God is only a fancy springing from an unwholesome, unhealthy exaggeration of the fears of conscience, which needs only to be overcome to enable man to live with free assurance in the gracious light of divine love. This religious fallacy has been once for all excluded and forbidden in the Bible by the terrible seriousness of its warnings concerning judgment, as they are found in the messages of the great prophets and in the eschatological discourses of Jesus.

[2] For this reason the parable of the prodigal son is safe on Israelitic soil from the misuse of the liberals who take refuge in the graciousness of God, which they regard as a matter of course, and whose existence Jesus simply reveals.

When Jesus brings forgiveness unconditionally He can only do so because He knows that He has come from the One Who is the source of the free decree of love and that He is in unity with Him; because He knows that He is indeed the coming Messiah, in Whom God anew approaches the humanity that has become estranged from His will. The miracle of His presence is the pledge that God has taken pity on the world. He has not constituted Himself the Reconciler but God has appointed Him. His word of the absolution is fully established on His absolute knowledge of His own mission; a consciousness of which even the Synoptic Gospels are fully aware. From the certainty that God, the living Lord of history, will create something absolutely new through His life and death in the world, comes the absoluteness of His claim by which He constrains both the individual and the whole world to make a decision concerning Himself, a decision that involves eternal consequences. With this consciousness of a mission that includes heaven and earth He bears the offense of His humiliation to the very end, and so abolishes all the standards of this present perishing aeon. The piercing "But I say unto you" of His discourses, the power of His miracles of healing as He conquers the demons, sickness and death, are alike pledges of divine reconciliation, as well as the eschatological assurance that the kingdom which has been established by His presence shall finally fill the whole earth. Bearing the burden and wretchedness of the sin of all mankind, He travels, in obedient love (St. John 4:34; Rom. 5:19; Phil. 2:8; Heb. 5:8), the way to the Cross, there to reveal to men God's judgment on mankind through the judgment that men pronounce on Him, and by His death discloses the justice of God, the injustice of man. He Who has been faithful unto death by conquering death rises out of the power of death with a glorified corporeal nature and has been made the κύριος by God (Acts 2:36); the promise of a perpetual Easter that has been given by God to His reconciled creation.

So we see clearly the profound contrast between Jesus' message and His works, and all other founders of religions. He makes the claim that as the Reconciler mediating between God and man, He is the turning point of the ages. He is not content to be one among many doors that lead to the Father's house, or one way among a number of possible roads, but He calls Himself "the door," "the way" that alone leads to true communion with God (St. John 10:7; 14:6). He is the only bridge on which man can cross the abyss of sin that separates him from God. He is the foundation that alone supports our tottering existence. This is in fact so unique, so overwhelming, so obnoxious, that we must either believe it or else be offended by it. Even for faith there often come times when the absolutely unconditional character of this bond threatens to become an offense; when it has to wrestle with the temptation of thinking that this might all be an illusion. But whether we adoringly believe in His plenary power to remit sins, or blaspheme it as insanity, much has been gained when we once clearly see that here are two opposite worlds of which it is necessary to choose one or the other because they have nothing whatsoever in common. On the one side are the unhistorical religions of salvation, whose founders are only significant as mystagogues and which, on that account, are tolerant and animated by a moral pragmatism and optimism. On the other side is the Gospel, whose founder not only obligates us to His teachings but also to the historical facts of His Incarnation, Crucifixion and Resurrection; Who makes His demands unconditionally; Who dashes us to the ground by the way in which He unmasks the supposed holiness of man, but Who also bestows perfect communion with God, through His pardon-bringing presence, to those who accept Him in faith. We can make this contrast between the Gospel and non-Christian efforts to attain salvation and sanctification still clearer if we include the messages of the Apostles in our comparison. We have already indicated the fact that wherever they went in the course of their missionary journeys they found themselves surrounded by a spiritual world that was filled with an extraordinary desire for deification. As Jews their opinions had been moulded in their youth by the moral strictness and zeal for the Law that was shown by great teachers like Hillel, Schammai and Gamaliel. Amid the filth of the modern cities of that day they saw the Stoic and Neopythagorean schools striving after divine purification through ascetic self-development. Wandering preachers of moral philosophy, at their sides, preached a new ethical reform and in Rome the ambition of the Caesars for universal domination was acclaimed as a means of saving the world. Innumerable cults by means of an exalted or refined stimulation of the emotions, by inflaming the erotic impulses as well as through purifying consecrations and rites were supposed to impart supernatural powers and a mystical deification. An elaborate mythology—dualistic in the Persian cult of Mithra, monistic in the Alexandrine school of wisdom, satisfied the urge for supersensuous knowledge and even made its appearance in the Judean homeland. The messengers of Jesus continually came into contact with these ecstatic possibilities. Nor did they treat them altogether with contempt. They saw in them, at least in their more exalted form, a manifestation of the longing and seeking of man's soul for its lost home, a pitiful striving and seeking after the unknown God (Acts 17), Who had never let mankind slip completely out of His reach, Who had given it this restlessness of heart and had filled it with the desire to come from shadowy appearances and delusions to full certainty and real communion with Him. One thing the Apostles understood clearly, that such homesickness and longing after God cannot find contentment through the heart itself, because it is in itself deceitful and desperately wicked (Jer. 17:9), and is continually being tossed back and forth between presumption and despair. So they had no intention of rivalling by their message that whole multitude of emotional mystagogues or the teachers of ethics and wisdom. What gave them the right, the courage and gladness of heart to go into all the world and pour out their lives, like a living libation, was the certainty that they were bringing something absolutely new, a εὐαγγέλιον with which no other message could be compared and which alone could bring peace to the deepest longings of mankind. With the grammatical forms that refer to actual occurrences (the indicative and aorist participles) they proclaim the marvel of a communion that has been established with God through reconciliation. What men have not been able to reach through any spiritual art or by their own wisdom and dexterity God has made possible by His sovereign intervention and has given it to all the world, and furthermore has done so while we were yet "dead in sins" (Eph. 2:5), quite independently of our spiritual condition, to say nothing of our cooperation. The "just dies for the unjust" and God Himself established a new rela-

tionship in Christ that is always and everywhere valid (Rom. 5:18 *seq.*;
I Peter 3:18). In this historic revelation of God in Christ, in the
historic fact of the Cross and Resurrection by which sin is judged
and vanquished in a real transaction, lies the certainty of their communion with God that the original messengers possessed, and this is
the source of their joy in carrying out their mission. Christ is more
to St. Paul than a mere symbol of a truth that is valid in itself.
Jesus is not simply like Osiris, a timeless myth that served in the
history of human thought to depict the coming of "life and death,"
but through the real historic fact of His death and through His
victory over the "principalities and powers of this world" He actually produces an entirely new situation through which judgment
is changed into salvation. The repeated νυνὶ δέ, the ἐφάπαξ of the
Epistles[3] is the clear proof that for the Apostles Christ is not merely
a universal truth manifested in historic form but that He is a *nudum
factum* which brings about a sharply defined transition from "once"
to "now," from the past to the present, and which gives a new turn
to the whole course of time and history in this eon. Between a theology
grounded on the facts of salvation and one that is founded on latent
truths that are superior to the events of history yawns an abyss that
we should never attempt to bridge by any sort of dialectic.

Paul brought this contrast between his message and all the categories of the systems of self-salvation into the sharpest and most con-
cise formulation in the dictum, the "justification of the ungodly" (Rom.
4:5).[4] It is true that this formulation that became of such significance,
the declaratory use of the word δικαιοῦν in the New Testament was
first used by St. Paul. The word had been furnished him by the Jewish
teaching of justification, which, however, understood it as an analytical
judgment of righteousness, that would be made at the last judgment
on the basis of demonstrated accomplishments. St. Paul retained the
declaratory meaning of the word, only for him the revelation of the

---

[3] Rom. 3:21; 6:22; 7:6; 8:1; I Cor. 15:20; Eph. 2:13; Col. 1:22, 26; Heb. 7:27;
7:12; 10:10.

[4] The quotation immediately following, from Ps. 32:1-2, shows the strictly imputative
character of this passage. The meaning of δικαιοῦν as a purely judicial statement of divine
grace is further confirmed by passages like Rom. 3:20, 24; 4:3 *seq.*; Gal. 2:16; 3:11.
Cf. also H. Cramer, *Die paulinische Rechtfertigungslehre*, pp. 45, 333, Gütersloh, 1899.

Lord which he had experienced, the basis of the absolving judgment of God, no longer lay in his own righteousness but wholly in the free determination of God's love outside the Law and beyond it. With the help of a judicial form of speech he produced a classic, perfect, sharply defined statement for this unique action of Jesus, Who, in the name of God, received as friends sinners who were enemies of God. It is impossible, on this account, to accuse St. Paul of debasing the Gospel through the introduction of rabbinical theology. Above all he is no Hellenistic syncretist. His doctrine of justification, the very center of all his theology, is solely a wonderfully clear confession of the gospel of the love of God for sinners. We might say it is a crystallized dogmatic recognition of the truth that the essence of Christianity is incarnation and not apotheosis.

What does this statement of the justification of the sinner, which is so fundamental to the message of Jesus and the Apostles, mean for the wide world of human strivings after holiness that we have passed in review? It is quite clear that the Gospel means its end—the end of all such bold, confident, proud aspirations. The very Word of God that imparts forgiveness tells of man's inability to help himself. God's very act of revealing Himself is a denial of our ability to penetrate to His hidden nature by our own creative efforts. Through the preaching of the covering over of sin He uncovers the burden of our guilt. As He grants forgiveness He makes us conscious of how deeply we have injured Him by our rebellion. The divine necessity of the Incarnation is the proclamation of human godlessness. When the Holy One of God has been crucified as a blasphemer by the pious leaders of a pious people the fact is blazoned forth that our holiness is still a blasphemy of God.

But the same word that has taken away the ground from under our feet, that shatters all our efforts and thrusts us down into poverty and emptiness, also includes in itself our complete salvation. The word that kills also makes alive. For this saving reality of Christ as the "absolute" salvation established by God does not simply convict us of the helplessness of all human effort. Just because this reality, which comes to us as an eternal gift, is completely unrestricted (*absoluta*), fully independent of the comparative strength of our occasional fitness, wisdom or emotions, it has that immovable, unconditional certainty and sustaining power. So long as the certainty of God and of our salvation depends in any way on what we have to furnish, so long man remains subject to the unstable, barometric changes of his subjective conditions. It is just the weak conscience that is in continual torment, wondering whether its ethical efforts are sufficient; whether love and fear (*contritio*) have been enkindled purely and strongly enough; whether the intellectual impulses (*motus rationalis creaturae ad deum, amor intellectualis*) are directed on the right way. True it is a "nullification" in the sense that we must cease to depend proudly on our own holiness, but it is also to an infinitely greater degree a "nullification" of the burden, the uncertainty, the disquietude that is continually being encountered on every road of self-salvation. The Word that places our works under condemnation removes the condemnation that rests on our works. God takes from us an imaginary certainty to give us complete certainty through His own "image" (Heb. 1:3). He takes away the merits by which in our presumptuous efforts we strive to draw near to Him, merits that can never truly justify, to establish a new relationship of perfect communion through His justification.

The Church did not guard the message of justification as carefully as she should have. The momentous dissolution and disintegration of that truth began very early and has continued to the present day as human activities and demonstrable experiences are mingled with the Gospel of the forgiveness of sins. Instead of the final, complete promise of God, that requires no supplementing, there is again substituted a gradual transformation reached by an habitual infusion of righteousness. Whether this infusion be of a sacramental, mystical or spiritualistic sort, in every case in the place of God's pardoning word, which establishes a new relationship, there is substituted a dynamic process by which our certainty of the possession of an unshakable basis of justification is again lost. In this connection we can place side by side Thomas and Osiander, Schwenkfeld and Weigel, Schleiermacher and the leaders of the "Christengemeinschaft." All too easily this view results in the accommodating idea of a meritoriousness that by the consequences of its teaching must of necessity completely destroy the *gratis justificari propter Christum.*

Even Martin Luther in his monastic life travelled the road of sacramental purification of the soul and of obligatory eucharistic offerings. When his awakened conscience had failed to find relief in the means of grace that the Church was offering he turned to the Bible in his bitter extremity and found there the solid rock of an unconditional divine promise of grace on which he could rest securely. Since the days of the Apostles no one had understood so fully as did he the uniqueness of the Gospel and its utter unlikeness to any form of synergism. In his conflicts Luther did not have to deal with an opposition from without, like St. Paul and St. John, who had to contend with the confident πράττειν of the strict legalistic Jew and the labored αἴσθησις and γνῶσις of the Greek sage. The medieval Church as well as the sectarians attributed a glorious part in the realization of human salvation to Christ. But in spite of that the Reformer breaks with the current sholastic teaching concerning justification and likewise combats the teachings of the fanatics concerning salvation because a grace whose efficacy is in any wise conditioned by human participation cannot assure him of real certainty. Augustine's *"Gratia vero nisi gratis est, gratia non est,"* has again come to life. What does the cumulative effect of an *inhabitatio essentialis* amount to, or what is the value of any self-augmenting mystic-meditative infusion of grace compared with the unbounded assurance of God's favor (*favor dei*) that comes to sinners in unrestricted mercy and enters into communion with them independently of all subjective presuppositions or preparations?

The teaching of a *justitia forensis,* as it was formulated by the reformers in many clear-cut theological statements, is nothing more than the Pauline position of a sincere thankful confession of Jesus Christ, Who sat down with the publicans and Who, as the Good Shepherd, by the offering of His own life had set out to seek and to save the lost. Neo-Protestant theology with its tendency to impressionism rejected such language. It no longer understood that all these "scholastic dogmatic formulas" were actually intended as a forcible expression of the paradoxical and realistic character of the Gospel that proclaims a reconciliation of heaven and earth which cannot be logically deduced nor ethically produced. It is worth our while to let the rich variety of these statements of reformation days pass in review. With continual new variations, that were splendidly stated by means of that classic medium, the Latin tongue, evangelical faith sought to confess the absolutely free and perfect action of God, because it was sure that just in these transcendental dealings with men the unconditional divine assurance of salvation became a certainty. So the gift of God is described[5] as *misericordia, benevolentia, vera et firma conciliatio, reconciliatio, acceptatio, adoptio in numerum filiorum dei, inscriptio in librum vitae.* Forgiveness is called—attention should be given to every word—*justificatio impii*; it takes place *extra hominem in foro coeli*; it is a *promissio gratuitae remissionis peccatorum propter Christum*, an *imputatio justitiae Christi.* The *justitia* produced by God is called *passiva, aliena, imputata, externa, extra nos posita;* it is the imputation of an *aliena sanctitas*; it is an *absolvere, salvare, non imputare peccata*, a *gratis justificari*,[6] *justum reputari seu pronuntiari.* Since the decree of justification is an *actus dei extra hominem*, a removal of the sentence and a promise of new righteousness, the characteristics of this operation of grace are: *certitudo, aeternitas, infallibilitas, perfectio*, qualities that require no addition or augmentation.[7]

The same objective clearness is found not only in these "dry" confessions but in the church hymns of that period as well. If the congregations had not accepted this teaching with such clear understanding and manifest sympathy poets and singers like Paul Speratus, Nicholas Decius, John Olearius, Paul Flemming and Paul Gerhardt, who all so simply and yet so clearly described the righteousness of faith, would never have come out of their midst. There is perhaps no interpretation of the *gratis propter Christum*, not even a theological one, that has such clarity and profundity as that found in the words of the hymn by the former monk and later preacher at Stettin:

[5] *Cf. Apology of the Augs. Conf.*, 108:112; 148:245; 94:43; 172:35; 139:184 *seq.*; 117:47; 226:19; 138:172; 145:219; 150:260.

[6] The *gratis* takes from the *justificare* the possibility of the Roman misunderstanding, which might result from its derivation and which is far less likely to occur in the corresponding Greek word than in the Latin.

[7] H. Schmidt, *Die Dogmatik der evangelisch-lutherische Kirche*, p. 342, Erlangen, 1853, English trans. by Hay and Jacobs, Phila., 1889 and subsequently.

> All glory be to God on high,
>   Who hath our race befriended!
> To us no harm shall now come nigh,
>   The strife at last is ended;
> God showeth His good will to men,
> And peace shall reign on earth again;
>   O thank Him for His goodness.

or:

> Our sins Thou bearest for us,
> Else had despair reigned o'er us.

Or we might recall the forensic strain in Flemming's hymn: "In allen meinen Taten," which reminds us of the beginning of Psalm 32. It is not a mere accident that these examples were taken from such different sources as a Trinity, a Passion and a traveller's hymn. We can see how, in the evangelical consciousness, the salvation that is produced by God alone and that consists in reconciliation with God, is not limited to the theological ideas of a small group of hymns that would be collected under the rubric, "Justification and the State of Grace," but that it permeates the whole round of Christian thinking. The certainty of possessing peace with God is a sort of *cantus firmus* that is confidently re-echoed everywhere, here in the hymns of the high festivals and of holy ministrations, on through those dealing with faith and life to the hope of the resurrection of the dead, which finds its basis in this justifying act of God.

In the faith of the reformers and quite in harmony with the testimony of Scripture, the pardoning act of God is ethically established, as it is bound to the *propter Christum*, the chief emphasis lying on Christ's obedient humiliation and crucifixion. Luther's hymns, letters, sermons, books and confessions all alike testify very clearly to the idea of Christ's meritoriousness that fills all his theology. The Large and Small Catechisms confess the *satisfactio vicaria* as emphatically as the Smalkald Articles. The great hymn on justification ("Nun freut euch, lieben Christen gmein") of 1523, praises the mercy of God that "cost Him the best He had" (v. 4). The words in Isaiah

53 concerning the suffering servant of Jehovah were "particularly dear" to him; his preaching had its beginning and ending in the "dependence on the extraneous work that was done by Christ."

The Gospel in its essence is a *gratia praeveniens*, that is a powerful intervention by God that springs from His unearned compassion, that is not bound by our habitual subjective state, that has not arisen from our attempts to save ourselves but rather in spite of them, and that, anticipating our needs, offers help to the helpless. Nothing shows more clearly the uniqueness and absoluteness of this gift, in contrast to all other religious efforts and promises, than an investigation of the evangelical understanding of Baptism, Communion, predestination and missions. In these four groups the New Testament conception of the exclusive working of God in effecting our salvation finds its expression in a unique and unmistakable way.

The rite of baptism is common to all religions. The idea of baptism as a single, never repeated act that brings a grace of eternal validity is first found in Christianity. In the apparently insignificant distinction between a single act and a number of repetitions of the same act, between baptism and baptisms (διάφοροι βαπτισμοί Heb. 9:10) the whole contrast between Christian and non-Christian faith and salvation is revealed. The Levite anxious to preserve ritual purity, the mystic devoted to his rites and ascetic practices, the spiritualizing intellectual who seeks enlightenment, and the Anabaptist who builds on acts of obedience, all alike in their hunger after purification will gladly submit to the *performance* of the act of baptism in the hope that thus, by means of a magical infusion and an habitual increase of power, the evil desires of nature may be destroyed more completely, and that they may be given more of divine power. The water of Baptism is classed as one of a great number of sacred means of purification, whose repeated use and continual multiplication are the most eloquent expression of the fact that man himself considers them weak and inadequate. (Hebrews 9.)

New Testament Baptism, on the other hand, shows its utter difference in two ways. It is a single, unrepeated act of grace, that is referred to as a completed action by the use of the aorist (ἀπελούσασθε

I Cor. 6:11), that needs neither increase nor repetition and that is a turning point of eternal significance by which the whole of life is divided into a "before" and "after." (I Cor. 6:11; Col. 2:13; Titus 3:3-5; Gal. 3:23 *seq.*) In his first letter St. Paul salutes the Church at Corinth as those "called to be saints" in spite of the fact that further on he pictures them as being anything but spotless and pure. Nevertheless he can address them in this fashion because they have been baptized and so, as those who have been justified by Christ, have been delivered from the bondage of guilt in God's sight and have been brought into a wholly new relationship to Him. If the Baptism of John had already pointed to the forgiveness of sins with prophetic symbolism (St. Mark 1:4), so the Baptism in the name of Jesus is the actual establishment by the Spirit of God of a new state of righteousness, the real pledge to the sinner of God's unconditional favor. Undoubtedly the Baptism into Christ (Gal. 3:27; Rom. 6:3; Col. 2:11 *seq.*) at the same time produces an emerging into the inmost, personal life communion with the risen Lord, Who thus becomes a present active possession, but we dare never forget that it is a union with One Who has been exalted and glorified, Who bears in His Body the wounds of the Cross, in Whom is life and Who has given that life for us on the Cross. It is our justification on the basis of the death of Christ and not the renewal that is begun in the Sacrament, that gives the act of Baptism its character of irrevocable validity. For this reason Jesus bade us find cause for rejoicing not because the spirits were subject to us, but because our names were written in heaven. (St. Luke 10:20.)

Because Baptism expresses the transcendental and synthetic character of the Gospel in such an impressive way the reformers always laid the greatest emphasis on the right understanding of this Sacrament. When Luther comes to speak of the *baptizatus sum* his heart overflows, for here he finds, as nowhere else, the most essential character of the Gospel most perfectly expressed. Here grace is offered that is nothing but grace because it is absolutely free; that is not conditioned by any scheme of cooperation between man and God; that is not limited by any ethical conditions in man. Here God's faithfulness is proclaimed, a faithfulness that is not destroyed by our faithlessness.[8] Here, and most of all in infant baptism, the Gospel shows itself in its purity and completely different character, in its uniqueness as it is contrasted with all other religions; as the *reditus ad baptismum* (the "creeping back to our Baptism") it becomes the infallible touchstone that proves whether the faith of justification has really been understood or not. One of the high points in the Large Catechism (which is the only one of the Confessions that has a special and extensive section on the baptism of children) is the "song of songs" concerning Baptism (part IV), that purely divine promise that is so great, both as a judgment and as a gift of grace, that "every Christian has enough in Baptism to learn and to practise all his life" (Müller, 491, 41). The second part of the book on the *Babylonian Captivity* begins with a prayer of thanksgiving because God has at least preserved "this Sacrament of the little ones" uncorrupted in the Church and that it has not been defiled by "the wisdom of the flesh." It is true that the lamentation immediately follows that here too men have known how to nullify the great gift, because, according to Roman teaching, they held that sin brings with it the loss of the grace of baptism. Therefore (according to a statement of Jeremiah) a "second plank" is necessary "after the shipwreck" for the maintenance of salvation, namely the sacrament of penance. In this way man is again led away from the consolation and strength of Baptism to the "countless burdens" of human requirements. In opposition to such ideas the Reformer warns against the "dangerous error" which imagines that through sin "the strength of Baptism was destroyed and the ship had become leaky. Baptism remains a strong, indestructible ship that is never broken apart into separate planks." For this reason Luther, quite in contrast to our own days, continued till his very end to preach unweariedly about Baptism, that it was not "to be regarded with contempt . . . but to be held in high honor and to be

---

[8] *Cf.* W. Ed. 34, I, p. 97, 18 *seq.* Large Catechism 497, 77: "Therefore our baptism abides for ever; and even though some one should fall from it and sin, we nevertheless always have access thereto (*regressus patet*)." Further, 494, 56, 57: Establishing the right of infant baptism: "Because we know that God does not lie: I and my neighbor, and in short all men, may err and deceive, but the Word of God cannot err." And: 495, 60: *"neque enim id, quod semel Deus ordinavit et locutus est, ab hominibus mutari sinit aut perverti."*

praised as our highest and most precious treasure." (*Sermon on Baptism preached at Dessen,* March 28, 1540.) Nor does he forget to impress on his hearers that the efficacy of this gift is never bound, as the Donatists imagined, by the subjective faith of its ministrant but depends alone on the sure and certain words of institution and on the command of the "invisible Baptizer."

Therefore a church that calls itself evangelical will hold fast to the objective validity of Baptism even when it has been administered by a representative of the *theologia irregenitorum* and not by a "converted" pastor. As opposed to anabaptism it will hold fast to the true character of Baptism which makes its repetition impossible, and it will maintain infant baptism in opposition to the Baptists, because both have distorted the character of Baptism as a pure gift from God. So in the care of souls and in the counsels given to those who confess their sins, troubled consciences are not to be consoled by referring them to a conversion that once took place or by the accumulation of a great number of completed penances, but by teaching the penitent to "creep back to Baptism." Any national Church that thus cherishes and offers Baptism, provided of course that it insists on an evangelical education, is incomparably truer to the *articulis stantis et cadentis ecclesiae* than some "little flock of the elect" that rails at the great ecclesiastical babel. We can endure such abuse with equanimity and in the cheerful faith that we are only bringing to the brethren the love which, according to God's promise and command, is to be brought to all the world.

Just as in Baptism, so in the Communion, the contrast between the universal religious use of such a celebration and the specific use of it in the New Testament is clearly recognizable. It is particularly when we turn from the "mystical atmosphere of antiquity" to the accounts of the institution given by St. Paul and the Synoptists that we notice the difference. The Greek and oriental cults had their holy meals where they sought to bring about a union with the divine by means of food and drink received in the temple. The researches of Mommsen and particularly of Reitzenstein have given us pictures of the many cults of the ancient world, where organized associations, with stipulated dues, assembled regularly under the direction of a *magister coenarum* for common meals (δεῖπνα κυριακά), in which they regarded themselves as the guests of divinity. These cultus meals as a φάρμακον τῆς ἀθανασίας were to plant in the soul the seeds of immortality and to produce a substantial increase and intensification of divine power. The common characteristics of these sacrificial meals are: (1) The attention is completely directed towards the transformation of the individual and the illumination of each one's own nature. (2) Their effectiveness remains the same without regard as to who the participant may be, whether it is a travelling merchant, a philosopher or a soldier who is the guest at the mysteries of Elusis, of Attis or Osiris. So the affirmation has been made that "this ancient belief in the union with divinity by means of eating and drinking" was shared by Paul; that he adopted such ideas from his Hellenistic congregations and transmitted them to the primitive Church. When we survey the history of the development of the doctrine concerning the communion as we find it in Ignatius, Justin, Origen and Augustine, its course seems rather to substantiate this syncretistic explanation. "Greek conceptions have settled down like a thick cloud" around the Communion (A. Schlatter). The oriental idea of the food for the soul that is the "medicine of immortality" is the predominant one, as a spiritual dynamic in Origen, as a realistic dynamic in the Apologists. But these striking parallels between Alexandrine mysticism and philosophy and early Christian theology are only a demonstration of the amazingly rapid and extensive spread of a tendency towards a syncretistic Hellenizing of the Gospel. The determination of the actual original Biblical view concerning the Communion is to be found in the Synoptic Gospels and I Corinthians 11. But here we find a twofold, clear-cut distinction that separates them from the sacramentals of the mystical cults.

For them the chief value of the Sacrament does not consist in a potential infusion but it is a divinely instituted gift of reconciliation, for the forgiveness of sins. (περί St. Matt. 26:28; ὑπὲρ πολλῶν St. Mark 14:24 and St. Luke 22:20.) And furthermore no individual salvation in a spiritistic sense is promised, no submerging into undifferentiated, pure being, but the Lord's Supper bears a decided eschatological character, that means it is a look forward towards a new world of

living communion with the exalted Lord, a communion that He gives
to the congregation by anticipation, which is apprehended by faith
and for whose complete realization He commands them ever to wait
and hope "till He come" (I Cor 11:26). The whole transaction first
becomes clear when we recall the time of its institution, a detail which
in this case is of tremendous importance. It was the Passover when
Jesus instituted the Sacrament, the day that above all others speaks
of satisfaction and of the parousia. Here again the truth has avenged
itself on those scholars whose investigations have attempted to find
a solution of this difficult question and at the same time have discredited its Old Testament origins. The sign of the Passover is the
atoning blood because of which the judgment of God "passed over"
His people. Under the same sign God had covenant with the delivered people through Moses on the Holy Mount. For this reason the
Israelitic father of the house, like a priest, celebrated the Passover as
a sacrificial and covenant meal. But the hammer blows of the prophet's
messages of judgment, which did not even spare the splendor of the
sacrificial cultus, produced a profound consternation and awakened
the realization that outward holiness, "food and drink," offerings
and sacrifices "could not make him that did the service perfect, as
pertaining to the conscience." Above the unsatisfied needs of the
Old Testament, which God had laid on the hearts and consciences of
His servants, resounds the prophetic promise of a "new covenant,"
which is "not according to the covenant that I made with their fathers
in the day that I took them by the hand to bring them out of the
land of Egypt, which my covenant they brake." The indication of
the new era will be found in the fact that the law is written in the
heart and mind, that "I will forgive their iniquity and I will remember their sin no more." After the proclamation of this message
of grace Israel knew in believing hope that when the Messiah came
the promised new covenant would be realized. Jesus connects Himself with this expectation. He knows that He has been sent from
above to establish this new relationship with humanity.[9] He knows
that as the old covenant became valid and effective only by a bloody
yielding to death, so the new covenant can be realized only if He, as

[9] Exodus 12:27; 24:8; Heb. 9; Jer. 31:31-34; St. Luke 22:20; I Cor. 11:23 *seq.*

both the Victim and the Priest, gives Himself to God as a sacrifice of reconciliation. (διαθήκη ἐν τῷ αἵματί μου.) As the One Who actually suffers death (and does not merely talk spectacularly about the symbolism of death) He gives His congregation not merely a sign of His death but the actual result of His death, which is the reconciliation of the world and the gift of a new relationship of peace with God that has been purchased through sacrifice.

The thought of the slain Easter Lamb is inextricably united with the celebration of the Passover (I Cor. 5:7). But for the Israelite an intensive feeling of renunciation was also associated with the recollections of this time. "And thus shall ye eat it; with your loins girded, your shoes on your feet, and your staff in your hand; and ye shall eat it in haste, it is the Lord's passover" (Exodus 12:11). It is the attitude of those who have broken with the affirmations of the old world, who are standing between the times, who are ready, like Abraham, to be led out into another country that God will show them. This is the *theologia viatorum*. This earnest, eschatological phase of the Passover pervades the Last Supper with increased intensity. The contrast to Neoplatonic cults and mystics cannot be stressed too emphatically. They are filled with the joyous, happy enjoyment of the divinity that is "close at hand," while here the terror of death and the agonies of Jesus, Who knows that only through the woes (ὠδῖνες) of a catastrophe, in which He is to be the sacrifice, can the old form of the world be overcome and only so can God's new world come to birth. So the Supper is for Him a Messianic anticipation (St. Mark 14:25; St. Luke 22:18) which He celebrates with His congregation and in which He permits them to look forward into the future, to the time of that "kingdom," when the world reconciled with God shall receive the gift anew from His hand. Of course primitive Christianity (like the ancient mystery cults) celebrated the Eucharist as a life communion with the heavenly Lord (I Cor. 10:16 *seq.*), however this was not a mystical uniting and absorption into the fullness of divinity but a real communion with the "crucified Lord, Who at the end of days would return" to make the earth the place of His dominion (L. K. Schmidt). So the recollection of the institution at the time of the Passover serves to demonstrate the "anti-mystical" character of the

Sacrament in the New Testament. There the mysteries of apotheosis tell of an ascent of man, here we find the forgiveness of sins, a condescension of God and his dwelling with men.

The greatness and richness of Luther's teaching concerning the Communion are due to the fact that he most clearly preserved this central Biblical idea. It is true he did not have to contend with a theological tendency that tries to tone down the Incarnation to a mere cult of mystery. His conflict was against the trends of moralism and humanistic rationalism, that in the end, however, were the same old foes. In opposition to the Roman teaching of the sacrifice of the mass (*officium*), as a continually repeated offering by which reconciliation was effected, he preached the gift of the Altar (*beneficium*), as the "venerable testament of God," through which full forgiveness was given to the believer. In opposition to the teaching of the Reformed confessions that in the Communion the aspiring soul seeks a fellowship in heaven, he held fast to the presence in the Sacrament of the glorified Lord, Who here descends to the earth and deals with His congregation and communes with it as He will do at the Last Day.

Baptism and the Communion according to the Scriptural ideas of the Reformers are clear, plain pledges of the mercy of God, Who, without seeking any return, invites sinners to be His guests. On the other hand the doctrine of predestination as an expression of the granting of grace presents far greater mental difficulties and is much more easily misunderstood, but because it contains such an emphatic denial of every effort at self-sanctification and of all humanly devised forms of self-development, all of the great witnesses of the Gospel have invariably returned to it: St. Paul in his conflict with Jewish teachings concerning the Law and works of merit; Augustine in his struggles with Pelagian confidence in a well-disposed will; Luther in his battle with the ethical confidence and virtuousness of the great leader of the Humanists. This very controversy between Luther and Erasmus clearly reveals the profound religious value of the idea of election. The diatribe *de libero arbitrio* (of the Fall of 1524) is not pure moralism after the pattern of Confucianism. It is rather a Paulinism diluted by Platonism, in which Jesus appears as the ideal pattern of humanity, surpassing all the spiritual leaders of ancient philosophy. The model has been supplied by God and the man who would please God needs only to do his "little bit" (*perpusillum*) of imitating, with vigorous, lively, practical efforts, the example of that teacher, according to the best of his ability. Against this pleasant harmony of our relation to God Luther places the experience of the complete helplessness of the natural will, which unless it receives the regenerative gift of the Word and Spirit is unable to rise to God, to do His will or to stand in His presence.[10] That man does not recognize this wretchedness but imagines himself "free, happy, unbound, strong, healthy and living" is in itself the strongest proof that the foundation of his nature is nothing but pride and self-love. If this unfree will, that is so blind that it cannot perceive its own blindness, is saved in spite of that fact, such salvation can never be gained by human cooperation but only through God's purpose and power. But with this knowledge comes the absolute assurance and unconditional comfort that it is really God who has forgiven us and called us out of death to life.[11]

So Luther's teaching concerning predestination, as we can see even in the title of his great controversial writing of 1525, grew out of his opposition to Pelagianism, scholasticism and humanism. He was not satisfied, however, with the mere rejection of the freedom of the will. None of the formulations directed against this opinion were

[10] "If I lived and labored till the Last Day my conscience would never be certain and sure as to how much it would have to do to satisfy God. For no matter what works I might do on earth the doubt would remain in my conscience as to whether that was satisfying to God or whether He required something more, which has been the experience of all who have attempted to find righteousness in their own works, and as I have learned myself by my own injury. But since God has taken my salvation out of my free will and established it in His own free will and now promises that I shall receive it not through my life or labors but through His grace and mercy, I am secure and certain that He is faithful and will not receive me. And furthermore He is so strong and mighty that no devil nor adversity can cross Him or tear me out of His hands." *Concerning the Bondage of the Will*, German trans. of Fr. Gogarten, p. 334 *seq.*, Munich, 1924.

[11] *Preface to the Epistle of St. Paul to the Romans*, 1522. "In the 9th, 10th and 11th chapters he teaches us concerning the eternal providence of God which is the original source that determines who shall believe or not believe, who shall be delivered from sin and who not, so that it is taken completely out of our hands and placed completely in the hands of God. And this is most necessary. For we are so weak and uncertain that if it depended on ourselves none would ever be saved, the devil would overcome everyone. But God is certain and His providence cannot fail, nor can anyone restrain Him, and so we have hope in spite of all our sins." Er. Ed. 63, p. 134 *seq.*

severe enough in excluding all human arrogance, presumption and
false security. So with his purpose clearly in mind he gladly used the
doctrine of election as the one theological statement that completely
assured the honor of God and the utter humiliation of man. It was
helpful, in proving the nature of faith, which is not our work but
which comes to us as a gift from above. But because it was only an
indirect necessity that brought Luther to this position he retained both
the complete inner freedom, the theological mastery and the necessary
theological certainty to place the doctrine of election in the background
when it became necessary to do so, as in the controversies with the
fanatics. If rationalistic moralism deprived Christ of His honor by
claiming an active cooperation in the work of salvation, so fanaticism
robbed Christ of His power as it separated the Word and the Spirit
and denied the continuous, active, objective redemptive power of the
means of grace over men's consciences. In opposition to the fanaticism
that awaited a special illumination from above, as a result of the
election of the Spirit, he shows that God "is always honestly serious
in what He does through His Word and His Baptism. But because
the Reformer's life-long conflict was not merely with Carlstadt, Thos.
Münzer and their associates but also with the Roman teaching of
work-righteousness, there was no reason why he should surrender the
book of 1525. In the evening of his life, as he looked back over the
rich fruitage of the years, he still professed its teachings as emphatically as those of the Small Catechism.

The revived study in our day of the Reformation message has again
led us to a new and living understanding of the theological significance of the doctrine of predestination. The understanding of its various details is, of course, by no means unanimous. The strict Reformed
theology again confesses the *gemina praedestinatio* as a *donum per-
severantiae ad salutem* and as a *reprobatio ad malum*, a "damnation
of those who are not worthy"; in each case for the glory of God.
Here the sole activity of God in effecting salvation undoubtedly comes
to the most emphatic expression but at a theological cost that is far
too great. The moral sense of sin and of responsibility is of necessity
completely throttled by the single objective solution of supralapsarianism. The reality of the choice made by faith is destroyed when we

are taught that in the preaching of the Gospel we must distinguish a twofold call, an effective one (*seria*) for the elect and one that is only apparent (*caduca vocatio*) for the lost (Calvin).

The Reformed teaching of a double predestination receives a peculiar modification in the theology of Karl Barth. In place of two clearly distinguished numerical divisions we find here (based exclusively on Romans 11:32) the duality of two conditions.[12] Complete rejection through judgment and unconditional pardon continue, in unsolved contradiction, to apply to every one simultaneously, to the individual as well as to the Church. While the Bible (though not apparent to our eyes) separates faith and unbelief, obedience and disobedience with terrible earnestness, so that a sort of ontological, "metaphysical" truth is established that concerns two eternally related spheres and whose final solution can most likely be found in the ἀποκατάστασις ἀπάντων. However much Karl Barth himself has safeguarded this "static truth" through an intense activity of conscience, the danger still lies close at hand, as a keen critic has rightly pointed out[13] that such a universal truth must finally work out into moral ineffectiveness.[14]

In contrast to these two there is a third position, that of Lutheranism, which thankfully uses the idea of predestination as a confirmation of the faith of justification, without falling into the possible misconceptions we have just considered. In place of a divine decree of rejection the universality of Christ's grace (*promissio universalis*) is accounted the only cause of salvation, which is always and everywhere efficacious and which brings a guilty responsibility on those who despise it. In place of a universally valid truth of simultaneous states of judgment and grace, we must hold fast to a belief in eternal death (with the rejection of the idea of a final restoration, as a philosophical postulate) as well as to a belief in the eternal life of the redeemed.

---

[12] *Der Römerbrief* p. 334. 2nd Ed., Munich, 1922. M. Strauch, *Die Theol. K. Barths,* pp. 35-37, 2nd Ed., Munich.

[13] Ph. Bachmann, Der Römerbrief und Barths Auslegung desselben (on the basis of Rom. 9-11). *All. Ev. Luth. Kirchen Zeitung,* 59th year, nos. 19-21.

[14] K. Barth, *Der Römerbrief,* p. 215: Man "must always be most exalted and most abased, he must be Moses *and* Aaron, Paul *and* Saul, one illuminated by God *and* one in ignorance, prophet *and* Pharisee, priest *and* parson. . . . He is always both, the first as he is also at the same time the second." (Italics in the original.)

Baptism, Communion, the doctrine of predestination are all mighty witnesses to the evangelical teaching concerning the righteousness of faith. Man does not lay hold on God through sacrifice or cultus, through any wisdom or spiritual talents, but God Himself, by His gracious interference, has created the needed help and so receives sinners. If Christian faith would confess what has here been theologically stated, in a purely objective way, through external actions it can do so most unmistakably by a living interest in missions. No charitable work of Inner Missions, no social sacrifice, no matter how necessary and blessed it may be, can so clearly demonstrate this fact to others as a living interest in the preaching of the Gospel to the heathen. That does not say that the work of Inner Missions, wherever it is properly understood and carried out, not as a mere Christian humanitarian philosophy, but as an expression of the fact and love of the Gospel, cannot be just as practical an expression of the revealed truths of Christianity as Foreign Missions. On the basis of Jesus' claim to universal supremacy, which is particularly affirmed by Foreign Missions and which is incorporated in its very existence, Inner Mission can likewise use the statement of Schlatter: "To carry on missions while the Church at home is being destroyed, to look on idly while Europe is being paganized and Africa Christianized is folly." The work of missions is the expression of a certainty in the absolute character of a gift that is given in revelation, that is given to the whole world. It is the primary work and the most essential expression of the life of a congregation that actually possesses the grace of Baptism and the faith of justification. It is not an appendage, a fad or a painful duty of faith but the free, inevitable expression of a conscience that really *lives* in the consciousness of divine reconciliation.

It is true that Mohammedanism and Buddhism are also missionary religions but in neither of them is the idea of missions something that is central as it is in the Gospels, or something that has grown organically out of the teachings and work of their founders. Mohammedanism has received the impulse for its monotheistic propaganda from Judaism and Christianity. How purely external this missionary spirit is becomes apparent in the sensuous and forcible nature of their propaganda. Similarly the greatest of the pre-Christian religions of salvation, Buddhism, did not originally develop the idea of a world mission out of its own teachings, for every pantheistic religion, of necessity, regards the toleration of other faiths as something to be taken for granted. The hard facts of history that demand a decision *pro* or *con* have no place here. Buddha (*cir.* 550-480 B.C.) did not give the group of ascetics who had become his disciples any commission to go to the ends of the earth. Only at a much later date and under the influence of political considerations did its expansion in Asia begin. How utterly different is the situation in the Old and New Testaments! Whosoever has once clearly grasped the Biblical idea of missions will cease talking about the "Indian" derivation of the "Baptismal commission."

The characteristic feature of the Biblical message is the way that men here talk about the world-wide and universally valid nature of the relation between God and man. In contrast to the narrow Jewish particularism with its feeling of national and religious superiority, the psalmists, prophets (Jonah!) and apostles testify not only to the universality of human guilt but they also tell of the promise and the reality of a world-embracing divine action that shall become known to all nations as the source of their salvation. The Prophet during the exile looks forward to the work of the Messiah, "the servant of the Lord," Who has been appointed by the Lord of all the earth. "It is a light thing that thou shouldst be my servant to raise up the tribes of Jacob and to restore the preserved of Israel: I will also give thee for a light to the Gentiles, that thou mayest be my salvation unto the ends of the earth." The hymns of divine service exhort them to say to the heathen: "The Lord reigneth and hath prepared his kingdom throughout the world, that it should not be moved." (Luther's translation.)[15] It is true that during the later days of Judaism the Old Testament expectation of salvation was in frequent danger of being corrupted by earthly and political motives. Jesus and the witnesses who followed Him in the obedience of the faith were the first to overcome the barriers of nationality, society

[15] Is. 49:6; 12:4; Psalm 96:10 and 3; 105:1; 18:50; 57:10; 68:32. "Princes shall come out of Egypt: Ethiopia shall soon stretch out her hands unto God." In addition, Isaiah 19:18-25.

and sex, and to proclaim to the whole world the dearly bought love of God, which reaches without distinction to all humanity sharing a common burden of guilt and which is offered to all alike. Jesus' immediate activity was indeed limited to the "lost sheep of the house of Israel" (St. Matt. 10:5 *seq.*) but the Sage in the Temple already greets Him as the Salvation which God has "prepared before the face of all people, a light to lighten the Gentiles" (St. Luke 2:27, 32). The prediction that was spoken concerning the child was fulfilled in the work of Jesus. In His personal activity He obeyed the law of God, Who always accomplishes the greatest results through faithful activity within the smallest bounds. But His message is world embracing, born out of the consciousness of His Messianic mission, that makes Him the consummation and salvation of the entire cosmos. The world-inclusive commission of Jesus to His Church is a certain fact, aside from all debates concerning the literary genuineness of the "missionary commission." Because those who were only Israelites "according to the flesh," in their unbelief despised Jesus' claims of authority: "Many shall come from the east and from the west" to sit down at meat with the patriarchs. After the people to whom sonship had been given had mocked and dishonored the messengers of the eternal King, the Kingdom of God was taken from them and given to the Gentiles who would bring forth the fruits thereof. Before the new creation of God is revealed "this Gospel of the Kingdom shall be preached in all the world for a witness unto all nations."

Here in the question of a missionary obligation, there is a complete organic unity between Jesus and Paul.[16] The message of the Apostle because it is concerned with the *gift* of God is likewise of necessity a missionary message. What has been revealed to the world in Christ for its salvation had for ages been concealed in the counsels of God, but now the "mystery" was revealed, namely "that the Gentiles should be fellow heirs, and of the same body, and partakers of his promise in Christ by the Gospel" (Eph. 3:1-12; 1:4; I Cor. 2:7). For this reason the Apostle contends with equally uncompromising determination against the narrow Jewish pride in their election and against the cos-

[16] St. Matt 28:18-20; 24:14; 8:10-12; 21:31-43; St. Mark 16:15; 13:10; St. Luke 24:26 *seq.*; 14:21 *seq.*

mopolitan syncretism of Hellenistic-oriental heathenism, because in either case the gift of reconciliation which has been given to the world and which alone can effect its salvation is trifled with and despised. If the guilt of humanity has been overcome and blotted out by an all-sufficient act of love in Christ, then the universal obligation of bringing it to all the world rests on the Church, which is His Body. Justification and a world-wide mission are interchangeable ideas for St. Paul. Whosoever has been "saved by grace" (Ephesians 2:5) has surrendered any particular claim of his own on God that might give him a preference over others and he recognizes and admits and helps to impart this saving purpose of God to *all* men.[17]

The Gospel blocks the way of all self-devised efforts to gain holiness. It deprives man of his self-confidence and of the idea that he has a rightful claim on God. Instead it proclaims through Word and Sacrament a free promise of grace which has been made available by an act of God, and which gives fully and completely (*rotunde et universaliter*) what could never be attained by self-devised methods. But if God is indeed the exclusive donor then the attainment of salvation cannot be accomplished through meritorious deeds or any other self-originated exertion on man's part, but only by faith which acknowledges the work of God in our hearts. So *fides* and not a *propria justitia* is the only ὄργανον ληπτικόν through which the communion with God can be established. The old Protestant theology described the marks of faith as *notitia, assensus, fiducia*. This definition is questionable in so far as it seems to separate faith itself into three actions. However when we understand the words in their original sense as a description of the logical sequence of an action that is essentially a unity, then this very order and relationship is a perfect definition of the nature of faith.

The description of faith as *notitia* makes it clear that the certainty of salvation is bound up with an historical event. Faith does not find its actual foundation in itself. It receives its content and power from a divinely produced happening *extra nos*. It depends on a synthetic,

[17] Rom. 1:14-16; 3:29 *seq.*; 5:18; 8:32; 10:12 *seq.*; 11:32; 16:26; I Cor. 15:22; II Cor. 5:15; Col. 1:20; I Tim. 2:4; 4:10; II Tim. 4:2-6; Titus 2:11; Acts 17:31; 26:16 *seq.*

freely made decree of God's will, that cannot be based on any moral or rational grounds. Thus the anthropocentric presumption that conceives of God and human receptivity as functional, correlative factors, that inexorably require each other like opposite poles, is put aside. The conception of *notitia* excludes the idea that God is somehow bound by the receptivity of man; it snatches him out of the sphere of subjective productivity and places him face to face with the objective, divinely established reality of Christ.

But this *notitia* remains *otiose, qualis est etiam in diabolis* (Apol. 130:128), a *falsa, mortua, vana,* if a subjective assent (*assensus*) and a "heartfelt trust" (*fiducia*) be not added. Without the acceptance of the offered grace and the surrender of our personality, faith becomes only an assent to an authoritative church teaching (*fides implicita*), a *cognitio historica* or the acknowledgment of a universal rational truth that can be objectively contemplated and understood by men, angels and devils without any serious upsetting of the central ego. If the *personal* confession of the power and guilt of sin be missing; if the thankful, eager, conscious reception of the forgiveness of sins be lacking faith will remain nothing but a "mere empty, idle, dormant idea concerning Christ."

But where the word of reconciliation has been heard, understood and accepted with implicit trust there follows an immediate, personal, spiritual certainty that pervades and dominates man's entire nature, his heart, spirit, understanding and all his powers, both conscious and unconscious. Just as the sinful burden of unbelief clearly cripples the joy and brightness of all of man's willing, feeling and thinking, so the remission of guilt and the imputed righteousness that is granted to faith affects his whole existence and manifests itself in all his actions. Faith itself, because it is divinely produced, remains a completely intangible reality, psychic in its nature, imperceptible to the senses, incomprehensible to mere reason, a miracle of creation that has come out of eternity; that has not come out of the treasures of man's own heart but is the result of the working of God's grace. It is only the transcendental power of faith that touches our ideas and feelings; its experiences are never the end in itself but they point to something beyond our subjective control, to something that has been done for us and to us. Even our emotions are affected by this subjective certainty of an objective fact; for the emotions have a part in the gifts the Creator bestows on His creatures. In this fallen world they are not more diabolical than the understanding and will that have fallen away from God. In the new creation of God's redemptive eternity they are not less valuable and important than the act of volition and understanding that is demanded by the Gospel. No theological tendency can afford to ignore what Schlatter has written in his anthropology. Two very different things are concerned when we talk of "God in our own heart," feeling an unbounded confidence about "God's dwelling in men," and when we speak of the possibility of experiencing the act of justification. For the faith that becomes active in apprehension and emotion does not desire to derive its strength from itself. The "experience" of grace does not put itself confidently into God's place, as it were the actual donor and mediator of grace; it does not depend on its own consciousness; it does not come out of some wellspring of the inner nature. It is something purely receptive, begotten and animated by the reality of the divine gift that is apprehended by faith. For this reason we cannot offhand reject the idea of an "experience" of faith as something suspicious and unevangelical, so long as the subjective experience we possess does not come out of some "little paradise of our own domain of the soul," but is begotten and mediated through an objective word of revelation that is accepted by faith. Beyond question the nature and greatness of the faith of justification is particularly shown by the way it continually learns to hold fast more and more firmly to the promise of forgiveness that was made to it without regard to the emotions and even in spite of them, but neither does it feel ashamed of the hours when the feeling of being accepted by God brought a conscious peace to the heart. It thanks God for the gift of such a helpful demonstration of the power of faith and from it derives an "unemotional" faith whose calm support is so needed for the hours of temptation.

It is well known how the Barthian theology has placed the words "occurrence, experience" on the Index and this taboo does not, as has so often been supposed, involve a mere dispute concerning more or less skillfully chosen expressions but it involves the question of the permissibility of the thing itself. In its pre-war development this theology, which was itself an offspring of Schleiermacher's subjective-religious ideas (Barth), suspects the hidden duplicity of man (who wants to enjoy visibly the development of his own powers) in connection with every attempt to describe the inner, spiritual consciousness. Faith is the surrender of all tangible perception, of all seeing. Faith is opposed to all experience and to all appearance. It is not difficult to bring many proofs for this position from the great wealth of Luther's writings.[18] From 1522 on Luther had to meet the opposition of the fanatics who, in the way we have described above, made man's subjective experience the actual foundation of his certainty concerning God. Here, where it was no longer the promise of an historically revealed grace, but the vividness of an experience that produced and established the soul's confidence concerning its relation to God, there was certainly reason enough for warning men against the overemphasis of the human factor. But whenever the reformers have in mind scholastic metaphysics, the dead authoritative teaching of a priesthood or a humanistic "historicism," they emphasize, in addition to the purely objective teaching of Scripture, the necessity of an inner confirmation and they do it with a magnificent carelessness of expression (that is positively painful for the critical theologian).[19]

[18] For example, the beautiful passage found in G. Buchwald's *"Predigten d. M. Luthers,"* I, 392: "If you are not ready to believe that the Word is worth more than all you see or feel, then reason has blinded faith. So the resurrection of the dead is something that must be believed. I do not feel the resurrection of Christ but the Word affirms it. I feel sin but the Word says that it is forgiven to those who believe. I see that Christians die like other men, but the Word tells me that they shall rise again. So we must not be guided by our own feelings but by the Word." *Sermon on I Cor. 15:1 seq., March 31, 1529.*

[19] "I have passed through so much *experientias divinitatis* of Christ that I must say: *Aut nullus est Deus aut ille est.* So that, God willing, I need not fear that I might become an Epicurean. I know full well what the name of Jesus has done to me. . . ." W. Ed., Tischreden, I, No. 583. Of the year 1533. *Ibid.* No. 518, p. 240, 5: "If God should take me away this hour or this morning I will leave this behind me, *quod Christum volo agnoscere pro domino, et hoc non solum facio ex scripture, sed etiam ex experientia, quid* the name of Christ has often helped me, *ubi nemo potuit juvare. Sic habeo pro me rem et verbo, experientiam et scripturam, et dedit mehi Deus utrunque* very largely *sed* it has also been made difficult for me *par tentationes*; which was good for me." *Ibid.* No. 448, p. 196, 26: "I have often found out by experience how the name of Christ helps, so that no one, God willing, shall shake my assurance. The same *experientia* makes me certain about Scripture." An extensive collection of similar passages is to be found in L. Ihmels, *Die christliche Wahrheitsgewissheit und ihre Entstehung,* pp.

We can see from the undeniably twofold character of their statements how clearly they felt the logical difficulty involved in the question of "faith and experience"; one that they recognized so clearly
that they did not venture to dispose of it by the simple expedient of a
deletion of the one or the other by means of an "either, or." It is
determinative for this as well as for all of the following questions that
we keep clearly before us the fact that fallen man in this present age
can easily stray to the right or the left of the road marked out for
him by God. The situation is so grave because security from falling
into one abyss by no means brings with it the assurance that we will
not slip into the other. Whoever has understood this twofold danger
that confronts conscience knows that because of the fall we always
have to use *two* statements, for with one we cannot express to the full
our grievous estate as sinners. Traditional orthodoxy without the accompaniment of faith and the lively assurance that "He is my Lord"
is as bad as the religious emotionalism of the romanticists. The possession of true doctrine without the accompanying faith of the heart will
save us as little at the final judgment as the "pious self-consciousness"
that lacks the foundation of a divine promise.[20] Only *fides* in the in-

---

10-37, Leipzig, 1914. "It is not enough that you say Luther, Peter, Paul have said so
but you must experience Christ Himself in your own conscience and feel that it is
unquestionably God's Word, though all the world opposes it. As long as you do not
have this feeling you have certainly not experienced God's Word." "We will also en-
deavour to experience this in the heart as well."

Calvin no less emphatically stresses this requirement of a subjective experience of the
divine Word: "Many falsely rely on their Christian knowledge when they only know
how to talk glibly about the Gospel. Christ's teaching has to do with life and not merely
with the tongue, nor is it grasped only by the understanding and memory like other
sciences. We only appropriate it rightly when it fills the whole heart and strikes its
roots in the deepest soul. It is true that doctrine occupies the first place as it gives us
the knowledge of salvation, but it must penetrate into the heart and life and so become
a part of us that it does not remain unfruitful." "The chief part of faith is that we do
not simply, in an external way, assent to the promises of grace that the Lord makes to
us, but that we inwardly appropriate them and make them our own." "So it is necessary
to take into the heart what the intellect has comprehended, for we have by no means
appropriated God's Word by faith if we juggle it around in our heads. It must strike
root deep in the heart if it is to be an invincible bulwark against all temptation. . . .
It is much harder to fortify the soul with inner certainty than to fill the intellect with
knowledge." Quoted from Karl Müller, *Joh. Calvin, Unterricht in der christlichen Religion*, pp. 345 *seq.*, 290, 293, 303.

[20] H. Bezzel: "True doctrine does not help where life itself does not shine forth."
"A satisfied, assured orthodoxy, sure in the pulpit and proud at the altar is not enough."
"Everything I have not experienced, grasped, appreciated for myself will desert me in

divisible unity of *notitia, assensus, fiducia,* in the inextricable bond of
the *quae* and *qua creditur* has the promise of life.

We might describe the entire history of Protestant theology down
to our own times as a continued striving after the correct logical relation of objectivity and subjectivity.[21] There are two poles; on the one
side the well-meant but utterly impossible "theocentric" attempt of
orthodoxy to discuss God in a purely intellectual, descriptive manner,
on the basis of single *loci* that have been derived from Scripture or
the history of redemption, and on the other side the attempt of the
school of Schleiermacher to make the experiences of the inner life the
sole norm and rule for the doctrine of God. Between them lie the
many tendencies, now veering to the right, now to the left, whose rise
can be explained as an attempt, in each case, to correct the exaggerations of the opposite tendency. Schleiermacher himself, in spite of a
too liberal inclusion of subjective sources, still understood and tried to
hold fast to the inseparable relation between God and the experience
of faith. The theology of comparative religions, however, that was
constructed on his ideas, leads by way of Biedermann and Troeltsch
to a purely imminent conception of faith as an intuitive, artistic, cosmic
vitality, whereby contact with the absolute is attained through the contemplation of the historically developing spirit that is everywhere active
in history. The God Who reveals Himself and Who creates faith
through the Word and the Spirit has here disappeared in the unlimited
existence of a universal permeation of the world by God.

If this development of Schleiermacher's theology leads to a complete dissolution of the transcendence of God, so the other development passes by way of Frank, Hofmann, Bezzel, Kähler, Ihmels,
Schaeder to an exactly opposite position, to an intense emphasis of the
theocentric position. The Erlangen theology, still following in Schleiermacher's footsteps, begins with the facts of Christian consciousness
and Christian experience (which it would be a mistake to regard as
something constant) but behind this tangible personal experience it

---

the hour when all pretence vanishes and all hypocrisy fails." Quoted by J. Rupprecht,
H. Bezzel, als Theologe, pp. 279 seq., 270, Munich, 1925.
[21] From this viewpoint E. Schaeder has attempted to write the history of theology
from Schleiermacher to the present time. *Theozentrische Theologie, Eine Untersuchung
zur dogmatischen Prinzipienlehre.* Erster, geschichtlicher Teil, 3rd ed., Leipzig, 1925.

clearly perceives realities that belong to the sphere of revelation and not to the wealth of our human attainments. The further development of those we have just mentioned leads them more and more to an unconditional exaltation of the justifying personality of God, Who through His emancipating Word creates the living contact with Himself. The latest systematic works have again begun to understand and consider the inseparable connection between God and a saving faith as that was always clear in Luther's mind. Because "no one ever passes beyond the limits of subjectivity" (Ihmels) and, on the other hand, because no faith comes into existence without a recognition of the benefactions of Christ, the Church can only hold a "theology of Faith," in the strictest sense of the word, which does not express the relation of God and man by "static formulas," nor limits itself to the judgments of faith that are based on religious experiences, but which always brings anew the whole wealth of God's condescension to us and our participation therein through faith to its paradoxical expression.

Faith and God belong together (Large Catechism, 386). In the *sola fide* our personality is attached to God in a relation of utter dependence. Man no longer tries to bind God to his own self-consciousness; he knows himself wholly bound by God and so faith brings humility with it. He no longer seeks to exalt himself but holds fast to the judicial grace of the Cross, which sustains him in the life that is there begun, continued and ended. He does not ask about the result or the reward, he does not expect or count on a future sanctification, he does not boast of a future transformation in which he will no longer need the grace bestowed on the dying thief; he clings to the promises of God, Whose favor he regards as a greater good than any self-imagined and self-made righteousness.[22]

But where man in seeking after the Kingdom of God and His righteousness has forgotten and discarded all his own righteousness, the opportunity comes for God to work something new in him. It is a fundamental law of life that where guilt is there is also bondage. When sin accuses, Satan has his hold and his rights. But when there

---

[22] *Cf.* Luther: "maius est deo soli placere quam sanctum esse." *Luthers Vorlesung über den Römerbrief*, ed. J. Ficker, II, 269, Leipzig, 1923.

has been a judgment of grace and the indictment has been destroyed, there is deliverance and freedom from the power of the accuser. The righteous man who has broken with the *fiducia operum*, who desires nothing more than *vivere in nuda fiducia misericordiae dei*, is able, just because he has become a *humilis, ex fide vivere*. Because God in the act of justification continually rejects the old, natural ego and lets it suffer death, He makes it possible for faith to become a new "I," that is free to serve, because God has freed it from itself. It is never a characteristic of the teaching of pure grace that it produces a selfish, self-seeking piety, as has so often been asserted (Schlatter, Schaeder and Holl, for example). Where there is a real living faith produced by the Word, and not a mere intellectual orthodoxy, it is bound to result in edification. The ego that has been delivered from its pride no longer refuses the recognition and confession of a common guilt. When selfishness has died and love is released through the preaching of the Cross there is bound to be a growing desire to bring this message of reconciliation to the brethren and to share it with them. So the article concerning justification is indeed the *articulus stantis et cadentis* ECCLESIAE.

CHAPTER IV

Sanctification as the Work of God in the Life of the Justified Sinner

EVERY ethics is confronted by a double problem; the question of the *content* and that of the *energy* of moral action. There is the material problem: What shall we do? And there is the formal problem: How are the obligations that we recognize to be realized? The great characteristic of all autonomous ethical systems is that they are supported by a belief in the possibility of a rational understanding of morality and the subsequent possibility of realizing what has been so understood. So evolutionary utilitarianism, the ancient family and civic morality of China, the Socratic and Stoic doctrine of virtues all presuppose that both the recognition and the performance of duty are human possibilities. In Israel the feeling about this double question was a different one. Here in every action they felt the stress of the question as to what was required and how it was to be done. Without the revelation imparted by the Torah it is simply not possible to understand the will of God in our present condition of sinfulness. Whoever does not learn it and observe its precepts must fall into error. But even the Jew who is faithful to the Law experiences a disturbing crisis. In the first place no law ever fully covers all the details of the new situations that are continually arising in life. Even the carefully developed casuistic aids of a long tradition, the "rules of the elders," cannot remove the torment of uncertainty and bondage. And in the next place, the exalted, pure requirements of the divine demands produce an uneasy conscience, that suffers from the painful realization that it never quite fulfills all of God's demands. "The law worketh wrath." The twofold evasion that is accomplished either by an ethical optimism or through a limiting of the obligation, which is so popular elsewhere, is not resorted to here because of a feeling of holy fear. So in its place comes a closer clinging to the hope that a time will come when this whole age of the Law, with its lack of clearness and power will finally be annulled. Faith knows that when the Messiah comes something entirely new will be begun. The Christ will be the end of the Law. Streams of water will then be poured out on the thirsty and barren land. Through the sprinkling of forgiveness there will be a cleansing from all uncleanness and a new heart and a new spirit will then be given that will rejoice in doing right and in walking in the way of God's commandments.[1]

We find this idea again becoming very vivid in the preaching of St. John the Baptist. When the Messiah comes He will baptize them with the Holy Ghost (St. Matt. 3:11); Christ knows Himself (His own teaching puts that beyond any question) to be sent from above for the dissolution and termination of that age that served God only in the fear and compulsion of the Law. He calls to Himself those who are heavy laden with the burdens of the Law[2] and while He puts the sinners to shame with His holy majesty, in the end a still greater love triumphs. He breaks down the ramparts of satanic power and restores anew the regal lordship of God. But at the same time the great change in the program (if we may call it such) takes place, to which neither the nation nor the Sanhedrim could adapt itself, which even the Baptist and the disciples could not at first comprehend. The transition from the old to the new did not take place in a smooth, natural, organically continous manner; instead the change occasioned a terrible conflict in which two irreconcilable opponents had to contend for the victory. Jesus did not simply, according to Marcion's ideas, introduce the great, free "Father thought" in place of the gloomy "Old Testament conception of an avenging God," as reassuring modern descriptions like to picture His activity. Jesus knows the Holy Scriptures of His people and acknowledges them. For Him the wrath of God rests as a fearful reality upon this fallen world and it gives the powers of darkness the moral right to enslave the world. That the Law is not fulfilled, that the question concerning the way

---

[1] Rom. 10:2; Is. 44:3; Jer. 31:31-34; Ez. 36:25-27.
[2] Cf. Zahn's *Kommentar zum Neuen Testament*, I, p. 442. Also *Handbuch zum Neuen Testament* 4. Das Matthäusevangelium erklärt von E. Klostermann, p. 103, and A. Schlatter, *Der Evangelist Matthäus*, p. 385.

(Whither shall we go? What shall we do?) has become so obscured is the manifest expression of the rule of an ungodly domination that must be broken. So long as the works of the devil have not been overcome in a sacrificial conflict (I John 3:8; *cf.* Col. 1:13; 2:14 *seq.*; Eph. 4:8), so long as no one steps into the breach, who shall fulfill the law and carry the guilty burden of the cosmos, just so long the work of a new creation cannot begin. So He travels the earth in lowliness. From the Manger to the Cross His life is a holy protest against the fashion of the world as He finds it. In His words and deeds with masterful anticipation He testifies to the new reality, which cannot be actually realized till the victory has been determined and assured by His death and resurrection. Above the Cross, on which sin has shown its might by a final exhibition of unequaled power, there is written the still mightier legend of grace: "It is finished"; the statement that God Himself attested on Easter Day when Christ appeared to the believing band of disciples as their first born Brother, the second Adam, Who comes to them as the master and beginning of a new world.[3] Though God, whose measure of time transcends all human comprehension (II Peter 3:8) may reserve the time of history's termination to Himself; though the worldly mindedness of men through their doubt, contempt or hatred may bring many persecutions and sufferings to the elect (II Cor. 11; Acts 2; 7; 26; 28), the believing Church still sees behind the stage settings of this cosmos the Kingdom of God, that is even now present and active, and that only awaits its final, visible manifestation. In that victory, once gained at so great a price, conclusion and beginning were united. The curse of the Law has been overcome, peace has again been established with God and the power of God, the living source of a new morality has been made free for the members of the Body of Christ. Thanks to the one sacrifice there are both deliverance from guilt and strength and understanding for moral action.[4]

As impossible as it is for St. Paul to speak of spiritual effects, in the sense of the Hellenistic mysteries, without the assurance of their establishment on the "judicially satisfactory" transaction of the atonement, so impossible is it for him to keep silent concerning the activities

[3] Rom. 8:29; Phil. 2:9; I Cor. 15:45; Rev. 1:5.
[4] I Peter 3:18; Heb. 9:28; Gal. 3:13; Rom. 8:2; Eph. 2:10; 2:14 *seq.*; Rom. 5:1; Col. 1:20; I Cor. 4:20; Gal. 3:4; II Cor. 3:5; Phil. 4:13; Acts 16:7.

of the new world after the historic atoning act of God had gained an eternal righteousness for all the world. For this reason the disputes between the Apostle and his enthusiastic opponents in Corinth as well as those he waged with legalistic Jews in the Galatian congregations take on such a passionate tone. If a sufficient redemptive action has not actually taken place, then all spiritual gifts are vain before God, then the entire extremity of sin's misery must overwhelm all humanity without any hope of deliverance (I Cor. 15:15 seq.). But if "death has been swallowed up in victory" it is the worst kind of unbelief and disobedience to continue to torment one's self with the fulfilling of works according to the exactions of the Law, when there are such full paschal powers ready for faith to use in the free activity of love. (Gal. 5:6.) In each case the attitude is a sinful one whether it be that we talk about life without considering the atoning death or that we contemplate with eyes of human wisdom the submission of the Lord to death and the lowliness of His Church, without believing in the life concealed behind them, that has been manifested in power. The Jew whom the letter kills and the Greek who has become intoxicated by his own natural endowments both alike need the preaching of the Gospel which in the preaching of the Cross is the power of God unto salvation. (Rom. 1:16 seq.; I Cor. 1:18.)

How intimately the substitutionary act of atonement and the δύναμις θεοῦ are bound together in the minds of the Apostles by their mutual requirement of each other is evident in the frequent overlapping of the expressions "faith and life" with the corresponding correlatives "death and resurrection." Ecclesiastical tradition has accustomed us to the distinction that would lead us to seek our justification in Jesus' atoning sufferings and our renewal in His resurrection.[5] But we are also compelled to acknowledge the frequency with which the righteousness of faith is associated with the events of Easter Day in the New Testament, and how again our renewal is based on fellowship with the Cross,[6] a clear indication that the New Testament knows only of a life coming forth out of forgiveness, but that it also acknowl-

[5] That this view likewise has a real basis for its existence is seen in passages like Rom. 5:10; Phil. 3:8-11; Col. 3:1-4; Eph. 2:4-6; I Cor. 15:21-23; I John 1:7.

[6] a. Rom. 4:25; 10:9; Col. 2:13; I Cor. 15:17; I Peter 1:3-5. b. Rom. 5:18; II Cor. 4:10; 5:14; 6:4-10; Gal. 2:19; Col. 1:22; Heb. 9:14; I Peter 1:19.

edges that what springs from this origin is a real *life*. Without the image of the love that offered itself up, human love always remains a cold and earthy work, impure, yea, dead. In the example of an Abraham, however, we can see on the other side what great things faith can accomplish. He trusted in the promise that God was able to cause the dead to become alive, even in this world, and his faith received its answer. St. John the Baptist believes that God is able to raise up children from the stones. In the same way the New Testament Church is to believe that God can make alive those who were dead in sins (Eph. 2:1 and 5; Col. 2:13) and that the works of the flesh will be displaced by the fruits of the Spirit through the almighty power of Him Who brought purification from sin.

The risen Lord proves Himself the personal head of His members by the operation of the Spirit.[7] There could not be such a real reception of the Holy Ghost if Christ were not risen. Then the old dispensation with the full burden of its Law would still be resting on the world. The gift of the Spirit can never be attained by the works of the Law for they affect only the realm of the flesh (*Cf.* Gal. 3:2 with 5:4). It is impossible to gain it through the increase of natural powers or spiritual exaltation, or even to demand it on the basis of a certain affinity to God. The New Testament not only does not interchange spirit and flesh but not even "spirit and ψυχή," nor like the Stoa, spirit and νοῦς. The leading by a demon, a vital gift, numinous dread, poetic inspiration, cosmic vision, intensified thought, all belong to the sphere of human, not of divine energy.[8] All that is no more "spirit" in the New Testament sense than eternity is merely indefinitely prolonged time. As God's creation was produced out of nothing, as the incarnation of the Son is an unearned, a free gift of divine revelation, so the Spirit of God is the *totaliter aliter* of all human spirituality, a creation *ex nihilo* that does not spring from the depths of man's own

---

[7] Rom. 8:9; II Cor. 3:17; Gal. 4:6; Phil. 1:19.

[8] We could continue much farther with the enumeration of the various forces in "the domain of the spirits that are not the Holy Spirit" (K. Barth, *Vom Heiligen Geist, eine Pfingstbetrachtung, Zw. d. Zeiten,* IV, 4). Genius, magic, occult or suggestive powers, the subconscious, the sensation of cosmic life, the perception of "the mother," whether they have ennobling possibilities or include the danger of degradation, or even are united with man's spiritual powers as useful assistants, are never the πνεῦμα ἅγιον but remain nothing but more developed psychological talents.

inmost being but descends on him as a purely miraculous gift of divine grace. If, however, a new era has begun with the exaltation of Christ from the Cross to the right hand of the Father, then there must be even now a πνεῦμα ζωοποιοῦν (I Cor. 15:45) as a pledge (Eph. 1:4; II Cor. 1:22) of the redemption that has been begun and is pressing on to its completion. According to the Scripture the "Comforter" (masculine gender) does not exist merely as an idea of "impersonal power" but as a personal activity that is now teaching, counseling, convicting, strengthening and manifesting the work of God in men, galvanizing them into action and filling their hearts with love for their neighbor.[9] The triumphant notes of St. Paul's spirit-centered theology may surprise us who have forgotten how to trust in the active reality of the Spirit. Every practical likelihood of such a mighty spiritual experience may be lacking in our times; we may make a virtue of necessity; we may pillory such a possibility of spiritual possession as a mark of theological romanticism, but the astounding fact cannot be ignored that St. Paul knows, both in his own experience and in the life of the congregation, of a being "filled with all the fullness of God," Who "is able to do exceedingly abundantly above all that we ask or think, according to the power that worketh in us." He ventures to speak of the beginning of a transforming and renewing in the image of God, that is a present reality, and to talk about a passing from one glory to another glory that is a gift of God, Who is the Spirit. Because the Lord has made His servants strong, "fashioned for every good work," they can even *now* show forth the praises of His glory, as before they had only been examples of the nature of sin and death that reigned in the world.[10]

What formulations should systematic theology then make on the basis of these New Testament statements? Because of the common and united operation of the Cross and the Resurrection the answer must always be a twofold one: reconciliation *and* salvation; the blotting out of guilt *and* deliverance; a liberating judicial decree *and* the maintenance of God's regal power; amnesty *and* victory. Both phases can exist only as a unity; they dare never be divided into two in-

[9] St. John 14:18; 16:8 and 13; Rom. 5:5; 8:14; 15:30; I Cor. 2; Col. 1:8.
[10] Eph. 3:19 *seq.*; 1:11; II Cor. 3:18; Col. 3:10; Gal. 4:19; I Tim. 1:2; II Tim. 3:17; St. Matt. 5:16.

dependent actions, separated in time, let alone distinct from each other. As the One Who has taken away wrath, Christ is also the Savior from bondage and Lord over the powers of the abyss. The forgiveness of sins carries with it the power of resurrection. *Remissio est regeneratio. Consolatio est nova et spiritualis vita (Apology Augs. Conf.* 98:62); the *justificari* is a *justum reputari et effici* in one, and both are grounded on the *certa promissio Dei*. The saving faith of the Gospel always receives both justification *and* sanctification. It always stands in the presence of the God "Who forgiveth all thy sins and healeth all thy diseases." Each is completely inseparable from the other. If Christ be *otiosus* He could not have been the true atonement, but if He is really the atoning substitute He cannot be anything else than *actuosissimus*. The humiliating fact that "without Him we can do nothing" is just as true as the proud statement that "We can do all things through him who strengtheneth us." To say the one without the other is blasphemous. To speak of "life" without remembering the death of the Lord is just as diabolical as to preach His death without witnessing to His life. What God hath joined together man shall not put asunder.

The history of Protestant theology contains a number of subtle or gross errors on either side. There was always danger of emphasizing either side at the expense of the other, or even of ignoring the one or the other completely instead of teaching both with equal emphasis.

Whoever makes the doctrine of the Spirit the central question and at the same time carries on a polemic against soteriological dogma should clearly understand how quickly the Church is led by such a theology to the brink of a pragmatic or enthusiastic abyss. Whoever reproaches the "old judicial dogma of salvation" too vehemently as being "a one-sided fourth of the Gospel" not only is not able to make any but the emptiest explanation of Baptism but in the teaching of sanctification is bound to run off on the wrong track. On the other hand, when the Gospel is preached merely as a forensic judgment that has been pronounced on us without regard to the "positive will that sanctifies us" then, to use Schlatter's words, "Christianity becomes inclined to verge into a meditation on sinfulness that evaporates into a comfortable feeling" that sin is no longer harmful because it is forgiven and so the Gospel finally becomes "sentimentalized." We have to admit that there was a forensic narrowing of the doctrine among the orthodox theologians. The same danger still appears occasionally today but, on the whole, those who warn us against it have no right to make such criticisms because their desire for progress has caused them to lose to a large degree all idea of the greatness and correctness of the Biblical teaching concerning the Atonement. Those who advocate an "undogmatic Christianity" are, of course, utterly incompetent to raise any objection.

How hard it is to keep within bounds in this matter we can see in the case of the great Württemberg theologians and preachers, men like Joh. T. Beck, Is. Aug. Dorner, Joh. Chr. Blumhardt. They all had the advantage of possessing a vital appreciation of the organic unity of religion and morality in Christianity. As a result they escaped the Melanchthonian danger of narrowing the doctrine of justification to a mere judicial process. But in their emphasis on the active realization of the divine righteousness they permitted themselves to be led into a questionable and blundering polemic against the emphasis on "pure doctrine," which could easily be misunderstood and which in fact was misused, as, for example, in the cases of Johannes Müller and Heinrich Lhotzky. After all it is really the "message," the teaching of the *aliena justitia*, that daily establishes and supports our relation to God. This is the source from which the much desired "activity" alone can spring. But the light should not find fault with the sun, the fruit with the root of the tree, nor "life" with "teaching." Naturally in all of these protests there is a justifiable nucleus which becomes apparent when we consider the development of the opposing positions in the history of theology. It is of fundamental importance, however, that we remember that any theology that is merely corrective of some other school of thought is always bad and in the end suffers from the same defect it attributes to its opponents, only on the opposite side. We have to break with both sides, with all disparagement of the soteriological confessions as well as with all misrepresentations of "Christian activity." Because every earthly testimony of the Spirit of God that we receive remains bound to the saving act of Christ on the Cross all statements that do not have a lasting relation to this act are only illusions. So forgiveness can never be merely a sort of entrance to renewal through which we pass only to leave it behind us. Because our "allegiance to God" in the "fullness of power" always depends completely on "God's favor to us" this must ever be the alpha and omega of all Christian preaching. Only the one who always holds fast to the repentance produced by the Cross, who always remains under the shadow of the gateway of justification (*justificatio cotidie iterata*) can be a recipient of the gift of the Holy Ghost.[11] Where, however, the *Christus pro nobis* is preached and believed on without reservation, the new creation is established (II Cor. 5:17). It is as the Church of the *Word* that Christianity has the promise that it shall become the Church of *deeds*. The *Credo remissionem peccatorum* is in the same article of the Creed as the *credo in spiritum sanctum et vivificantem*. The risen Christ with the wounds of the Cross and not the Docetic Christ, nor even the Christ of the Pieta, belongs on the altar of an evangelical Church.[12]

---

[11] *Haec poenitentia in Christianis durat usque ad mortem, Sm.* Art. 318, 40. *Christus non desinit esse mediator, postquam renovati sumus. Apol.* III, 41.

[12] EXCURSUS. All the possible relations of justification and the *nova vita* came to the fore at least once during the period of the Reformation. Historically they can be designated by the names of Melanchthon, Luther, Osiander and the Council of Trent. What was produced later was partly a deepening, partly a mixture of the previous positions in which unfortunately the most successful solution, that of Luther, was the least considered.

In the *Apology* Melanchthon still kept the *justum pronuntiari et effici* side by side, though the emphasis is already completely on the pardoning judicial decree of God. Following the publication of the *Commentary on Romans*, 1532, however, the word justification more and more loses its double meaning and at last receives an exclusively forensic character. It is possible to claim that without this sharpened, "disjunctive" form the *sola fide* teaching could not have been maintained in the difficult crises of the following centuries. The rejection of every amalgamation not only brought to Melanchthon's theology the advantage of greater systematic clarity but it also really avowed in a unique way the central thought of the Reformation, "Thy lovingkindness is better than life" (Ps. 63:4). On occasion there are men to whom we must be grateful for having always said only one thing. This gratitude is owing to Melanchthon in the second half of the sixteenth century and to Herman Cramer and his spiritual kindred in the nineteenth century. It is true that both Holl (*Rechtfertigungslehre des Protestantismus*, pp. 18 *seq.*) and Hirsch (*Die Theologie des A. Osiander*, pp. 267 *seq.*) have pointed out, not without reason, that this separation of justification and renewal in the course of time brought with it questionable consequences. The preservation of the "article of a standing or falling Church" in the school of Melanchthonian orthodoxy cost something, for in time wide circles sought to satisfy their desire for renovation, that was here inadequately presented, in Pietism or Roman Catholic mysticism. Because of its great historic significance, however, Melanchthon's teaching should always be criticised with moderation. As a systematic *solution* it is certainly not satisfactory.

The desire of a "religious" man is always directed towards the increase of his inner powers, which is something to be effected by God. The question of guilt he passes by. So he errs in his attitude towards God and remains devoid of the possession of the Spirit. But the man

---

With Luther the primary question was likewise not that of making holy but of being accounted holy. The communion with God that has been interrupted by guilt can only be again restored through the removal of guilt (*Cf.* the Heidelberg disputation of 1518). But besides Anselm and Occam, Luther was also influenced by Augustine and the Mystics who alike (under the influence of Eastern theology) emphatically placed the effective overcoming of the power of sin in the foreground. Besides the idea of the imputation of the righteousness of God we always find associated with it in Luther's ideas the belief in the commencement and continuation of a progressive renewal of life, but with the righteousness of faith ranking above the renewal. For in quite a unique way Luther understood how to distinguish in thought ideas that were for him a real unity; an evidence that he was not so careless in systematizing as men like to picture him. He wanted to distinguish between "external" righteousness and "inner" sanctification but without separating them from each other. His linking together of the two while at the same time maintaining their correct inner sequence will always remain the ideal solution of the problem. So, and only so, will justification be preserved from the danger of quietism and sanctification from the danger of perfectionism. If, on the other hand, the attempt is made to divide the *remissio* and the *regeneratio* into two separate acts, occurring at different times, each will waste away with mutual injury.

A closer examination will further be able to distinguish three periods in Luther's development, each having a different emphasis in the treatment of the constituent parts of this relationship. There is a first period in which he so strongly emphasizes the *effici* alongside of the *reputari* that he interchanges them without any scruple and even speaks of a *magis et magis justificari*. Otto Ritschl (*Dogmengeschichte des Protestantismus*, II, 1, Chap. 28 *seq.*) includes the lectures on Romans in this period. Then, however, the emphasis begins to fall ever more strongly on the *Christus pro nobis*, which, definitely given the pre-eminence, is combined with the *Christus in nobis*. Here (say in the commentary on Galatians of 1522-35) is the real climax of Luther's creative activity. In the latter part of his life, as a result of his experiences, he approaches closer to the attitude of Melanchthon. The *justitia aliena* which we already find clearly indicated in the writings of 1520-21 is more and more placed in contrast to renewal. It is certain, however, that Luther at all times, though with varying degrees of emphasis, held fast to the essential connection of justification and sanctification, while at the same time marking clearly the theological difference between the two conceptions.

What Luther so vigorously welded together was again split apart by Melanchthon as he gained consideration for a purely imputative view of justification. While the wealth of meaning in δικαιοῦν was thus narrowed, through this one-sidedness, the free, pardoning operation of God's grace in behalf of the sinner was given powerful expression. In this way the central thought of the Reformation was not weakened but actually strengthened. Far more serious were the results on the other side, when the emphasis was laid on the effective aspect, when instead of the promise of God the moral change was made most important for the establishment and maintenance of the relationship with God. This was the case with Osiander. He too started with Luther's teaching but instead of stressing its forensic aspect, like Melanchthon, he turned to its effective, immanent aspects. He was strengthened in this position, as E. Hirsch first clearly pointed out, through linguistic, philosophical Logos speculations of Cabalistic and Neoplatonic

whose conscience realizes the eternal requirements of the omnipresent God forgets the desire for exaltation in his fervent prayer for forgiveness. Through justifying faith the terrified conscience finds rest. But since there came from that Cross, to which faith looks, not only an atonement but also a new beginning, all these other gifts and blessings are added to the one who seeks first after righteousness. As faith seeks refuge in the *nudum factum* and trusts alone in its imputation, its possessor is placed at once in the spiritual world of Eastertide, where he is made fruitful unto good works. Two momentous conclusions follow from this fact. First: the idea of the *ordo salutis* must be relin-

---

sort, which he had acquired particularly from Reuchlin and Pico della Mirandola. In so far as he made the external word of Scripture the vehicle of the inner *justitia essentialis* he remained a Lutheran, but when he opposed the teaching of imputation without rightly understanding it, and made the certainty of salvation depend on a progressive *qualitas habitualis in animo* he became a Thomist. So the certainty based on the forgiveness of sins became a merely subjective assurance that, because it required continual augmentation, was always insufficient. The effects became the cause; the extent of inner experience supplanted the assurance of a divine promise. Infusion took the place of forgiveness; the *sanatio* that of the *imputatio* and a quality of the soul supplanted a divine objectivity. Luther too had taught the activity of the one who was justified but for him that was too uncertain and variable a basis to permit faith to be grounded on it; the righteousness that enters into us is only a beginning and therefore only fragmentary. The righteousness, however, that is imputed *coram deo* is *tota et perfecta.* Osiander's ethical protest against the academic externalizing of justification was well meant but his view of the essential infusion of the divine nature of Christ alone, as the means of attaining righteousness before God, not only upset a correct christology (*perfectus deus, perfectus homo,* Athanasian Creed) but it also distorted the reformers' message of free grace into an ethical-rational sphere. A teaching so strongly reminiscent of the *gratia infusa* of Roman sacramental theology was no weapon for a Church that had just learned by hard conflicts to find *vera et firma consolatio* in the *gratia extra nos posita.* (*Cf.* Hirsch, p. 271 and the Formula of Concord, Sol. Decl. 623, 59 *seq.*)
We can perhaps formulate it thus: for grace, Melanchthon says forgiveness; Luther says forgiveness and sanctification; Osiander, sanctification and forgiveness. The Roman Church for grace, says only sanctification. The use of the word to describe a purely divine act and a valid promise of grace is expressly forbidden. *Si quis dixerit, sola fide impium justificare . . . anathema sit* (*Trid. sessio VI, can.* 9). Justification becomes exclusively a process of justification (*transmutatio*), the *gratia forensis* becomes a *gratia habitualis,* that through sacramental power is poured into the will. If in Osiander's teaching the renovating power of grace that establishes salvation was still bound in its operation to the *viva vox dei* in His Word, here, under the influence of Greek theology and a conception of God as substance, that had been drawn from ancient philosophy, the operation was conceived of as something naturally substantial and consequently magical (*actio dei physica*). The freely promising, personal working of God is here dissolved into an inner dynamic, an operative function. With such a conception of grace it is no longer possible to speak of a real assurance of salvation. *Cf.* H. Rückert, *Die Rechtfertigungslehre auf d. Triedent. Konzil,* II part, pp. 100 *seq.* Bonn, 1925.

quished, if it is regarded as anything more than a logical and psychological description of the processes of faith viewed from various angles. Though in the inception of faith the external manifestations of the various steps of the process, as it is usually described, do not become apparent, yet fundamentally where there is faith all the operations of the Spirit are given simultaneously. There is no illumination that does not immediately unfold itself as renovation, no God-given penitence and conversion that does not include a new obedience. That the "sudden conversions" which were not infrequent in the New Testament and in the history of the Church, often, in spite of their sudden beginning, display an unexpected stability and active obedience is understandable in the light of that fact.

The other and more important result is the fact that sanctification must also be understood as an exclusive act of God. Just as forgiveness is exclusively God's work and every cooperation or conditioning activity on man's part is completely excluded, so regeneration is an energy that comes simply out of Christ's victory and does not require our supplementary efforts. It is not fitting to teach justification evangelically and then in the doctrine of sanctification to turn synergistic. Nowhere can we see the gruesome power of "devout" sin as active in theology as at this point. If the "flesh" had to surrender all credit for the origin of faith it again asserts itself all the more emphatically in the continuation of the Christian estate. Man is unwilling to give his honor and gratitude to God alone. From the fact that he is and may continue to be a tool of God he would like to take some credit to himself or even aspires to assist the *gratia operans* by his own works of penitence and love. The statements of the New Testament, however, make the gift of sanctification dependent, in the same measure as the forgiveness of sins, on faith in Christ, and commands that the message of deliverance be heard and accepted just as gladly and assuredly as the promise of pardon.

Among the theologians of the "Gemeinschaftsbewegung" Th. Jellinghaus has made the most careful attempt, though in a homiletic rather than a systematic way, to develop the thought of the "sanctifying power of the death and resurrection of Christ" along Biblical lines. But even in this sympathetic and sober leader of the German Holiness

Movement, even more than in the closely related Oxford Movement or in English Methodism the great danger becomes apparent that the unity of justification and sanctification given in the act of faith becomes mingled in a confused promiscuity, instead of keeping justification in a place of clear logical pre-eminence over the sanctification that is given with it. As we have seen, neither can be separated from the other. But that does not mean that faith can be regarded as a sort of arithmetical equation with two factors of equal value that are to be combined with each other. Luther was quite right in his repeated warnings against "mingling and stewing together" faith and works "so that it is impossible to know what is done or what is contributed by faith or by works." Justification, as the moral condition which is essential in God's sight for the new life, must always be given the first place. We might say that the former is related to the latter as creation to preservation, as birth to growth, or as the sealing of a covenant to the subsequent life lived in the fellowship. The one is (we are reminded of the close connection of justification and Baptism) unrepeated, absolutely valid, complete and possessing the character of a final decision as it eternally determines our whole existence with a majestic, unchangeable actuality. The other is something growing, not a being but a becoming, not a receiving but an increasing, not a state but a movement. Though both atonement and renewal come from God, though both are given together in Christ, a difference still remains that dare never be erased. It consists in the fact that the sin that *condemns* us is completely blotted out by the grace we are given (*favor dei*), while the vivifying that then begins has still to overcome the sin that *binds* us. *Deus in Christo regenerat hominem generatum sanatque vitiatum a reatu statim, ab infirmitate paulatim* (Luther). The decree of justification establishes a new relationship between God and man, the spiritual gift introduces a new vitality. The first is an act of divine compassion (*misericordia*) the second is the beginning of the activity of divine training. So without detracting in any way from the reality and divine power of sanctification we can truly say that justification is complete, sanctification is always something incomplete.

If the Darbyite teaching concerning sanctification were correct the difference would cease to exist, for according to Darby's view the sanctification of the regenerate is something that takes place at once; that is completed in an instant. Those who through faith have been endowed with holiness are completely saved and need no further ethical development; the fifth petition of the Lord's Prayer has become superfluous in their lives. Even in the case of Jellinghaus, more enthusiastically in John Wesley's view and most definitely of all in the statements of Pearsall Smith[13] the "fuller" and "complete" sanctification supplants justification in importance. Either accompanying faith like a sudden stroke or as the result of a second sudden act of God, pure passive, "continuing without bounds," victory begins over the gross or subtle allurements and temptations to sin. Just as in the Roman Catholic teaching concerning grace a sacrament, so here a sanctifying faith produces a condition of transformation in the organic growth of the soul, a perfection that actually far surpasses what is bestowed in forgiveness and no longer requires daily repentance.[14]

It is not surprising that those holding such views should have criticised the teachings of the Reformers very sharply. Quite aside from the fact that it ill becomes the tower to disdain the earth on which it rests, as soon as any one begins to speak of "stages in Christianity" as they actually do (Jellinghaus) the basis for the certainty of salvation has been removed even for these theories of perfection, for the moment we speak of a spiritual development there is an admission that something has not yet been attained, that there is still something lacking in holiness. But this lack (even if it were only a provisional one) accuses the dilatory one anew every hour in the sight of God, Who has the right to require complete love and complete devotion at all times. This is what is so deceptive and unevangelical in every sort of teaching concerning sanctification that would attempt in some way to reach a point in which the communion with God no longer depends completely on the gift of justification, that it turns what is partial

[13] E. Kalb, *Kirchen und Sekten der Gegenwart*, p. 322. "He asserted that for 27 years he had committed no sin and stated that his little son Frank had received the grace of justification when four years old and of sanctification when he was seven."

[14] Jellinghaus, p. 548. The statement that "a believing Christian must always remain in a state of continual repentance" would have been unintelligible "to the Christians of Apostolic times."

into something that is complete and what is complete into something
only partial. It is true even of the *vir sanctus* that only *ex fide vivit*.

However, we must not pass judgment too precipitately but must
consider seriously what New Testament trait runs through all holiness
movements and has given them such great influence in the course of
the history of the Church. The religious feeling behind every "revival" rests on a perfectly correct understanding of Scripture that
teaches us that it is God's will that we should be freed from the defilement of sin and that He provides the needed means to this end.
But since God is perfectly serious in this matter of sanctification men
have concluded that it must take place unconditionally through an
infused power coming from above and by that power must come to
perfection.[15] Here we find the main reason for the belief in a complete renewal and here is where the opposition to the Church of the
Reformation arises, the opposition that so bitterly accuses her of holding fast to a universal and all-pervading sinfulness of humanity only
because it is necessary for the retention of her traditional teaching
concerning a forensic imputation of grace! Is an understanding between them possible, or do the two ideas completely exclude each
other?

We have not proceeded far enough in our investigation to give the
final answer to the opposition that here becomes apparent. We have
only a presentiment that if Christ, the Holy One of God, had to die
because of human sin, then sin is such a terrible reality that its power
of involving men in guilt cannot be pictured too intensely. Since we
are a part of that world that crucified Christ and still crucifies Him
afresh, our whole life depends on an act of divine forgiveness. But if
the Cross is the pledge of victory, it is also the manifestation of God's
will and power; the assurance that we are to be raised to life through
what transpired there. If Jesus in the prayer He gave directed us to
pray for the forgiveness of sins *and* for deliverance from evil in that
order and connection the believer perceives a connection between the
two that has been indicated by the Lord Himself, and that is continually being proved anew both by other portions of Scripture and by

[15] *Cf.* E. Cremer, Das volkommen gegenwärtige Heil in Christo, eine Untersuchung
zum Dogma der Gemeinschaftsbewegung, *Beitr. zur Forderung chr. Theologie,* p. 321,
Gütersloh, 1915.

his own conscience. It is the connection of inescapable guilt, which requires daily forgiveness, and of an effective salvation that has been promised him. It is the connection of an indispensable justifying faith and the certainty of renewal proceeding from it.

From what has preceded it is evident that a justifying faith, according to the teaching of the Reformers, includes the certainty and reality of renewal, that is, it confesses the reality and living activity of the Holy Ghost in the world. How we are to understand this real presence of the Spirit, according to evangelical teaching, whether He is manifested by His creative and directive power in the life of the believer and, if so, in what way and to what degree, we must now consider in its various aspects and with a critical examination of dissenting views.

The first problem that then confronts us is to consider both from a theological and from a philosophical standpoint the relation of the transcendence and immanence of God. Two utterly different answers have been given to this question in the more recent discussions of philosophy. The two positions which have been maintained down to the present times are associated with the names of Spinoza and Kant, but philosophical systems have always influenced the form of theological statements and all too often have made of theology the *ancilla philosophiae*. That has been the case in this connection.

In 1656 Spinoza was excommunicated from the synagogue by his fellow believers. It was the identification of God with infinite substance (*substantia una infinita*) that seemed blasphemous to the minds of those who had been trained under the influence of the ideas of the Old Testament. The "Short Treatise" was regarded as high treason to Judaism. But this very apostate became the "church father" of all the philosophy and theology of immanence. Here the existence of God within the world is an ontological, timeless truth. In every place within "the all" an immediate mental contact can take place between the finite and the infinite spirit. Like a stream God overflows the cosmos, which is His body, and every soul is a breath of His being. This timeless, unhistorical monism reappears in Goethe, in Lagarde and A. Bonus and in the writings of Rudolf Steiner that deal with natural science. Long before Spinoza's time it had been seen in the Indian mystical identity of the *Tatwam asi*, and it lives, only feebly restrained by the New Testament idea of revelation in the mystical theology of the Areopagite, in the fanatical spirits of the period following the Reformation, and in the quietism of the Molonists. The rapturous enjoyment of the fullness of divinity in the depths of the soul, the confident, unquestioning "possession" of His presence is fundamentally only another way of expressing the truth of the *finitum capax infiniti* as it has been reached in the case of Spinoza by the way of speculation.

In sharp opposition to this naturalistic philosophy is the critical philosophy of Kant. Here there is a complete break with all naïve empiricism as well as with all rationalistic metaphysics. Within as well as without the bounds of experience we have no knowledge, in the strictest sense of the word. God, above all, remains incomprehensible to our thought, bounded and determined as that is by the various categories. This epistemological doctrine of the absolute transcendence of God has also borne its theological fruit, though in a less uniform fashion than in the intellectual tendencies that came from Spinoza. The idea of the complete unknowableness of God led, by way of the Neo-Kantian school, to skeptical illusionism and agnosticism (Feuerbach, A. Lange, Vaihinger); in the Ritschlian theology it came to an anti-mystical moralism that completely lost the Christian idea of the Spirit. The most forcible theological expression of the ideas of Kantianism is to be found in Karl Barth, Emil Brunner, and Frederick Gogarten. Here we are told that God is to be found nowhere in this world, neither in nature (Spinoza), nor in history (Hegel), nor in the soul (mysticism). He cannot be produced by any religious technique whether it be called knowledge, temperamental state or effort. As the One Who dwells on high, He is fundamentally separated from all these realms. Our first two chapters tried to show that in this decisive negation of all natural religious attempts to reach God there is a correct expression of a Biblical idea.

However, the attacks of the dialectic theology as they are made from the standpoint of God's transcendence are not restricted to the "heathenish extravagances" of theology but are directed with equal severity against "the pietistic corruption of orthodoxy" (Gogarten), which, on the basis of the Incarnation and Ascension of Christ, ventured to speak of an experimental consciousness of the presence of God and of a contact with Him taking place in time. Even in Christ the temporal does not compass the eternal, even in the New Testament the separation of God and man is maintained and the *non capax* that was applicable to the Old Testament is not modified one particle in the New. Every theology of experience (Hofmann, Frank, Ihmels, with their favorable attitude towards the starting point of Schleiermacher's theology, not excepted) discloses itself as a subtle and therefore all the more dangerous betrayal of the Christian *hope*, because the gifts of the Spirit that are purely otherworldly in character and only to be expected as an eschatological possession are here appropriated in this present world. God, however, "is never identical with what we call God, what we experience, grasp by intuition or worship as God." Even in Christ He only works as One Who only touches us in a deadly crisis and so brings His infinite, qualitative remoteness sharply to our consciousness. How does the evangelical Christianity that draws from the rich treasures of Luther and his Church estimate these two great tendencies of pantheism and critical philosophy, and, as a result, what is its judgment concerning the theological schools that have been so largely influenced by one or the other? Which is most closely related to the New Testament, Kant's utterly unapproachable "thing-in-itself" or Goethe's pantheism?

To make a long story short, it can be said that Lutheranism would take its place, for the time being, with the one against the other, but in the end would reject both alike, not for the sake of taking a mediating position but to follow a new road lying beyond these two possibilities. Lutheran missions have always understood the fact that in the heathen glorification and deification of nature there lies a last, concealed longing for the lost paradise. It is the shadowy recollection of that state when "God saw all that he had made and lo it was very good." It is all very much distorted and yet contains an unconsciously Biblical element, for example, in the present devotion to sport, in its opposition to the suppression of everything earthly and corporeal in the interest of an exaggerated spirituality and a "monadological" doctrine of immortality. Whoever has grasped this fact can hear in the songs of the romanticists the sighing of the creature that longs for the restoration of its original glory. But after the fall which is the thing that separates us from all naturalistic idealism, there can be no thought of a naturally given presence of God in the world under any conditions. To chatter about the revelation of "God in humanity" apart from revelation is an irreverent and illusionary undertaking. Here in the unyielding differentiation between the Holy Spirit and the cosmic spirit lies the great strength of the Barthian theology. How much we have learned from it and how deeply we are indebted to it the reader has been able to see clearly in what has preceded. In opposition to the lawless presumption of the verse:

> "Tis not without, where fools alone do seek,
> It lies within, thou ever bring'st it forth,"

Christian faith takes its decided stand on the side of the *Critique of Pure Reason* and translates it into the Old Testament statement: "As the heavens are higher than the earth so are my ways higher than your ways and my thoughts than your thoughts" (Is. 55:9). However, it does not stop there but in opposition to the philosophical teachings of immanence and transcendence alike, it turns to the miracle of the Word made flesh, to the incarnate Christ, and sees in Him, and in Him alone, a breaking of the barriers between God and the world that had once been established by sin.

In opposition to a static, intramundane consciousness of God the Bible affirms, what is such an offense, that the fact of "God among men" is tied to the place and time of a redemptive event of history; in opposition to the critical, transcendental philosophy there is in the lowliness of the crucified and the concealment of the risen Christ a distinct indication that faith is to believe in the actual surmounting of transcendence.[16] The Greek spirit feels itself disturbed in its im-

---

[16] Ph. Bachman, Der Römerbrief und Barths Auslegung deselben. *All. Ev. Luth. Kirchen Zeitung,* Nos. 19-21, 1926. "The true super-rationalism, the super-rationalism of the Biblical Gospel lies elsewhere, lies in an exactly opposite direction from this thesis (namely that God, as contrasted with the world, is the utterly different). It is to be found in the unheard of, daring statement, so completely surpassing all human comprehension, that God, the ever living God, is completely ours. That is the 'foolishness of the Gospel' that was preached by St. Paul." *Cf.* Luther: "It is a mighty and incomprehensible fact that a man should be a shrine, a church a domicile for the One Who here speaks. It cannot be comprehended by reason, we must grasp it in the Word." On St. John 14:23 *seq.* Buchwald, I, 417.

mediate progress by the strong anti-mystical, Judaic spirit of the New Testament and the critical dialectician is no less disturbed by the "absolutely un-Judaic" views of a Paul, which seem to sound so "Hellenistic" that a purely historical and psychological scientific investigation can find no solution for the riddle except the convenient device of syncretism. But in actual fact the New Testament is just as hostile to every form of religious apriorism as to the Kantian dualism.[17] Both, Greeks and Jews, though each at a different point, must break with their dogmatic presuppositions if they would comprehend and experience the saving power of the Gospel. Because neither wants to receive anything as a pure gift, the one because of pride, the other because of unbelief, neither has any advantage over the other. To desire to be with God without God's invitation is just as presumptuous and disobedient as denying God's presence after God has spoken. To boast of our possession of the Spirit without remembering the Mediator Who has interceded for us, is just as much "an approach to a blasphemy of the Holy Ghost" as His denial and refusal after God has promised Him in His Word, as a pledge and seal of the inauguration of His kingly rule. Historically considered theology will have to lean now more to the one side, now towards the other, according to the variations in the history of thought, but it dare not in doing so lose its balance. In times when mysticism, pious intoxication and romanticism flourish luxuriously we have to write "anti-Schleiermacher." In an era of positivistic skepticism and of a purely intellectual moralism it becomes necessary to speak all the more emphatically of the promise of Pentecostal activity (though with a simultaneous warning against the possible danger of confusing the psychic and

[17] It is therefore probably necessary to relinquish the formula *finitum capax infiniti* as an ambiguous statement because it may awaken the idea that man through his natural religious or spiritual activities is in a position to compel God to reach after him and draw him to Himself. But just as unsatisfactory an explanation of what is given to faith through Christ is the statement *finitum non capax infiniti*, because it only states correctly what is impossible to the natural man but does not include the rich treasures which faith through God's condescension in His Son receives in this life by means of Word and Sacrament. In place of both impracticable formulas the statement (first used, as far as I know, by Brunstäd) *infinitum capax finiti* should take its place among Lutherans. By this statement the Old Testament—Reformed transcendentalism and the aprioristic immanence are alike rejected while the complete transcendence of God as well as His real communion with the sinner are clearly expressed.

spiritual domains). In all events it is always fundamentally necessary for theology to keep in mind the danger of deviation in *both* directions and to guard against it. This is particularly the case with the Church of today that has continually to fight attacks from all sides.

Lutheranism has built its dykes on both sides. To ward off spiritualism and Spinozism it has made the statement: *"deus non dat interna nisi per externa, deus spiritum sanctum non mittit absque verbo."* The Word with its judicial claims, with its power of establishing and maintaining communion with God, excludes the idea that the reception of the Spirit has to do with some essential condition based on an existing divine relationship. But in opposition to the abridgement of the Gospel into a purely transcendental faith the Formula of Concord taught just as emphatically in its christology as well as in its pneumatology and doctrine concerning the sacraments the personal, indwelling of the *deus ipse*, and even rejected the teachings of those who declared that only the gifts of God were present in the believer (*quod non Deus ipse, sed dona dei duntaxat in credentibus habitent*).[18]

How little the presence of God that is assured to faith has to do with pantheistic immanence theology has shown most effectively under the four viewpoints of the condescension of God, the reality and amissibility of faith and of eschatology. How far the possession of faith reaches beyond a supposedly impassible transcendence of God theology shows most clearly through the maintenance of the doctrine of the *unio mystica* in Word and Sacrament.

It is due to the creditable work of John Rupprecht on Hermann Bezzel that attention has again been drawn to the theological significance of the idea of condescension, which had already been stressed by Hamann. God's "condescension" to the world in creation, preservation, incarnation and sacrament does not come from any rational or natural-philosophical relation between God and man. The humiliation of Christ in the "likeness of man," in the insignificance of "wretched, every-day natural agencies" He used, is an utter paradox; it is the gift of a love that freely gives and sacrifices itself. God's pardoning Word is a real word of pardon on which man has no natural claim. His

---

[18] III, 65, p. 624. *Cf.* also John Gerhard: *Spiritus Sanctus non est seperatus a donis suis, sed in templo illo, quod donis suis coronat, etiam ipse habitat.*

entrance into the limitations of human speech in Scripture and preaching, with the possibility of being thus despised, is a deep abasement which He has freely chosen for the salvation of the world. This truly evangelical idea of the condescension of God, in which all of Luther's *theologia crucis* lies hidden, should be applied, as Bezzel does (ch. 5), to the inspiration of men, not because the finite is able by itself to appropriate the infinite, even though it does possess spiritual abilities, but because the Spirit, as well as the Son, humbles Himself in His ministering love, therefore man can become a partaker of contact with the divine. *Infinitum capax finiti.* God, Who in freely exercised omnipotence has reached down into time through the sending of the Son, still imparts Himself everywhere where men believe in Jesus Christ.

By means of the idea of condescension the sovereignty of God is preserved in the evangelical conception of immanence. The emphasis on the real nature of this "in-dwelling" gives to every statement a still stronger note of reverent dependence. As we have already pointed out, mysticism describes the union of God and the soul in sentimental naturalistic terms. It speaks of a substantial marriage of the human and divine spirit that ends in an act of union where all distinctions cease. But wherever the *Deus in nobis* is affirmed on the basis of the *Christus pro nobis*, Who is accepted by faith, there can be no talk of an absorption and submersion into a state of static being. When the Word becomes the vehicle of the Spirit the ideas of judgment and guilt are not excluded, then the awakened conscience discards the presumptuous idea of identity, and the ecstasy of a being-like-God. Only in the attitude of simple faith can the nearness of the Lord be received, for in all His gracious surrender to man He is never absorbed by him, any more than the Creator disappears in His creation. We only have to compare the descriptions of the in-dwelling of God that are found in the accounts of the ecstatic confessions of a Catherine of Siena, Theresa, Madam de Guyon or in the last chapter of Bonaventura's *Itinerarium* with the communion hymns of our Lutheran Church[19] to recognize the profound difference between the idea of

[19] For example Joh. Hermann's "Herr Jesu Christe, mein getreuer Hirte." We find this holy restraint particularly in the hymns of Paul Gerhardt. We need only to compare the lines "Make Thee within my soul a place, That I grow fruitful through Thy grace," or

mystical identity and the evangelical view of immanence; a very far-reaching difference that it seems to me has not been properly appreciated by Brunner and his friends because of their indiscriminating rejection of every form of divine in-dwelling. How modestly and with what an exalted tone Luther, in his *Freedom of a Christian Man* uses the picture of the bride and bridegroom that is so common in mystical literature, and how unsensuous are the descriptions of the "exchange" that takes place in faith as we find them, for example, in the letter to the Augustinian monk, Geo. Spenlein! The real reception of exchanged possessions is maintained but the erotic taint is no where to be found. To receive the "wedding ring of faith" is a "joyous exchange", a "joyous business," not an ecstatic love union. Faith, even when endowed with God's richest blessing, continues in a state of pure humility.

If the personal communion with Christ is bound to God's freedom and the activity of faith, then the possibility of losing it is also admitted. As soon as man ceases to live in the surrender of justifying faith heaven is again completely closed against him and is finally hidden from his sight. A permanent philosophical and religious nearness of God "without means or price" is an utterly unjustifiable subjective fancy. Uncertainties and the severest shocks will then not be lacking. In the end unbelief always reveals its own natural condition of separation from God, a separation which always continues till through faith in the Gospel the hidden God is transformed into the *deus revelatus*.

The preceding statements should be sufficient to show the fundamental difference between the Christian and the philosophical conceptions of immanence. But the contrast becomes still more apparent when we recall the eschatological character of all the statements concerning the divine presence found in the Gospels. While, of course, the Spirit as the hidden motive force of this new reality is already at work in believers, since a new era has begun in Christ, on the other hand it has pleased God to delay the final visible revelation of the "other" world that lies beyond the old world. The Kingdom of God is still "veiled by

---

"So let me e'er Thy dwelling be, Come, come and enter into me" with the amorous longings of St. Gertrude; "Lo my heart burns with desire for the kiss of love, Open to me the beloved bedchamber of Thy love. Lo, my soul thirsts for the embrace of the most intimate union with Thee." (Heiler, *Das Gebet*, 2nd ed., p. 338.)

the Cross." The present condition of the world as a painful reality, full of suffering and guilt, still oppresses and humbles even the spiritual man. As yet there is no actual vision of eternity, but in the face of such evident visible facts it is necessary to *believe* in the hope of the already accomplished resurrection. So long as the cosmos that is destined to perish still casts its heavy shadow over the congregation of the redeemed so long they will only venture to speak of the possession of perfection with a "secret, hidden, yea," and not with a loud triumphant note, while the tribute exacted by daily sin still continues to stand in such terrible contrast to that ultimate expectation. The intoxicated enjoyment of God found in Bernard, under the influence of the language of the Song of Songs, is as impossible for those who are awaiting the consummation as would be the hopelessness of the two disciples on the way to Emmaus. The mutual exclusion of possession and non-possession is here overcome by the paradox of "having nothing and yet possessing all things." Between the *beatus possidens*, who no longer needs to hope and the one without possession who thinks that he dare not accept the "now in this time" (St. Mark 10:30) is the Pauline νυνὶ καὶ οὔπω that casts down the one and raises up the other. "So it is comprehensible how we can be both those who have attained and those who wait, resting and hastening, loosed and bound, singing triumphant songs and sighing at the same time."[20]

Whether the Spirit whose donation takes place in this way be described as the bestowal of pardon, as faith that can be lost or as a pledge of hope, in any case its confusion with the immediate experience of God or with a philosophical-religious contemplation of truth is out of the question. Whoever makes essential righteousness the actual basis of the knowledge of God, apart from the Word or the outward sign of the Sacrament, speaks of the Spirit in entirely different terms from those used in the Gospel. But when faith has sufficiently secured itself from the neighboring *finitum capax infiniti* of philosophy it dare not be afraid of affirming, on its side, the evidence of the presence of the Triune God in faith. Luther did so frequently, often almost recklessly in view of the dangerous nearness to the deifying ideas of the fanatics and to humanistic intellectualism.

[20] P. Althaus, *Die letzten Dinge*, 3rd ed., p. 73 *seq.*, Gütersloh, 1926.

In the realm of faith even Calvin thought in more immanent fashion than his former or present followers care to admit.[21] The "mighty rushing stream of Luther quotations" with which Brunner, Barth and Gogarten have sought to overcome this situation is smothered by the great mass of statements that tell how faith "brings Christ into the heart." If we wanted to show how the *adesse Christi in cordibus* was an indisputable reality for the Reformers it would be necessary to begin with *Glosses to the Psalms* and continue through the *Lectures on Romans*,[22] the *Commentary on Galatians*, the exposition of St. John's Gospel, 1537-40 (Er. Ed. 45-47), Luther's sermons and treatises, Melanchthon's *Loci* and would have to copy the Third Book of Calvin's *Institutes*, concerning the *insertio in Christum*.[23] If only

[21] *Instruction in the Christian Religion*, ed. of E. F. K. Müller, p. 389. "We confess that God has not only reconciled us to Himself through the righteousness of Christ and that He regards us as just through the forgiveness of sins, but there is united with it the further gift of faith, namely that through His Holy Spirit He dwells within us and that through the Spirit's powers the lusts of our flesh are daily killed more and more. So we are sanctified, that is, consecrated in the Lord to a truly pure life and our hearts are fashioned to the obedience of the Law of God. Now our will is directed principally to serving the will of God and to advancing His honor in every way." (*Cf.* K. Barth, *Vom Halten der Gebote, Zw. d. Z., V.* 3, p. 227: "The statement that in our conscience we can become conformed to His will is false.") Further, p. 377: "With the greatest emphasis we teach the connection of the Head with the members. The in-dwelling of Christ in our hearts, yea, His mystical union with us. As Christ becomes our possession He makes us partakers of the gifts that He has acquired for us. We do not dream about a distant Christ, Who remains a stranger to us while His righteousness is imputed to us: much rather because we have put on Christ and are incorporated into Him, yea, because He has made us worthy of becoming one with Him, we dare boast that we have a part in His righteousness." P. 305: "It is a mark of wretched blindness when men undertake to brand with their disapproval those Christians who claim the presence of the Holy Ghost." Further, pp. 313 *seq.*, 397, 562, 564.

[22] It is significant that Luther during the years in which the lectures on Romans were given issued several editions of the *Theologia Deutsch* because he had "not seen a more salutary theology or one more in conformity with the Gospel, either in Latin or in our own Language." (Letter to Spalatin, 1516.) The young Luther was opposed to mysticism in the sense of philosophic speculation, human cooperation or a Neoplatonic weakening of the conception of sin, but not to the idea of the impartation of the Spirit of God, imparted through the Word. *Cf.* Frank-Grützmacher, *Geschichte und Kritik der neueren Theologie.* 4th ed., Leipzig, 1908, p. 348. Calvin's aversion to the *Theologia Deutsch* is well known.

[23] The statements of the *Apology* are in full accord with this position, "Faith is not a mere empty knowledge of the historical accounts but is a new light in the heart and a powerful work of the Holy Ghost by which we are born anew and the terrified conscience is again revived and we attain to life" (108). "*Abacuc 2:4, Justus ex fide vivet. Hic primum dicit homines fide esse justos, qua credunt Deum propitium esse, et addit, quod eadem fides vivificet, quia haec fides parit in corde pacem et gaudium et vitam*

the "want" without the riches of the possession of the Spirit were the mark of the Reformers' faith then the "pietistically degraded neoprotestantism" would have had its roots in their time. For Luther, however, human emptiness and the fullness of God were not mutually exclusive but rather became one. Because the Word of God is regal, mighty and efficient (*regnum, potens, efficax*), it produces in man that complete submission, that "vacuum" which God can and always does fill,[24] for it is His will that His supreme rule shall be actively maintained at all times and in all places. Since faith is the penitent acknowledgment of sin, it also shows itself as "a divine work within us, that transforms us and begets anew in God and kills the old Adam, making us utterly different men in heart, disposition, understanding and in all our powers, and brings the Holy Ghost with it."[25] That the sinner confessing his guilt, in the reality of this confession, actually becomes a new spiritual man, not only eschatologically but in the present, is a paradox in which is contained the unique greatness of Lutheranism in contrast to all other confessions that have tried to remove the paradox either in favor of transcendence or of immanence.

The Shibboleth that shows whether this paradox has been maintained is heard in the attitude assumed towards the Lord's Supper.[26] Only in this connection can we understand the fidelity that Lutheranism has shown towards this article of the Confessions and the way it has held fast to it even in the times of deadness. Only in this way can we understand the unyielding intensity of the conflict as it was waged at various times not only against Rome but also against Crypto-

---

aeternam." To which the German text adds: "Peace and joy and eternal life, which begins in this present life." (105, 100.) *"Quia vero fides affert Spiritum Sanctum et parit novam vitam in cordibus, necesse est, quod parit spirituales motus in cordibus. . . . Postquam igitur fide justificati et renati sumus, incipimus Deum timere, diligere, petere et exspectare ab eo auxilium, gratias agere et praedicare, et obedire ei in afflictionibus. Incipimus et diligere proximos, quia corda habent spirituales et sanctos motus"* (109).

[24] Albrecht Bengel: "What is man to do except provide an empty place which the power of Christ shall fill and completely occupy." (*Weisheit im Staube, ein Lesebuch der Schwabenväter*, pub. by Joh. Herzog, Tübingen, 1927.

[25] *Preface to the Epistle of St. Paul to the Romans.* Quoted from the Form. Conc. Sol. Decl. IV. *de bonis operibus*, p. 626.

[26] *Cf.* E. Sommerlath, *Der Sinn des Abendmahls*, Leipzig, 1930.

Calvinism and the Prussian Union. Here we have to deal with something more than confessional controversies, for it concerns an essential factor of the faith, yea, it involves the very destiny of the Church. Dare I be certain that even now, on this earth, I am given the nutriment of the New World, with the forgiveness of sins, as an anticipation of the coming Communion of the Kingdom of God? Is it possible to receive today, through communion with the risen Lord, not only deliverance from guilt but the gift of strength as well? Can the brotherly love, which makes the Eucharist a bond of union between those who celebrate it, be received now? The answer does not depend on considerations of natural philosophy as Neo-Lutheranism in dependence on its church father Martensen has attempted to do. It is not theosophy that separates us from the Reformed in the question concerning the Lord's Supper, nor is the way we regard the question concerning a magical transubstantiation the real cause for the separation from Rome, but it has to do, in both cases, with this question: Does the Lord, Who will return in the future, come into the darkness of our hearts today so that faith neither despairs because of the hidden nature of God nor exalts itself in false self-assurance but can console itself with the immediate presence of its holy and sanctifying Lord?[27]

Besides the ubiquity and voluntary multiplied presence (*Multivolopräsenz*) in the doctrine of the Sacrament, Lutheranism has a second dogmatic locus that just as clearly shows its special attitude towards pneumatology as it is expressed in the Confessions. It is the teaching of the *unio mystica*. At first we might think that the expression, a mystical union, could not have found acceptance in this company, after Luther's exceedingly harsh rejection of the Areopagite had thoroughly discredited it. Following the publication of Ritschl's *History of Pietism* it has been taken for granted that this idea and its manifestations were lapses, of the post-Reformation period, into medieval (Bernhard) and Jesuistic (Labadie) mysticism by which genuine Protestantism was deformed and corrupted. When we examine John Arndt in whom we find unrelated Lutheran and medieval mystical influences existing side by side, this thesis appears to be justified. Here the marriage of the soul with a heavenly spouse, with

[27] Cf. Fr. I. Stahl, *Die lutherische Kirche und die Union*, p. 148, *seq.*, p. 75.

Christ the loveliest Bridegroom, is related in fervent language. The toying with the *fruitio dei*, where the soul becomes "intoxicated by the superabundance of eternal desires," if it did not exclude the stern seriousness of the idea of justification certainly supplanted it. That Tauler, Val. Weigel, Thomas à Kempis and the *Theologia Deutsch* were its sponsors cannot be denied.

There are, however, two considerations that must make us reject the assertion that there was a mystical secularizing of Lutheranism. The one is that the impulse which started this accusation came from the Ritschlian school, which had so little understanding for the living self-witnessing presence of the exalted Lord in the heart of man, and the other is the observation that in Lutheranism just the most noteworthy supporters of the theology of justification and the most pronounced opponents of the Reformed teaching professed the *unio mystica*.[28] We think of the great line that descends from Stephen Prätorius, Ph. Nicolai, Val. Herberger, Habermann, Chemnitz, John Gerhard, Quenstedt, E. V. Löscher, through Philippi, Vilmar, Thomasius, Rocholl (Realpräsenz!) and Löhe on down to Bezzel. All these men were earnest, mighty preachers of the Cross and yet they felt the real, perceptible union of the members with the Head, without departing even in the slightest degree from the essentials of the Reformation faith. They knew that in the *Deo uniri per fidem ex promissione* (St. John 14 and 15) they were on firm Scriptural ground, even if it was not possible for each one to realize the essential connection of *justificatio* and *unio* as vitally as Luther, or later on, Quenstedt. Their conviction of the doctrine of justification preserved them from falling into exaggerated talk about a magical transformation. The article of a "standing or falling Church" was not robbed of its importance by a second, independent principle that excelled it. On the other hand it was equally important to assure a living in-

---

[28] If Lutheranism at the very time it was guarding itself most anxiously against Crypto-Calvinism, used in the medieval devotional literature, that had been transmitted through Erasmus and Schwenkfeld, for its prayers and hymns (P. Althaus, Sr., *op. cit.,* pp. 14-27) that is a sign that the Old Testament bondage was felt to be a danger to the faith at least as great as the false language of mysticism, though men were not blind to the latter danger. The way to the *unio* and its form were manifestly very differently described but still there was a certain feeling of kinship that was based on the recognition of the fact of the sharing of a living presence of Christ.

dwelling of God, through Word and Sacrament, since the denial of that fact would endanger not only the whole christological dogma but also the teaching of the Confessions concerning Scripture and the Sacraments. The narrow way led between spiritualistic mysticism and Socinian rationalism. It was necessary to guard against both, against a presumptuous mysticism by an anti-mystical, forensic emphasis and against a superficial moral intellectualism by the entire living force of the Lutheran views concerning grace.

The task is exactly the same for the orthodoxy of today. Mystical religiosity, "German piety," Indian teachings concerning salvation, cosmic transfigurations demand a theology of "contrast." In opposition to utilitarianism, the mechanizing of life and critical skepticism, however, it is necessary to proclaim the Gospel of inspiration through the Spirit of God. The paradox of Lutheranism, "the more external—the more inward" (*extra nos—in nobis*), is always incomprehensible to natural thinking or party feeling. The one who contends against the dangers now on the right, now on the left, because he understands them, may be accused, by those who fail to understand, of a lack of steadfastness; they will class him now among the mystics, now among those of a Judaizing tendency and then again among the mediating theologians, who travel in "an uncertain twilight." It is the burden of faith that to be obedient to God it can only express itself on earth by means of two contradictory thoughts.

If such a curious paradox of concealment *and* manifestation, of the distance *and* nearness of God, of hope *and* the present possession of the Spirit, exists for faith, what are we to say about the application of the word "mysticism" in the theological language of the present day? It is well known that a number of theologians have advocated the retention and use of this term. It is not only among theologians of the philosophy of religions type, like Deissmann, R. Otto, Albert Schweitzer, Beth, Heiler and Söderblom that we find this opinion, but even systematic theologians of a pronounced Lutheran position like Girgensohn, H. E. Weber, Keopp, Sommerlath and Schaeder, and for some time Althaus. By coining new words like "justification-mysticism, faith-mysticism, historic-mysticism, eschatological-mysticism" ("personality-, spirit-, Christ-mysticism") they have sought, especially the last named, to manufacture intentionally paradoxical, antithetical formulations in which the possessing and non-possessing, the real presence of the Spirit and the revelation mediated by the Word, forgiveness and vivification should come to a living expression. Whoever has read H. E. Weber's splendid work on the subject, where in opposition to Roman Catholic mysticism with its superiority to the Word and faith he so convincingly advocates the word "faith-mysticism" (*Glaubensmystik*) with its paradoxical sound, will find it hard to kick against this goad. In view of the preceding course of our investigation we can only take our place with those who in their advocacy of a "mysticism of faith" are solely concerned about the preservation intact of our inheritance from Martin Luther, in opposition to Ritschlian moralism or the Neo-Kantian, modern Reformed transcendence. Only in so far we would dissent from them and agree with their opponents, Barth, Brunner, Heinzelmann, Schumann, Peterson, H. W. Schmidt and others, as we, more emphatically even than Weber, feel that the word "mysticism" is so loaded down and distorted by extra-Christian syncretistic elements that it would be decidedly better to exclude this word, once and for all, from the vocabulary of an evangelical theology because of the "hopeless confusion" (Heinzelmann) it brings with it. The origin of the idea in non-Christian religions, the Roman Catholic reminiscences, the fondness for a neutral conception of God, the absence of the idea of guilt and judgment, the Platonic avoidance of eschatology, the lack of comprehension of anything historic, all give occasion for such fatal substitutions and distortions, and have always done so, that the renunciation of the expression seems necessary, however much the fact of a "mystery from above" (Barth) must have its place in our understanding of the Christian faith. Of course the linguistic sacrifice at once places before us the task of describing the nature of faith in a fuller way and with new expressions that will make it clear that the Third Article of the Creed is not dealing merely with an *actio extra hominem, quae non potest hominem intrinsece mutare* (Hollazius). Of the terms that have been proposed, though none are, nor can ever be, adequate, it seems to me that the expression, the "mystery of faith," is the best fitted for the description of the fact, which passeth

all understanding, that the miracle of the actual presence of the Lord
is accomplished in the anti-mystical faith in Christ's vicarious surrender to death.

But now the insistent question is raised, one that is more warmly
disputed than the one we have been considering, concerning the
psychological possibility of experiencing the promised forgiveness. The
question is whether the new life in the Spirit can be made a matter
of experience, and if so, in what form it takes place.

If the Spirit (*Pneuma*) is the activating force of the new world
then it is evident that it can never become perceptible as a tangible
reality of the old world. As long as the flesh (*sarx*) that is at enmity
with the Spirit (Gal. 5:17) has not been abolished, so long the activity of the new world cannot appear in a visible form that is convincing to every one. For life is still shrouded in the mortal forms
of the present age and it does not yet appear what we shall be. To
affirm that the Spirit is universally comprehensible and tangible in
this fallen world would be to deny the fall and to question the origin
of the Spirit from the Father and the Son. Secularization of the Spirit
is a mocking of God. But this is only dealing with one side of the
question. If the Spirit of Christ is already at work as the Creator of
the new world and as the One Who undermines the old, it follows
that He must continually manifest His victorious power. Utterly hidden Himself, psychologically intangible, incomprehensible to the
reason, He must manifest Himself in His operations (καρποὶ τοῦ
πνεύματος), judging, drawing to Himself and rewarding men. If the
triumph over "principalities and powers" has already taken place (Col.
2:15) then this event must throw its shadow across the earth for
whose liberation the warfare was waged. To use Karl Heim's apt
comparison, it is as though a three-dimensional body were casting
its shadow from above on a plane surface. The projected shadow
appears at first as a bit of the entire plane and those who do not know
any better might confuse it with the latter or entirely overlook it.
And yet the shadow points the inquirer to a dimension of a higher
sort which cannot be fittingly expressed by the measurements of a
flat surface. This comparison has been most appropriately chosen because it illustrates two things at the same time: first, the "completely

incommensurable relation" (Brunner) of cause and effect, of God's absolute spirit and our own experience of Him, and, at the same time, the perceptible deeds that testify to another reality as does the shadow to the body which is always something apart from it. When we speak of the invisibility of the Spirit man is referred to faith which the Epistle to the Hebrews calls the "evidence of things not seen." When we speak of the possibility of the gift of the Spirit and of His activity among us we are holding fast to the assurance that faith is actually vitalizing men at the present time. To deny the visible actualizing of the gift of the Spirit and still to affirm His living existence is an offensive contradiction for natural reason; for faith this double aspect of the *nova vita*, its hidden nature and its manifestation, in spite of that fact, on earth, is the living expression of the fact that "we have here no continuing city" but that the future one is already prepared for us.

What then are the concrete effects of the Spirit of God on men? Man's willing, feeling, thinking, when it is centered in itself knows only one spirit, as we saw in the first chapter, the spirit that says: "Go to, let us build us a city and a tower whose top may reach into heaven; and let us make us a name." If in this self-exaltation it is just man's fall that finds expression, so the Spirit of God begins His work of renewal by causing this exaltation to collapse, and by teaching a complete self-knowledge that penetrates to the very root of all things. He carries as His sword the sharp, quick and powerful word, that is "a judge of the thoughts and intents of the heart." Before Him "every mountain and hill shall be made low and the rough places plain." Here no trust in the righteousness of man's own accomplishments is any longer tolerated. The Spirit demands that man put no dependence on his own works of righteousness. With the birth of faith every form of self-approval must perish at its root. Faith that yields obedience to the Word is no human merit; something that could take the place of many holy efforts as a *causa meritoria*. It is the gift of the Spirit solely and alone that creates faith, without our desire and even against it, through the urgent pressing call of God within us that overcome us (*conversio passiva*). Where there has been a rescue from death all the merit and praise belong to the rescuer and not to the one who has been saved. *Per fidem* (not *propter fidem*), *propter Christum salvamur* is the statement of the Confession. To demand here a merit even though it be only a *meritum de congrue*, in connection with the gifts that have been given us would be the very climax of presumption and hypocrisy.

As the spirit of God destroys our confidence in our own works so He becomes the turning point of all emotional and spiritual feelings, whether in the natural or religious spheres. Spiritual pride and melancholy, voluptuous emotions, agonies of abasement manifested in mass gatherings are neither means of grace nor ways to salvation. To cultivate the technique of producing them or to build on their results is mere folly. The Spirit does not intoxicate and stupefy but produces a holy sobriety. He does not occasion depression but arouses serious thoughts concerning the end; His speech does not revel in satiated feelings of beatitude, nor in sentimental sweetness and softness, but is marked by a wholesome virility. Presumptious erotic phrases, the soft strains of nuptial mysticism, a twilight enjoyment of God, indecorous contortions of the soul must all pass away where the noontide brightness of Jesus Christ shines forth. It is exceedingly significant that just in those passages that refer to prayer (I Peter 4:7) there is an admonition to be "sober and watch"; here, where "pious agitation" has always been so prone to pass all bounds. Nor can any one preach about the Cross and justification, where the understanding and will bow before God, and allow the emotions to flare with words of unbridled passion. As long as the realm of feeling is not purified so long subjective individualism has not been overcome and so long a real congregational fellowship is impossible. Above all, under the discipline of the Holy Ghost there can be no sort of inwardness that imagines that it can ignore the content of revelation, as though it were enough to talk in a purely formal way about religious movements and "experimental qualities" without continually referring to the Gospel as the true source of all "life." The Spirit does not establish the certainty of God through the violence of certain agitations of the soul, fervent terrors, by the standards of a stronger or weaker personal experience or on the excitement of an act of surrender, but on the promise of God. The Word must first bring us to the reality of God. This reality, however, is infinitely wider and greater than the participation in it that is possible to our own anthropocentric, and therefore so variable, fund of experience. It continues to be valid and in fact shows itself most powerfully when the ardor of spiritual youth has been dampened by age, sufferings and death. The *testimonium spiritus sancti internum* tells of God's unchangeable faithfulness, not of the constancy and fervor of our own spiritual estate.

The Spirit says faith, not works; He says faith, not activity, and He also says faith, not knowledge. That is the criterion of His activity, that the reason to which He has spoken ceases "to flutter up to heaven" (Luther). "It ceases trying to climb up into heaven by its own thoughts and speculations, and to form its ideas about God independently of the Word," because, "apart from Christ He is much too great and exalted for it." The confident self-glorification that provides its own law for itself is deprived of its leadership and the Spirit takes its place as the Regent. Our own ways, devised by our own cleverness and choice, because of their unruliness are given the hard names of "deception, misleading, betraying" ($\pi\lambda\acute{a}\nu\eta$, $\alpha\pi\acute{a}\tau\eta$), by Scripture. The attempt of reason to comprehend God's wisdom *a priori* is called an "arrogant proud endeavor" ($\delta\psi\eta\lambda\acute{a}\,\psi\rho\text{o}\nu\hat{\epsilon}\iota\nu$), born out of foolish vanity of the mind ($\mu\alpha\tau\alpha\iota\acute{o}\tau\eta\text{s}\,\tau\hat{o}\nu\,\nu\text{o}\acute{o}\text{s}$); a most remarkable contrast to the conceited Pelagian self-confidence of men. While on the Gnostic mastery of the world, monistic spiritualism, the philosophic deductions from the combination of opposites and evolutionary optimism all of them products manufactured "out of the depths of our own being" descends the hard judgment of the Bible, "Thinking themselves to be wise they became fools."[29] For the Logos is not identical with our reason; He is the speech of the Holy Ghost that circumscribes our thinking and reveals its uncertainty, so that we learn at last to look for help outside ourselves.

To sum up the results of our discussion thus far, we can say that the activity of the Holy Ghost is manifested when the man who has been touched by Him in his entire personality ceases to make any claim on God and gives Him all the glory. It is a dying, into which God in mercy drives our will, against our will, and which our con-

[29] I John 4:6; Col. 2:8; Heb. 3:13; Eph. 4:17; Rom. 1:22.

science must approve as holy, just and good. If the nature of sin consists in *crimen laesae majestatis,* παρά-βασις, ἀντι-νομία, denial of our limitations and disregard of all restrictions, then the return to God is a sharp self-judgment of this hybrid thing, with a modesty that understands itself, with a reverent, renewed recognition of His greatness as that is presented to us in the First Commandment. In none of these three particulars dare we venture any longer to attempt a secret evasion. There is no last island of refuge that the destroying storm of the Spirit would not overwhelm.[30] To be humble in works but proud in thought, modest in knowledge but confident in action, critical of the theoretical or practical reason but puffed up in spiritual affairs are all "false, self-righteous, wild ways of salvation" (Luther) that lead past Christ, Who only condescends to dwell with sinners who know their own estate. The "no" of the Spirit is spoken over the gross and refined lusts, over the lack and the defectiveness of good, over blindness and doubt to the point that we are forced to despair of our own reason and strength. It is the very man who most highly regards moral virtue and spiritual knowledge who learns to recognize and assent to such a judgment.

But we must not forget that where there is a dying with Christ there is also a living with Him. True, it is a *hidden* life, but a *life* hidden in *Christ,* Who is the head of the body and Who will transform all His members.[31] πιστὸς ὁ λόγος ἐι γὰρ συναπεθάνομεν, καὶ συνζήσομεν When the Son walked in lowliness on earth they esteemed Him "stricken, smitten of God and afflicted" but through word and deed the glory of God shone through the veil of His servant's form. This paradox of the unrecognizableness and, in spite of it, the perceptibleness of God incarnate can also serve as a type of the disciple endowed with the Spirit, provided we make the necessary allowance for the difference between the two. The resurrection life of believers is veiled just as Christ after His ascension vanished from view into the hidden glory of God. Weakness, sin and health are visible in all those parts of the lives of the disciples that come into our view. And yet that we are risen with Christ is a truth and not a delusion; rather "everything

---

[30] *Cf.* Fr. Gogarten: "Belief in God is disbelief in man and in all his possibilities and capabilities." *Von Glaube und Offenbarung,* p. 49, Jena, 1923.

[31] *Cf.* Gal. 4:19; Rom. 8:29; Eph. 3:16.

that would conceal this truth is a delusion." Therefore the participation in the new world of glorification is bound to show itself, as salt and light, as a contrast to the old life and as its purification, as the attacking, disturbing and purifying of the old world. The Spirit will fill the vacuum He has created, so that above the sounding negation of the world the secret affirmation of Eastertide becomes audible. "Just as a carver while he takes away that part of the wood that is not needed for the image at the same time develops the image itself, so the hope that forms the new man grows through the fear that the old man cuts off" (Er. Ed. 37, 423). The will that has been separated from sin by judgment is able to serve. The emotions that have been purified by "chastising" grace have received, through its "teaching" power that overcomes the hostile egotism of our nature (Titus 2:12), the ability to love one's neighbor. Because the Holy Ghost "is no skeptic" (*Concerning the Bondage of the Will*, Gogarten, p. 13) the fear of the Lord is the beginning of wisdom. Because Zacchaeus thinks he is not worthy that the Lord should enter into his house the Lord enters in. The limitation of the Barthian theology is found just at this point. It results from the failure to emphasize the New Testament living with Christ with the same vigor with which it speaks of the dying with Him; the living with Him that God does not refuse where men speak seriously of that dying, as surely as God is not a God of the dead but of the living. To make the mountain-removing, world-conquering faith a purely future matter; to substitute a future *spes* for a present *res* is nothing more than a denial of the historical resurrection of Jesus Christ.[32] The Spirit of Christ witnesses the power of His death and resurrection in us through the *mortificatio* and *vivificatio*, in the defeats *and* victories which He has prepared for us, by wounding *and* healing, by making poor *and* making rich (John 15:5). We can never receive only the one factor from Him. It must either be both or neither. But today, since the "Theology of Crisis" has proclaimed the judging power of the Spirit in our will, emotions and intellect while maintaining an

---

[32] The Augsburg Confession (Art. III: *De filio Dei*) confesses of Him Who sits *ad dextram Patris* "that He sanctifies them that believe on Him by sending the Holy Spirit into their hearts to rule, comfort and quicken them, and to defend them against the devil and power of sin."

intentional reticence concerning the healing effect of redemption on these three fundamental factors of our existence and believes it necessary to warn others against such statements, a further discussion is necessary.

The statement was made at the beginning of this chapter that the fundamental problem of ethics was that involved in the question as to the content and power of moral action. Where the recognition of the work of the Spirit is not complete or is not considered seriously the answer can only be legal prescriptions and the enforced effort to fulfill such regulations. But where there is faith in the Holy Ghost, there, in place of the Torah, is "the perfect law of liberty" (St. James 1:25), and in place of compulsion there is a glad readiness to do God's will. Next to the localizing of divinity in holy objects and holy places the natural man in his sluggishness desires nothing so much as a fine meshed casuistic, a puritanical regulation of the course of his life, in which he is relieved from the burden of making moral decisions by a strong external authority that prescribes his conduct for him. The Roman Catholic conduct of the confessional is very ready to meet this requirement. It is well known that her great power of attraction and fascination does not stop finally with this concession. The natural man in his desire for unbridled freedom wants a freedom of conscience resting on his own standards; a freedom like that proclaimed by the Renaissance and as it found a Christianized continuation in Kantianism and Neoprotestantism (through a humanistic falsifying of Luther's ideas of freedom). His self-glorifying, self-creative spirit provides its own inner law for itself; in its *"Daimon"* he seeks the stars of destiny that shall indicate the way of his journey. A Whitsuntide prayer like:

> "O counsel us upon our way,
> And let Thy presence with us stay,
> Who cannot walk unguided,"

is unintelligible to him. But neither of these ways, the heteronomous or the autonomous one, can really solve the ethical problem. Consequently both are impossible in evangelical Christianity. Why?

It is impossible for any code of rules to prescribe down to the minutest details what shall be done in each new situation that may arise in the continually altering circumstances of life. In the care of souls the pastor is continually confronted with entirely new problems and with the most momentous decisions for which he can nowhere find any specific written guidance. But at such times a freedom that reaches its determinations and decisions only according to the ability of our natural reflections, inclinations and general attitude is even less satisfactory. The lack of a reliable compass and of inner certainty prevent us from acting with any real assurance. The final result of such self-direction is always capriciousness as has been shown in so terrifying a way in the ethical relativism of our day. In cases like these, that are continually recurring in our personal business and in ecclesiastical and political life, it would only be possible to help if there were a mandatory center possessing a twofold function: that it would be a binding norm that would free us from the burden of arbitrary action and that would have such direct contact with life that it could give us fresh directions in each new situation. Only in this way could the question concerning the *content* of ethics be solved. Above the vain gropings of a fallen humanity that is seeking the right way, ring the glad tidings of the Spirit "Who leads us into all truth." Jesus actually pledges that whosoever continues in His word shall know the truth and the truth shall make him free. Accordingly, besides the inadequate human attempts of legalism (ὑπόνομος) and relativism (ἄνομος) there is a third possibility, though it is one that no one can acquire unless it is given him from heaven, and that is the possibility of guidance through the divine Spirit by the lifegiving law of the Spirit; where constraint and freedom have become an indissoluble unity, where the service of God has become perfect freedom.[33] This means, of course, that man becomes completely dependent on God and all human crutches, all self-dependence, has been taken away. Only in the continual hearing and obedience (ἔννομος χριστοῦ, I Cor. 9:21) of the revealed Word do we receive guidance from eternity. The same

[33] *Cf.* St. Matt. 10:19 *seq.*; St. John 16:13; 8:31 *seq.*; I John 2:20 and 27; Rom. 8:2 and 14; Gal. 5:18. Further, the many prayers for right guidance found in the Psalms, 32:8 *seq.*; 73:24; 31:4; 27:11; 139:24.

Spirit that assures us of the adoption of sons is the guide of our actions.[34]

But if the Spirit is "a spring from which all wisdom flows" then Christian ethics can never stop with a merely formal description of morals. The mere contemplation of the climax of our work is too comfortable to permit us to remain there. The description of the paradox of grace and judgment that lies over all our actions is not yet the complete fulfillment of what is required of us. True, he should refrain from producing a Christian ethics who does not know a "crisis of ethics" as it is found in the Gospel, but the spirit of God wants more and gives more than that. He is *near* to the contrite heart. He is ready at all times to give to each life an understanding of the content of His will, as well; is ready to interpret the meaning of a particular commandment in a particular hour, whether it be that He commands us to speak or keep silent, to run or to rest, to fight or to heal and bind up the wounds. And while God must repeatedly break down what we have tried to build up, because we have heard badly, that does not release us from our task but rather obligates us to renewed attempts to describe the content of Christian ethics as it must be newly grasped, when the mysterious changes of history continually alter the situations that arise in wedlock, school, Church, nation and state. Beneath the hammer blows of the Spirit, as He continually de-

---

[34] Luther, *Sermon von guten Werken:* "From this it follows that a Christian living in this faith does not need a teacher of good works but what occurs to him he does, and it is well done. . . . So a Christian who lives in this confidence towards God knows what he has to do and does it cheerfully and freely." "For every one who so lives as to secure for himself all graces before God, is well pleased with spiritual purity, consequently it is much easier for him to resist carnal uncleanness and the Spirit instructs him in this faith how he shall avoid all evil thoughts and everything that is unchaste. For the faith in divine favor, as it is continuous and always active, does not cease to admonish those who possess it concerning what is pleasing or displeasing to God, as St. John says in this epistle: 'Ye need not that any man teach you but the same anointing that is the spirit of God, teacheth you all things' (I John 2:27)." Er. Ed. 16:127 *seq.* A Christian "can distinguish between the spirits of error; power over the devil and the world has been given him, so that he is not only himself the temple of God but through his works he can instruct the world, which nevertheless has to be so unthankful that it persecutes him and cannot endure him." Buchwald, *Lutherpredigten,* I, 417. *Cf.* also Holl, *Luther,* p. 223, notes 2 and 3; p. 226, note 2, p. 234: *"affert gratia iudicum omnium rerum; perfectus Christianus plenus spiritu potest decalogum quendam ordinari et de omnibus rectissime iudicare."*

stroys the old, the warming fire of a new understanding and a new love will grow brighter.

The brother of the Law is compulsion, the sister of freedom is gladness. When the Spirit is the teacher He leads on to a cheerful spirit. The one who walks in the "flesh" brings a grudging sacrifice, but he who is led by the Spirit finds gladness in sacrifice and surrender.[35] The servant moils and toils in trying to do his duty; the son serves *ex hilaritate et amore.* The evil guests of greed, envy, vindictiveness, licentiousness and the fear of death, even the one who is armed cannot drive out of his house. "But when a stronger than he shall come upon him and overcome him he taketh from him all his armour wherein he trusted, and divideth his spoils," (St. Luke 11:22). Genuine self-denial, fearlessness in witnessing, patience in suffering, fervor in prayer (to say nothing of the endowment with extraordinary gifts of holiness and prophecy) cannot be secured forcibly, even by the most ardent zealots or most strong willed ascetics, for all their sacrifices are defiled by unspontaneous coercion, and the effort they have cost them. But where the breath of the Spirit bloweth the graves are opened and that which was withered becomes alive.

Any one who knows but a little of what is being accomplished out on the mission fields through the operation of the Gospel; any one who knows something of the strength of faith and sacrifice that is shown by the baptized heathen who so shortly before were still in fetters, will be inclined to be ashamed of this "European theology" which, as a result of scholastic investigations and almost a century of submersion in materialism seems to have forgotten how to trust in God's greatness or how to ask great things of Him. Here the "paralytic Christianity" (Blumhardt) of the West must turn back and

---

[35] Luther: "In the old man there is nothing but error through which the devil leads him to destruction. But the new man possesses the Spirit and the truth by which the heart is enlightened and which brings holiness and righteousness with it so that he follows God's Word and takes pleasure in doing good and in a godly life and conversation etc. So, on the other hand, the desire and love of sinning and all manner of vice proceeds out of error. Such a new man is created after the image and likeness of God; he must be a new man, different from those who live in error and evil lusts, who exist without the knowledge and obedience of God, for if he is to be the image of God he must possess the true divine understanding, knowledge and purpose and he must live a godly life, following after righteousness and holiness like God Himself." *Sermon for the 19th Sunday after Trinity.* Eph. 4:22-28. Er. Ed. 9, p. 311.

again learn to become like the little children; it must learn from the foolish how the first shall be last and the last first. The thing that impresses every student of missions is the striking parallels he finds to the accounts given by St. Paul of his missionary experiences. Here, as there, we find the evidence of "actually existing and easily demonstrable operations" of an external power. We see a great break with the heathen past, as for example, in the case of the "great repentance" on the island of Nias in the year 1917. In these fields the fear of demons and the tyranny of sorcery lose their power over enslaved men, as happened once at Ephesus. Shame and repentance, modesty and fervor in prayer appear in hearts before barren and hardened. And all that takes place not as the result of some sort of moral compulsion but through the overwhelming conviction of the Spirit working through the Word. In the same way the work of Inner Missions has its Pauline parallels. Here we can see how through the spiritual power of the preaching of the Cross and Resurrection the specific and very real vices of the great cities (ἀκαθαρσία, πορνεία, πλεονεξία) are overcome, now as then, and how the Easter power of purity becomes manifest.[86]

The work of the Spirit is directed towards positive ends. God does not stop with the eradication of the evil root; the planting and fruition of a new seed is equally His concern. The will that imagines itself free (*liberum arbitrium*) is shown its bondage, and the enslaved will (*servum arbitrium*) is liberated (*liberatum arbitrium*). Even the world of the emotions is subject to the progress of this holy regulation. The confusing intoxication of all the senses, the soft, luxurious enjoyment of religious feelings, the painful melancholy, the passionate desires are deprived of their disturbing insubordination and willfulness. It is not for the purpose of producing virtuosos of Stoicism. The ancient ideal of an anxiously regulated temperance, the Stoic ideal of freedom from desire are neither expected nor required of faith. The deadening of the feelings to the point of insensibility is not the end of the ways of God. "God does not want to destroy nature through the Gospel, what is natural He lets remain but directs it on the right way" (Er. Ed. 34, p. 250 *seq.*). If the powers of emotion

[86] I Thess. 1:3, 4:9; II Thess. 1:3; I Cor. 6:9-11; II Cor. 8:1-5; Col. 1:4; 2:11-13; 3:5-10; Phil. 2:13; Eph. 2:1 and 5; 3:20.

are an integral part of the whole psychic organism created by God
then the sanctifying power of the Spirit cannot pass by without affecting this domain whose disorders can distort both mind and will.
The Spirit judges the desires and passions of licentiousness, but He
does not demand emasculation; only the disciplined regulation of the
erotic impulse to its pure use. The words of the suppliant are not
to burn with wild ardor, they shall not be allowed to die by being
choked by their own superabundance but neither should he be anxiously or despairingly silent, but should speak like a dear child to his
affectionate Father. The one tormented by sufferings, under the discipline of the Holy Ghost, dare not simply writhe under his pains
or perish through them; not because he attains the insensibility of
a stone but because he gains the obedient strength of those who are
called blessed because they *endure* suffering. The stormy power of the
desires, which so quickly destroy fellowship, must die, not to make
way for loathing and dull joylessness, but to become the quickening
and beneficent bond of our fellowship when we have been justified
by faith. Even the Christian has a burning heart, only its fire comes
from a pure altar. When the emotional life is subjected to the purifying and sanctifying discipline of the Spirit it becomes a wonderful
instrument for the praise of God Who has given it faculties of hidden
depth and beauty that are not a natural endowment of human willing and thinking. The life of every noble woman who suffers herself to be led in the obedience of Christ is a living demonstration
of that fact. The mistrust of the inner life that is so characteristic
of our modern thinking has some justification in the over-valuation
and over-stimulation of the emotions that has always had such disas-
trous moral results for the life of faith. But the abuse dare not carry
us to the opposite extreme, to a point where the dulling of the emotions and their negation seems the end to be striven after. God rather
separates us from the errors and confusion of the emotions which
sin has brought with it, so as to set them free for their original pure
purposes by uniting them to Himself.

We have ventured to speak of a renewed willing and feeling in the
life of the believer on the basis of the vicarious and organic communion with Jesus. In contrast to the assumptionless views of philoso-

phy we have limited the testimony of the Spirit by God's freedom and the "not yet" of an expected fulfillment. The "yes" of the quickening was based on the hardest "no" which was stamped on the creative pride of man but by such presuppositions we have committed ourselves to the acceptance of a new birth that begins in an act of faith. Is it then likewise permissible, on the basis of revelation, to speak of a renewed knowledge or does faith have to content itself with a sort of critical agnosticism? Perhaps the attempt to distinguish here between a σοφία σαρκική and a σοφία πνευματκή, a "wisdom of regeneration" (Vilmar) will seem to many to be simply another case of pious presumption. However, it is hard to see why we should restrict our statements concerning the renewing work of the Holy Ghost just at this point. As in Adam the entire nature of man, in his actions, feelings and thoughts was corrupted, so, according to Scripture, this corruption shall be completely removed through the second Adam (Rom. 5), indeed it is to go beyond a mere reparation to new days of creation. But if a redemption of feeling and will is to take place in this present age through the gift of the Spirit given from above, so a wisdom from above must take the place of the wisdom of this world (σοφία ἐπίγειος, ψυχική). If there is a power in sin that darkens the understanding, so in Christ there is a power illuminating the Spirit. The New Testament leaves us in no doubt on that question. It makes four clear statements on the subject.

1. For the Christian the renewal of his mind (Rom. 12:2) means the surrender of his own human wisdom, which derives the materials for its constructive thought from the elements of the world. The divine wisdom is not merely an intensified human understanding. The two actually vary in an inverse ratio so that the one nullifies the other (I Cor. 1:18 seq.).

2. The illumination of the knowledge of the glory of God arises in the face of Jesus Christ (II Cor. 4:6), which means that it is not to be gained by means of intuitive, clairvoyant abilities but is a wisdom that has been produced by God Himself, is mediated by God and consequently is restricted to His revelation. "Not that we are sufficient to think anything as of ourselves; but our sufficiency is of God" (II Cor. 3:5). Only a "trinitarian" relationship; only in the triple har-

mony of a revelation that comes to us in creation, redemption and sanctification is the charism of renewed understanding to be gained (I Cor. 12:8).

3. The illumination of the understanding goes hand in hand with the renewal of the will. The thought of love and sacrifice is not endangered in this way, whereas the questioning of worldly wisdom easily leads to conceit, serves to produce self-glorification and admits the attitude of a proud observer. The wisdom that is from above is always to a certain extent bound and knows that it is obligated to service (I Cor. 8:1-7; 4:8-10; 13-2). "Rethinking" always means a new birth of the moral as well as of the intellectual concepts.

4. The present perception, even of the man who is spiritually minded, remains incomplete in comparison with that which is "perfect" and which is yet to be revealed (I Cor. 13:9-13). Where the "eyes of the understanding are enlightened" they are directed to "the glory of his inheritance" (Eph. 1:18). The natural reason, on the other hand, regards its results as absolute, believes in an immediate apprehension of the truth by the reason or will and despises the *Credo ut intelligam* of a God-fearing humility.

So we can see clearly what a radical difference exists between the "new thinking" and every rational metaphysics. An ontological realism that seeks to grasp the nature of being in the act of perception is no "devout" thinking in the view of the New Testament. For there God is reached by the autonomous reason that does not need His grace. The immediate knowledge of God in nature can never lead to the goal because the curse of Adam's transgression operative in nature confronts the observer with a harsh dissonance which can only be understood and endured when seen against the background of the Biblical ideas of judgment and hope. The praise of creation is only possible when the Creator is recognized as the One "Who forgiveth all thine iniquities, who healeth all thy diseases." Only where *deus in mundo incarnatus* is loved is it also possible *amare mundum in deo*. Every attempt of the philosophy of history that would ignore the second article of the Creed must fail. The spirit that is active in the history of peoples and nations may be regarded now in an idealistic, optimistic, now in a critical, pessimistic way, according to

circumstances, the march of events or personal experiences, so long
as the eschatological solution with its thoughts of judgment and grace
is not applied to all that has taken place. G. E. Lessing, Herder,
Hegel, on the one side, Schopenhauer, Spengler, Theodor Lessing on
the other may serve as examples. Wherever we seek to arrive at the
understanding of the world, be it in nature or in history, in the glorification of the body or in pure reason, it can never succeed apart
from the blessing of Christ. Why?

If according to the view of the New Testament our conscious woes
are only the theoretical expression of our practical guilt; if our judgments are all too largely determined by the prejudices and advantages
of self-love, then there can be no true knowledge so long as the guilty
load of prejudicing and enslaving sin still rests upon us. This hard
truth always becomes most evident by contrast with the person of
Jesus Himself, and in the light of His teaching. The one held in bondage by passion denies the reality of Christ and regards that reality as
a delusion and folly. The thinker wrapt up in the conceit of his own
wisdom despises the poor words of the Bible. The restless soul that
is pursued through life by the guilt and torment of wasted years
seeks in vain for the significance of their meaningless history (St.
Matt. 6:22 *seq.*). To the eyes of the lecherer all nature is a place of
wild desire and pleasure that destroys itself. Back of the sentient ego,
as Karl Heim has so convincingly shown in his *Glaubensgewissheit*,
is the volitional ego, which can only be separated from it by artificial
distinctions and which whispers to it its judgments of value. But if
this impure will that obscures our ideas is erased by the word of
forgiveness and itself is renewed through the power of the Spirit the
burden of doubt and blindness must be removed from our processes
of thought, and reason, once a "wise fool," enlightened by faith, becomes "a beautiful and splendid working tool of God" (Luther). If
it be pride and an ignoring of the limitations imposed by our own
guilt to try to give a final answer to the ultimate questions of the
world by philosophizing apart from Christ, so it is pure cowardice
not to accept the "depth of the riches, both of the wisdom and knowledge of God" (Rom. 11:33) through the *Christus pro nobis et in nobis*,

"Who of God is made unto us wisdom and righteousness and sanctification and redemption" (I Cor. 1:30).

What we have in mind is shown most clearly by the attitude of the
Christian towards nature. The Greek and Spinozian symbolic thinking sees in nature, from its beginning till its final destruction, the
working of eternal power.

> "When in the infinite recurring,
> The same forever floweth forth.
> A thousand different shapes unfolding,
> Combining brings new forms to birth,
> The joy of life from all is pouring,
> From largest star and smallest orb,
> And all the effort and the striving
> Is endless calm in God the Lord."

Goethe's feeling for nature, that finds its culmination in the devotion of love to the eternal feminine,[37] the hylozoism of the Ionic
nature philosophy, Laotse's Tao teaching as a cosmic-mystical intuition of the order ruling the world's totality, Gust. Th. Fechner's
"day view" in antithesis to the night view of science, Anker Larsen's
dreamy vision of nature, where in blissful states of unconsciousness the
secret of the All is unveiled ("Stein der Weisen, bei offener Tür),
are all attempts at a clairvoyant, artificial intuition and espionage of
the divine control of nature. Here the finite is already swallowed
up in the infinite and needs no hope of a future perfection. Not
very far removed from it is the Roman Catholic understanding of
nature, which has always gladly united with the mystic-pantheistic
transfiguration of nature as held by the romanticists. Certain circles
in the Roman Catholic youth movement of the present day are proof
of that fact. Above all we have to remember the Roman Catholic
teaching of the Sacraments and the sacramentals. Even though the
transformation of the earthly into the divine is coupled with the historic mystery of redemption, at the moment it is consummated the
heavenly becomes objectively visible and can be placed on exhibition.
The contemplation of faith has become superfluous through the static

---

[37] Tobias Poelmann, *Goethes Naturanschauung in neutestamentlicher Beleuchtung*, p.
31 *seq.*, Berlin, 1927.

presence of what is Holy, in finite nature. The completion has been anticipated, eternity made material on earth, only in a far grosser way than in the artistic vision of nature.

To this the Reformed view of nature furnishes the most complete antithesis. Here everything is dominated by the sharpest dualism between nature and grace. Max Weber has spoken of the "great historic religious process of exorcising the world" that began with the Hebrew prophets and was concluded in Puritanism. The tendency towards Nestorianism in Reformed Christology, the division of the Communion into two acts, one in heaven and one on earth (*cibus mentis*), we may venture to say are only the theological expression for the rigid separation that we find here between the corporeal and the spiritual, between nature and grace. In contrast to the unrestrained attempts of romanticism and vitalism to erase all boundaries it possesses a wonderful Old Testament view of the majesty of God. But it also possesses an unbiblical separation of heaven and the earth that is a result of divine creative power. In contrast to the New Testament testimony of the incarnation of the Word and in contrast to Jesus' attitude towards nature it has a repellent coldness and hardness. Though the resurrection of the body and the renewing of the earth are included in the Reformed Confessions yet there is missing a real basis of Christian hope in the true Biblical valuation and judgment concerning the present creation. Cultus and art, picture and music, the natural pleasures of the senses, in fact everything corporeal in creation had to die in the face of this suspicious, hostile condemnation of the earth. They believed that the only choice was between the honor of God and mere carnality, that there was no third course. It was inevitable after such a deflation of creation, after such a "hygienic rationalizing" of nature that God was either ethically rationalized or mystically spiritualized. Man isolated in a state of pure spirituality had nothing left except the choice between an obedient cultivation of the earth and its resources, as the tools that God had provided for the discharge of duty, and a world-renouncing soaring upward, from a godless earth to a pure spiritual existence on high. Unsacramental legalism and ascetic mysticism in the course of time both developed by an inner necessity out of Calvinism. In this way Schleiermacher's theology could be regarded as philosophical Calvinism.

For Lutheranism all these ways are alike untenable; the transfiguration of the senses in a naturalistic romanticism, the magical idealism of Goethe and Novalis, as well as the complete spiritualizing through a contemptuous elimination of the earth and its corporeal forms. For Luther all the reflections about the wisdom of God that have been gained from nature, apart from Christ and His Word, are only "inquisitive fables," "but since Christ has been born He has hallowed all things that we do in our natural life." What was natural in the eyes of Christ, by virtue of His union with the Father, this Martin Luther possessed by virtue of the atonement and his renewal through the Father. As Jesus' similitudes express the most intimate relationship of heaven and earth so Luther held the same faith and was appreciative of the divinely ordained congruity of nature and the Holy Spirit. In the presence of Christ he possessed that renewed knowledge which made him perceive in all that was God's creation, both large and small, a mark of His grace and sincerity. The flowering trees in the garden became Easter preachers for him. "Blessed be God, the Creator, Who in the springtime awakens these dead creatures to new life! . . . Here we have a beautiful picture of the resurrection of the dead. Winter is death, summer the resurrection of the dead when everything becomes alive and once more verdant."

But the graveyard aspect of nature, whose recognition distinguishes Christian symbolism from general religious and aesthetic ideas, is likewise present to his observation. The bounds and limitations of our knowledge of nature remind Luther of the lost Paradise. "The sun is a beautiful work of God but we are unable to contemplate it or steadily fix our eyes upon it. We have to turn our backs to it. Ah, dear Lord, if we had remained in Paradise we could have looked with open eyes upon the sun, without hindrance or pain." "Alas, if only Adam had not sinned man would have recognized, praised, lauded and loved God in all His creatures, so that even in the tiniest flower he would have seen and called to mind God's omnipotence, splendor and grace." But in spite of the appreciation of all the splendor and beauty of nature there is no losing sight of the fact that we are only "strangers and pilgrims" who are on our way to a more perfect home. The reminders of our departure and pilgrimage are constantly recurring. Paul Gerhardt's "Lo! I deem it here so sweet" we already find in Luther: "If God created this perishing kingdom so beautiful, how much more beautiful will He have made the imperishable and eternal kingdom!" And in May time he cries out "O that we could rightly trust God! What will that life be like when God can give us such joy in this time of our pilgrimage?"

The figurative possibilities of creation as they are unfolded to faith are not exhausted by the few comparisons we have selected from the riches of Luther's writings. Morning and evening, the seasons of the year and the ages of man's life, seed time and harvest, our bodies and our daily bread, time and space, all speak the holy and gracious language of God to those who have ears to hear and eyes to see. We are here dealing not only with artificial metaphors which can be constructed when a sufficient poetic talent and imagination and the necessary inclination are present, but with God's personal message directed towards us; a message which faith is able to perceive in the language of His works and which it thankfully recognizes. "Here," we are moved to say in the words of Augustine, "we have rather to adore than to understand." Whosoever has looked into the heart of God through His Son, may look upon His face in His creation. If Christ is "the beginning, middle and end of all His creatures" (Er. Ed. 45, p. 324), "through Whom, from Whom and in Whom they have their life and being" (St. John 1:3), then the soul that trusts in His *revelatio specialis* will be led by Him to His *revelatio generalis*. Faith then sees no longer merely the "workday clothes" of a fallen creation, but "rejoicing in hope" (Rom. 12:12) also sees the "Sunday clothes" which the pure world of God wore at the beginning and which it will again assume in still greater beauty and purity at the end of days. Not Goethe, Keller, Dehmel nor Thomas, nor even Gellert, but Luther, Dürer, Paul Gerhardt, Joh. Seb. Bach, Hamann, M. Claudius, Claus Harms and Loehe possessed such a vision of hope.[88] While those first

[88] It was the same Paul Gerhardt that wrote the *Güldene Sonne; Geh aus, mein Herz* and *Nun ruhen alle Wälder*, who, although he was "not a contentious nature," preferred to demit his office rather than sign the declaration demanded by his Reformed Elector. The customary explanation of his stand has been the assumption that "unfor-

mentioned placed God and nature in one plane or rose by cosmological proofs from the world up to God, the others met God in the incarnate Christ, then progressed to the Third Article of the Creed and there found again the First Article, by virtue of that Biblical organism that unites corporeal and spiritual in one redemptive unity.

The New Testament conception does not know the Greek immediateness of knowledge that comes from an immediate perception of God in the world, but just as certainly it also rejects the dualistic separation of body and spirit by which Christianity would become a spiritually attenuated other-worldliness. But it does know a change of mind, an illuminated reflection concerning the cosmos that is made possible by the statements of a transcendental revelation. It is hardly possible to estimate how far reaching the results might be if a believing theology would muster up courage enough to speak authoritatively about a renewal of thinking, just as it speaks about a renewal of the will and of the emotions. We can best discern the grievous consequences of a view of nature, apart from faith, of a habit of thought that has not felt the influence of Pentecost, by recalling the practical results which have resulted from the rational, formal division of the world into a purely physical-material and a purely spiritual sphere.

If man has no place before God as a corporeal-spiritual unity but only as an intelligent, ethical personality (Kant), then the body is degraded to a mere material product and as such is misused. Then all bodily activities, eating and recreation, labor and art become wicked, sink into mere technique and mechanism, or are degraded to the satisfaction of the lowest sensuality. Only on such soil can a "philosophy of pride" (Sartorius) or a "theology of rhetoric" (Vilmar)

---

tunately" alongside the "warmhearted" poet there existed a "harsh theologian" Gerhardt. But this ignored the fact that it was only as such a confessionally faithful son of the Lutheran Church that he could write such morning, evening, and summer hymns. This is especially true of Joh. Seb. Bach. A Schweitzer once asked the significant question what would Bach have become "if he had first seen the light of day in Zurich or Geneva"? Such a spirit could only unfold itself in the atmosphere of Lutheranism; in the Church of a Meyfarth, Eber, Hermann, Matthesius, Herberger and Benj. Schmolk. It was the same master musician who would not permit his children to attend the Reformed school in Köthen, who had in his library two complete editions of Luther, as well as copies of Tauler's sermons, Arndt's *True Christianity*, and a strikingly large number of Lutheran devotional books, the so-called "ancient consolers."

come into existence. Only from this standpoint is it possible to forget that our entire thinking is continually bound to our corporeal nature, which is a daily gift to us, and that without the miracle of creation the very act of thinking is itself inconceivable. The Biblically minded man, who is convinced of the completeness and unity of body and spirit knows that as a consequence of his created nature, even in his very mental activity he is in a continuous physical dependence on the Lord, Who can bestow both or deny both. For this reason, if for no other, he does not assert the autonomy of knowledge. For the same reason he thankfully acknowledges his indebtedness and responsibility to the brethren whose labors in gathering the fruits of the earth have alone made possible the flights of his fancy. To forget the physical basis of spiritual activity is to deny reality and to be arrogant and unlovely. All uncorporeal-abstract, spiritualistic philosophizing individualizes and isolates men, while the recognition of the earth as God's dwelling place can bridge over social class distinctions and exert a unifying force.

We have learned to know the threefold office of the Spirit in His reproving and blessing activity. As the Spirit omits nothing from man's extremity, so He omits nothing from his renewal. Just as every one is abased under His judgment, so under His uplifting grace everyone who is abased becomes exalted. "He hath put down the mighty from their seats and exalted them of low degree, He hath filled the hungry with good things and the rich He hath sent empty away" (St. Luke 1:57). In the weak the power of God is mighty so that with renewed thoughts, feelings and purposes they are enabled to accomplish what before was sought in vain. "The Holy Ghost changes the person and turns him into a new man who then possesses a new understanding and a new will that are both inclined to good" (Luther).

The Church of Christ has never lacked men and women who have honored God through the penitent confession of their sins and weaknesses and who in doing so became rich in the "fruits of the Spirit," in power, in love and in clearness of knowledge. So it is impossible to see why there should be any objection to mentioning as examples the names of those in the history of the Church who believed in the

pardoning and sanctifying power of God in His Word and whose conversation, according to the testimony of many witnesses, became
streams of blessing, fountains of living waters. According to the
Apology of the Augsburg Confession (223, 4) we are to thank God
because in His saints He has shown examples of mercy; because He
has shown that He wishes to save men; because He has given teachers
and other endowments to the Church. And these endowments, because they are so great, should be highly exalted and the saints themselves who have faithfully used these gifts should themselves be lauded,
just as Christ in the Gospel praises the faithful servants. The Confession adds as a further ground for thankfulness the strengthening of
our faith and the encouragement to discipleship through the example
of those who were loyal in faith, love and suffering. The absolute rejection of the invocation of the saints (Augs. Conf. XXI) never destroyed the thankful commemoration of the example of the great
teachers and servants of the Church in Lutheranism. Historic references to the blessed activities of such men dare not be sneered at as
"little litanies of all saints." On the contrary, it would be very desir-
able if theology as a science, as well as in the preaching of the Church
and the teaching of the school, would make larger use of the rich
treasures that lie hidden in the history of Christian piety and in the
biographical literature of the Church. Evangelical Germany does not
have to go to Rome or to England to seek living examples of justification and sanctification. Any one who is familiar with the lives of
Bengel, Rieger, Hofacker, Blumhardt, Löhe and Harms, just to make
an arbitrary selection of a few names, sees before him figures who are
certainly not of immaculate purity; who according to their own confessions are "inclined to hate God and their neighbor" (Heidelberg
Catechism) but who through the mighty workings of grace have been
enriched with a fullness of the Spirit that makes it profitable for us in
our poverty to draw inspiration from them. True if the question had
been asked whether "any inspired person were present" who could
assert that he loved God and his neighbor, not one of them would
have stood up. Men do not brag about gifts that have been given
them, nor do they place them on exhibition. The one who has no
fruits of his own but only what he has received from God does not

proclaim his holiness nor does he make it the object of calculating and proud contemplation. "Only by its fruits shall it be manifested; we shall not strive to bring it to light by self-contemplation and self-observation; that would only grieve the Spirit and hinder the growth of love" (Kierkegaard).

But it is by just such a humility that is daily born anew in the crucifying fires of justification that man becomes skilled in the service of God. The same powers with which he dishonored God when he was dead in sins are now liberated to the praise of His glory. Out of the insolent natural will comes the fidelity of a strong, courageous obedience. The pursuing persecutor now follows. Weak sentimentality can be changed into a sympathetic understanding of the neighbor's needs. Consuming doubts may become mighty spiritual reflections concerning the wisdom of God's thoughts. If the understanding, will and emotions have been alike fully developed as a result of the great change that has taken place under the influence of the Spirit, then such great personalities are produced as Paul, Augustine, Luther, who deeply humbled themselves and yet could give forth so superabundantly that it is hardly possible to grasp the full extent of their life work. But even the smaller gifts and talents that come as a result of the vivifying power of the Spirit of God, may attain to an undreamed-of purity and fertility (St. John 15). The feelings of the heart, the spiritual maturity, the discipline of the will that we can find among faithful Bible readers in the humblest circles, among the peasants and workingmen, are a living proof of that fact. Contrary to all claims it might make, contrary to and above all comprehension and understanding, a faith that humbly awaits God's judgment, experiences such acceptance and giving of life, with such liberation from the double burden of guilt and power of sin that every possible expression of gratitude remains insufficient for the greatness of the grace that has been bestowed.

CHAPTER V

Sanctification as the Answer of the Justified Sinner

WE HAVE spoken in most emphatic tones, perhaps too emphatically for some, concerning the renewing, sanctifying power of the Spirit of God. We have undoubtedly had the right to speak and have needed to speak emphatically because our attention was directed exclusively towards the *Deus semper agens*, and the "superlative greatness of His power over us," and not towards the heart of man. God's will desires a complete communion with us. For that purpose He effected in Christ a universal and actual atonement and vivification, and placed the power of awakening faith in the word of the Gospel. Why then is God not victorious on earth? Why then do unbelief and alienation from God, the bondage of sin and enmity towards God, continue to rule so widely and mightily, as though Easter had meant nothing but the appearance of a phantom? Why do weakness, timidity and backsliding prevail so extensively even in the camp of the confessors, rather than God's certain peace and victorious power, in spite of the fact that the will of God is our sanctification and the risen Christ is on the field with His good gifts and spirit? It is not possible for the Church to excuse herself in all cases with the objection, "Have they not heard?" What Paul wrote to the young congregation in Rome applies still more forcibly today: "Yea verily, their sound went into all the earth and their words unto the ends of the world."[1] If, however, God causes His will to be proclaimed that we might live[2] and, yet, more die than see life, the reason cannot be found in God Himself but must be found somehow in the attitude of men. *Cum promissio sit universalis nec sint in deo contradictoriae voluntates, necesse est in nobis esse aliquam discriminis cau-*

---

[1] Eph. 1:19; I Tim. 2:4; Heb. 4:12; I Thess. 4:3; Rom. 10:18.
[2] *Cf.* Ez. 33:11, quoted in the Formula of Concord, 600, 49.

sam, is the statement of Melanchthon's *Loci*. But here we have reached the central point of our investigation. It is the question concerning the relation of grace and freedom, of the relation of the divine and human wills both in its beginning, in its continuation and in the preservation of faith. All that can be further said about justification and sanctification will depend on the correct description of this relationship. We will begin with the most important question, that concerning the relation of divine grace and the freedom of the human will in the *awakening* of faith. It is well known how many different answers have been given in theology for the solution of this problem. The very multiplicity of such answers as Ludthardt has given them with approximate completeness in his well-known work[3] is sufficient proof that we are here confronted by one of the most difficult problems of theology. We will consider only the three most important views, as closer examination will show that all the rest can be included under one of these. They are deterministic monergism, Pelagianism and synergism.

A simple unquestioning confession of God's sole activity, of the irresistibility of grace in the bestowal of salvation would seem most in conformity with the Biblical testimony concerning man's deadness in all that is good. Here an end has been made once for all of every theory of human freedom; with the Roman Catholic teaching of the *infirmata libertas* and still more emphatically with the Socinian idea and that of the romanticists of a creative autonomous power residing in man. As a result of the fall there is no freedom left. To use St. Augustine's figure of speech: the coin that has fallen from the hand of the king into the dust cannot return of itself into the hand of its owner. So it is with the soul, even though it may retain the traces of its original image and may desire to return to its lost home. But the case must be stated still more sharply. The fearful situation does not merely consist in our resting in a state of separation from God. Even after his fall man has continued to possess a creative capacity but this is now only able to show itself in a degenerative activity that separates him further and further from God. But a falling body can never halt

[3] *Die Lehre vom freien Willen und seinem Verhältnis zur Gnade in ihrer geschchtlichen Entwickelung*, Leipzig, 1863.

its own descent, to say nothing of reversing it into an ascent. Such a change can take place only through a forcible interposition from without. But that means that conversion and renewal depend wholly on the sovereign interposition of God Who "deals with men."

Powerfully as this expresses the Biblical concern for the expression of man's helplessness and God's exclusive omnipotence, it is nevertheless not possible to suppress certain serious misgivings. There is the danger, that Lutheranism has always seen more clearly than Calvinism, namely that in the exclusive emphasis on God's election and His forcible operation the personal, moral responsibility of man, who has been awakened to faith, will be overlooked and its real importance despised. "In this respect it might well be said that man is not a stone or block. For a stone or block does not resist that which moves it, and does not understand and is not sensible of what is being done with it, as a man, as long as he is not converted, with his will resists God the Lord."[4] Our endowment with faith is under no conditions to be described as a gift that is "magically imparted to us," forcibly impressed on us (*necessitate physica*) and is only endured by us with helpless unwillingness: "We do not want it but cannot escape it" (Schlatter). Wherever such compulsory, deterministic statements are used to describe God's activity we come dangerously close to supralapsarianism, which ultimately makes God the author of sin. The absolute supremacy of God's call and election dare never suppress the feeling of human guilt and responsibility. The gift of regeneration coming from the hand of the personal, divine Creator and Redeemer is too great to be accomplished in man unconsciously and without regard to the personal will, like some physical process, as if "water were poured into a barrel," or as "a statue is cut in a stone or a seal impressed upon wax, which knows nothing of it." Faith as the result of an act of God's majesty dare not be so described that the "*gratia trahit non cogit*" and the "*nemo credit nisi volens*" is excluded.[5] "God's Spirit bestows Himself, but He does not surrender Himself." He urges a choice but He does not thereby exclude our decision. He gives us

[4] Form. of Concord. 602, 59; 608, 82 *seq.*
[5] Form. Con. Sol. Decl. II, *De libero arbitrio:* 609, 89; 603, 60. *Apology,* 95, 48; 125, 106; 139, 183.

courage for the affirmation of faith but still leaves us the freedom to choose the unhappy negation of unbelief.

To have brought the fact of moral responsibility very emphatically to its rightful place is the real contribution of Pelagianism and it probably owes its long life only to this fact. It is the "perpetual brother" of predestination; its great antagonist that is always bobbing up in history whenever dogma threatens to suppress ethics to a point where it is meaningless; a demonstration of how "an eternal truth is wrapt up in every great historic occurrence" (Wilhelm Preger). The Pelagian emphasis rests on the simple proposition, that seems so apparent to natural reason, that each one must save his own soul and die for his own sins. But behind this optimistic, magnanimous feeling of personal responsibility lurks such a superficial idea of freedom, such a philosophically untenable, abstract autonomy of the soul, such a naive confidence in personal ability, that both Scripture and personal experience have always very quickly corrected such a theology.

The final "solution" that usually resulted as a consequence of dissatisfaction with both views was synergism. For the "either—or" there was substituted a "partially," a division that still permitted two varieties to exist as either God or man, received the pre-eminence. As far as the final result is concerned, it is true, it makes little difference whether man makes the beginning (*naturalibus propriis viribus incohare*) and God comes to his assistance (*adjuvare*) in completing it, or whether God approaches a certain distance towards him and man thereupon advances from his side. In either case man is an efficient coworker in effecting his own salvation. Whether or not God accomplishes His work of salvation, according to this view, is decided even for God Himself by man's preparatory willingness (*se disponere, se ad gratiam dei praeparare*) or by his loving cooperation (*cooperari*). This view which makes God an obligatory rewarder of His own creation is found not only in Semipelagianism and the Thomistic theology but it has always found adherents in Protestant theology and has retained its influence on the pulpit to our own day.

Melanchthon and the Philippists (for example Pfeffinger and Strigel) were already afraid that as a result of Luther's harsh deterministic statements concerning the bondage of the will ("the condemnation

of those who have not deserved it"), the practical-ethical side of faith
as an inner decision might be lost. So his followers formulated, with
the greatest caution, the teaching *de tribus causis efficientibus, concur-
rentibus in conversione hominis non renati.* The Word, the Spirit
and the will they said must be united if the act of faith was to come
into existence. In this connection the third factor, the human will, was
described with evangelical modesty as a *non repugnari verba dei* ("in
so far as man does not reject the Word and strives against his own
weakness"). However when the assenting decision of man was re-
corded as a *tertia causa* in regeneration, equally as important as the
forces of divine operation (*verbum, spiritus*) then man was no longer
a *subjectum convertendum* but his assent became a *causa salutis.* It is
true that the description of faith as a *non spernere sed assentiri* conformed to the Biblical facts but by the coordination of a completely
receptive act that was produced in man with a free productive action
of God immediately brought them again face to face with the scholastic declaration: *Hominis voluntas in conversione non est otiosa, sed
agit aliquid.*[6] Of course it was only a minimum of cooperation that
was here required; an exceedingly small requirement compared with
what was asked by the medieval practice of penance. As the synergists
stated it: God gave the dollar, man only the farthing but, as the
Gnesio Lutherans saw with irrefutable clearness, salvation was thus
once more placed in the hands of man. Even the subtle synergism was
recognized as a late offshoot of Pelagian teaching and the Formula of
Concord with sharply defined, clear-cut statements excluded this whole
tendency in its gross and subtle forms alike. Man is not in a position,
*viribus suis propriis aliquid, ad conversionem suam vel ex toto vel ex
dimidia vel minima parte conferre, agere, operari aut cooperari (ex
se ipso tanquam ex semet ipso, 589, 7).*

We have seen the chief answers that have been given the question
as to the relation of grace and freedom in the inception of faith. None
of them has seemed to us to be wholly satisfactory. While each contains some element of truth none of them includes the truth in its
entirety. Absolute monergism avows with unmistakable emphasis the
justificatio impii, the calling and invitation by God of a hostile and

[6] Form. Con. 610, 90; 608, 86.

antagonistic humanity, but with its hard and fast formulas it over-rides the personal character of the human spirit and makes God a tyrannical, mechanically operative force. The idea of autonomous freedom is indeed animated by a serious feeling of moral obligation, but it is ensnared by a dangerously blind optimism concerning the extent of its ability. The mediating solution of synergism leaves to man a modest portion of responsibility in the attainment of salvation but in doing so it again makes the individual's worth and merits a cause and condition of blessedness before God and finally reveals itself as nothing more than a somewhat more tenable variation of the theme of the freedom of the will. So none of these three does full justice to the facts of faith. Neither does it make a statement that really conforms to the Biblical teaching, which holds fast, without any qualification, both to God's sole activity in the work of salvation and also to man's full moral responsibility. So it is evident that a really Scriptural answer must of necessity bear a paradoxical character that can be affirmed only through the deepest experiences of the con-science. Only through the feeling of guilt, by which man perceives himself as a part of a fallen world, is it possible to comprehend that we have to speak in contradictory terms and with statements that it is hard for the reason to understand if we would rightly perceive and possess the truth that is to make us free.

The essence of the Gospel may be described in two statements: God in Christ seeks the lost through His Word, and quickens what is dead. Even where He is not sought He addresses men and where He is avoided He yet faithfully speaks and acts. God shows the will its contrariness and the understanding its darkness. Through His state-ments in the Law He terrifies our conscience and crushes our pride. But in the Gospel of Christ He pictures to us His heartfelt mercy, and through the Spirit gives us the courage to trust in His Word. In con-version God forcibly turns our rebellious minds to repentance, tears the hard heart out of our breast and as it were by a miracle gives us the new spirit and understanding of faith. It is not as though man through the Word received certain powers from above by whose assistance he could then freely decide by himself to accept grace, to surrender and obey. No, what precedes conversion is nothing but darkness and opposition, enmity and death. Man *suffers* the merciful kindness of God in his heart, will, understanding and emotions; it is God Who awakens the stones so that they become children and Who fills the broken and contrite hearts with the consolation of forgiveness. It is true man must hear, receive and permit God to hold and fill his resisting hands, but here the old, keen definition of the fathers must apply: *receptio alicujus rei non est actio sed passio*. The reception of anything is not something active but passive. The act of reception is necessary, however it is not the receiving hand but the food that is given which saves and satisfies. The man who is converted and has come to believe always finds himself face to face with an incomprehensible, unearned happening that has come upon him as a blessed, saving experience; that he has neither produced nor selected by any natural or higher capabilities, and that is nevertheless not felt as a compulsion but as an unspeakable joy, which he thankfully accepts.

If faith is an *actus passivus*, something that God does to me and effects in me, that does not exclude my personal participation and my willingness to be used as an instrument but rather includes both, then unbelief is an *actio rebellis*, a conscious, intentional and responsible decision against God, a fixed decision not to permit myself to be judged or saved by Him. As men we have the sad possibility of a freedom to do evil. The freedom to do good must be given us. We can destroy the image of God in which the Creator fashioned us as His creatures, but we cannot repair it. We cannot move God to call us, but we can stop our ears to His call when it comes to us. None of us can bring about the "drawing of the Father," but we possess the fearful ability to withstand the breath of the Spirit when He breathes upon us, and so to rouse the wrath of God against us. He who allows himself to be fed with the bread of life receives life, he who refuses it compasses his own death. Man cannot save himself but he can destroy himself. My faith is produced *sola gratia*, the *repugnare* is *mea maxima culpa*. The *bona opera* are God's work, the *mala opera* are our work. The "I will" comes from God, the "I will not" from man's own free choice. Acceptance is not earned through merit but is a gift; perdition is not the result of fate but of sin. In the final judgment men are placed at the right hand of the Judge; they place themselves at His left.

It is quite evident then how our statements differ from the three historic positions of theology that we cited above. There we saw that for the monergist both salvation and rejection come from God; for the autonomous spirit both salvation and damnation come about through man himself, while the synergist cautiously divides what is done into two parts because he trusts neither the power of God nor that of man completely. The division that results from our description of faith is utterly different. Here the positive results are attributed to God alone, the negative consequences to man alone. To rational and rationalistic-ethical thinking it will always remain incomprehensible and to the highest degree offensive that under the same circumstances the failure to reach the highest objective brings punishment with it, but in its attainment the "negative cause" (Stahl) brings no corresponding merit to man, and that in the final judgment on life salvation is regarded as something unearned, while its loss has been earned. Yet faith can never surrender this paradox, for thus alone the entire strength of its conviction and its holy sincerity can reach its full expression: our surrender to God does not come out of ourselves but from God's promise to us and from the renewing power of His Spirit, Who bears His own witness within us (Autopistie). Our rejection in every case is a renewed and guilty exclusion of ourselves from His call and life-giving activity for which we are fully responsible; it is a renewed departure from Paradise, without occasion for it in the happenings of the world, after God has again opened its gates.

Far-reaching consequences for Christian preaching spring from this paradoxical experience that conscience has made of God's sole activity in effecting salvation and man's sole responsibility for his own destruction. If preaching is to do justice to this paradoxical combination it must always speak both in dogmatic *and* ethical terms; in the indicative *and* imperative, not in the sense of synergistic combination but in the sense of that incomparable antinomy: "Work out your own salvation with fear and trembling, for it is God which worketh in you both to will and to do of his good pleasure" (Phil. 2:12). This Pauline "for" which cuts through all human logic is secure both against the reproach of quietism and against the possible misunderstanding that our salvation was effected by the combined cooperation of two equal partners. This γάρ makes it impossible to call the conversion a joint work of God *and* man; to speak of a cooperative activity or of a contribution on our part. We are not active in our regeneration as though we had helped to bring it to pass, for both the impulse and the power to believe come from God. So there can be no thought of self-praise (Rom. 3:27). We do not thank ourselves for the gifts we receive from others. The credit for deliverance from the danger of death belongs to the rescuer and not to the one who has been saved. So the Pauline statement in Phil. 2:12 *seq.* does not call in question but rather substantiates the *justificatio impii*. But the other thought, "Today if ye will hear his voice harden not your hearts," likewise retains its full significance. If we are lost it is our own personal guilt that is responsible. It is not because of God's specific election. Neither is it the fault of the Word, as though its light were not strong enough. "That not all but only a small part of humanity are illuminated," remarks Luther, "is not the fault of the Light, our Lord Jesus Christ. For He is called and really is the Light of the world and of all men; He shines forever and ever and for this purpose He has been appointed by God. . . . Because men do not want to be enlightened by it, but deride, persecute and condemn it as lies of darkness and of the devil, it does not follow that Christ is not the light of all men. They feel the brightness and light of our teaching but do not want to see it. It is not the fault of the light that they do not accept it" (Er. Ed. 45, p. 378 *seq.*).

The theological significance and justification of the doctrine of eternal damnation is to be understood in this connection. That Luther approved and affirmed it is in full agreement with the opinion we have just cited and with what continually recurs in his writings. A Biblical eschatology cannot omit this dark thought of judgment because just here the decisive character of faith is carried to its logical conclusion. Helpless man is still so powerful that he can defy the Almighty—even beyond the gates of death. By his continually hardened self-will he is actually able to accomplish the fearful result of ruining God's tireless efforts to save him and of fulfilling in himself the words of the Apocalypse: "He that is unjust let him be unjust still" (Rev. 22:11).

If such a terribly serious retribution rests on man's rejection then theology as a science, and not simply the practical care of souls, is concerned in discovering what are the grounds for this refusal and what hindrances prevent the acceptance from coming to pass. Why will men not come, though the invitation of divine mercy, "Come, for all things are now ready" is presented to them? In the parable Scripture cites eroticism ("I have taken a wife"), and mammon ("I have bought a field"); the desire for pleasure and the desire for might as the two great powers man does not want to surrender nor yield to judgment. According to Scripture, however, these are not the only causes of hardening. Besides them there are the limitations created by the pride of reason, the self-indulgence in an effete emotional life, by the desires as well as by the weakness and pride of the will. This is not yet the place to discuss them in detail but of this there can be no doubt that for the overcoming of unbelief a real knowledge of its various causes is one of the most essential theological and practical tasks of the Church.

At the conclusion of the first question we look once more into Scripture and find that this paradox of exclusive divine action and of entire human responsibility, as we have been describing it, has not come out of a fondness for toying with paradoxes but springs out of the Word itself that so clearly states both facts: salvation is by grace alone without human additions, but that does not permit any resentment against their fate or a dull resignation to it on the part of those who have erred. Even the prophetic words of the Old Testament tell of freely offered grace: "Lo, every one that thirsteth, come ye to the waters; and he that hath no money, come ye, buy and eat." God provides wells in the wilderness. Immediately beside them, however, are the most terrible judgments pronounced over the nation that has despised God's freely electing love and become a harlot. The Gospels portray Jesus as the Good Shepherd, Who goes out to seek the lost sheep that neither can nor wishes to find its way back. He seeks, invites, persuades and induces, wrestles and prays for each human being. "Ye have not chosen me but I have chosen you." So He manifests the power of the Father that alone can bring salvation. But besides testifying to the love of God He proclaims the holiness of God, which no one can mock and go unpunished. God rewards the one who holds Him in contempt by granting him his desire so that he forever separates himself from the source of life. None of those men who refused His invitation shall taste of His supper and it is said of Jerusalem, that had ever and again hardened herself with a "would not": "So your house shall be left unto you desolate." St. Paul does not know of any work of the flesh that could effect salvation; he proclaims a righteousness availing before God, that has come through Jesus Christ, "without the works of the law," and that possesses the power of producing faith. "But they have not all obeyed the Gospel."[7] There are refined (Galatian) and gross (Corinthian) vices by which man suffers shipwreck of the faith God has produced and by which he loses Christ.

In Scripture we find both David and Herod. Both commit adultery. Both receive a warning from God, the one through Nathan, the other through John the Baptist. The one breathes forth the psalm of penitence, the other kills the annoying preacher. Together the Gospel portrays the thieves, the one on the right, the other on the left; the Roman centurion and the hierarchy of Israel. The Cross preaches its message to all. All see and hear the suffering, praying and dying Christ. A part are carried by His death to God, a part remain nothing but spectators, to their own damnation. Paul smitten down by God on the road to Damascus does not speak "with flesh and blood" and through the grace of God becomes what he is. The Lord "opens the heart" of the jailer at Philippi, but alongside of such as these, who have permitted themselves to be saved, the story of the Book of Acts passes before our eyes a multitude of persons who destroyed themselves with their own freedom. The judges of Stephen "were cut in their hearts," but "they gnashed on him with their teeth, . . . they cried out with a loud voice, and stopped their ears and ran upon him with one accord." Felix, the governor was terrified when he heard St. Paul's sermon concerning righteousness, temperance and judgment

[7] Is. 55:1; 65:2; II John 15:16; St. Luke 14:24; St. Matt. 23:37 *seq.*; St. John 5:40; Acts 7:51 *seq.*; Rom. 10:16, 21.

to come, but he got rid of him with a polite lie. The resurrection and world power of the Messiah is preached to King Agrippa. He yields in a measure to the preaching of the Apostle but destroys the work God has begun in him by the smooth and wretched excuse: "Almost thou persuadest me to be a Christian." Thus Scripture denies to man any credit for the beginning of faith but does not absolve him from his own responsibility. It bestows salvation to man but it does not credit him with any merit.

Is this paradoxical relation of grace and freedom that we have encountered at the inception of faith in any way altered when we come to discuss the progress and maintenance of faith? Here the older Protestant theology made a very decided distinction. The attitude of the natural man (the *homo ad bonum prorsus corruptus et mortuus*) in his conversion is *pure passive*, there is no cooperation on his part in producing faith. It is different in the case of the regenerate who "through the power of the Holy Ghost can and should cooperate, even though it be still in great weakness" (Form. Con. 604, 65 *seq*. and 609, 88 *seq*.). At the same time two important cautions were at once added. Once there is an explicit statement that such a "cooperation with God" exists only so long as "God rules, directs, guides with His Holy Spirit." "As soon as God withdraws His hand" it ceases. In the next place there is an explicit denial that the regenerate man "cooperates with the Holy Ghost in the same way that two horses harnessed together draw one wagon." How are we to regard these doctrinal statements of the Confession?

We have seen that the word of forgiveness possesses the power to produce in the hearer through faith a new life force—the Pneuma. It is not the support and strengthening of the old will as it already exists but a completely new creation. "The stone is not merely lacking in softness, so that it is now sufficiently softened, but it is exchanged for a heart of flesh."[8] The believer who does not withstand the Word but rejects the natural evil condition of life, is permitted to receive in secret the newly aroused impulses of the Spirit. He then receives new spiritual powers and abilities not only in his will but in the totality of his existence, including his powers of emotion and understanding.

---

[8] Calvin, *Unterricht in der christlichen Religion*, pp. 142 and 146.

Freedom is attained in faith (II Cor. 3:17). With a power of volition that has been awakened to new life by the Holy Ghost he is able to love and serve God, and this freedom grows, when rightly used and exercised, just as its misuse brings about the destruction of faith, according to the rule that to him that hath shall be given, so that he may have abundance, but that from him who hath not shall be taken even that which he hath.

So the Confession is perfectly correct in its statement that through the Word and faith a liberated will (*arbitrium liberatum*) is in fact imparted to the one who is justified. It possesses a new activity and with a new ability to act also a new sense of obligation. A God-given will is begotten within us that unites itself with the will averse to sin and that is accepted by our personality, and makes itself felt in all our being. But in spite of this, in spite of all its caution, the Formula was mistaken when it called this liberated activity, that after all is no part of us but proceeds from God, a "cooperation." When neither the incentive to action nor the power of accomplishment, nor the perseverance that leads to completion comes from ourselves, then every expression must be scrupulously avoided that might awaken even the appearance of any creative participation on our part in the process of renewal. So sanctification as well as regeneration must be guarded against every form of synergistic misunderstanding. What is true of justification is also true here. It is a *sanctificatio impii*; an *actio dei gratuita*, that is, the vivification as well as the continuation and preservation result from grace, without our being an associated cause for their existence. Of course Scripture speaks of the disciples as "fellow workers with God" but perhaps hardly any of its statements are handled with greater flippancy than this one. There is a vast difference between these words when they are used by St. Paul, the humbled witness of Jesus Christ, who has been consecrated to His death, and when they are used by some orator of zealous piety who wants to help God "build His kingdom." Cooperation would presuppose that we do not everlastingly hinder, spoil and destroy the work that God is trying to accomplish in us, when in fact the truth is that in spite of much indolence, opposition and despondency He nevertheless succeeds in us through the power of His omnipotence, that does not need the assistance of our supporting activity. So the same strict law that determined the beginning of the life of faith also determines its continuance. We can and we will act but in our activity all autonomous independence and significance is lacking. "We do what is done by the Spirit of God within us" (Calvin). Or to express it in the classic words of the Epistle to the Ephesians: "We are his workmanship, created in Christ Jesus, unto good works, which God hath before ordained that we should walk in them" (2:10).

But the other side of our relationship in renewal is equally serious. Every lapse from the new life into our old nature is our own grievous guilt. Because there is a quickening Spirit present, Who gives the impulse and the ability for prayer and service, it becomes a sin for which we are accountable when we do not pray, do not obey, do not hold fast to our "first love." To state it according to the order of the steps in the *ordo salutis*; we cannot call (*vocare, trahere*) ourselves but we can despise the call that has come to us. God converts us (*regeneratio*) and we turn ourselves away from Him. God causes us to be grafted into Christ (*insertio in Christum, unio mystica*) and we tread under foot the seed corn. We are hallowed through the charism of the Spirit and lose that holiness through uncleanness. God gives the power to run (*bona opera*) and we stand still. God alone preserves us in fidelity (*conservatio fidei*) but we are able to reply to His long-demonstrated faithfulness with thanklessness.

The paradox of God's sole activity and man's responsibility which is found in sanctification as well as in justification, brings with it an entirely new conception of the New Testament imperatives whose importance and frequent occurrence cannot be emphasized strongly enough.[9] In no case are they to be regarded, like the Old Testament commandments, only as schoolmasters to lead us to Christ (*usus elenchticus*). Undoubtedly they always serve to uncover mercilessly the separation that exists between us and God. But that is not their sole purpose. The numberless exhortations of the epistles, for example, are not in the first place addressed to unbelievers, who are thus to be driven to a decisive ethical choice. They are actually addressed to those who are baptized, to the regenerate and to those who have be-

[9] παρακαλεῖν occurs fifty-four times in St. Paul's writings, παράκλησις twenty times.

come members of Christ in His Church, who on the basis of their communion with Christ already possess what is being required of them. For men who are in the unregenerate state of the natural man the high points of St. Paul's exhortations are as unintelligible as they are unattainable. Without the reality of the presence of the Holy Ghost such commands would be utterly meaningless. But since God has turned tasks into gifts in the Gospel, the believer can understand and accept such great things. The statement, *"Da quod iubes et iube quod vis"* becomes a reality. The "Thou canst because thou shalt," becomes a "Thou shalt because thou canst." Christ gives what Moses commands. *Fides impetrat, quod lex imperat.* For this reason the New Testament commands are always preceded by the clear statement of some divine action, frequently with a connecting causal particle, "therefore" or "so" to show whence the strength for the action comes. All the great deeds of God are enumerated, not in order that they might be supplanted or completed by human actions, but as finished and completed realities that are the basis of faith, its sure possession and its source of life. Even in the Old Testament in its Messianic anticipations that connection is occasionally indicated. The commandment "Thou shalt have no other Gods before me" is preceded by the miracle of the deliverance; the "Which have brought thee out of the land of Egypt, from the house of bondage." What in the old covenant were "shadows of things to come" are found in the new covenant as "the very image of the things" themselves (Heb. 10:1). The *debere* becomes a *posse.* Jesus has sanctified Himself for those that are His in order that they may be hallowed in the truth. The obligation to fight the good fight of faith, to serve in love, to sacrifice, exists because "we have such promises" and because we "are called to eternal life." Because Christ has taken hold upon us we are already partakers of His resurrection, and for this reason the call comes to us to awaken the gift of God that is in us. Because Christ died once unto sin and we have died to sin in Him, sin needs no longer reign in our members. The one to whom the Pneuma has been given can and shall walk in the Spirit. The expectation of the day of Jesus Christ makes strangers and pilgrims in this world of those who abstain from its lusts. The great hope has a purifying power.[10] So the commandments of the new covenant become proclamations of the Gospel and witnesses to the sanctifying, regenerative power of the Spirit. To the burning question as to whether sanctification, growth and constancy are actually possible here on earth there is hardly a clearer answer than the New Testament imperatives that are spoken to congregations existing in a corrupt and perishing world.

But the problem of the New Testament commandments also receives new light from the other side of our paradoxical statements concerning sanctification. Some one might ask, if *dare* and *jubere*, if description and prescription thus coincide in faith, why is there any further need of commandments that demand action? This objection is only possible when the opposite pole of the double relationship is overlooked, the fact that while we can neither create nor maintain the new life we can always lose it.

When God accepts a man and endows him with the Spirit He does not destroy the evil within him in an instant, but he is like a dead twig that is grafted into a living tree, to grow and quicken to the increasing mastery of evil. "All sins have been remitted by grace but not everything has been hallowed by the gift." Sin is indeed forgiven but "it has not yet been completely swept out, destroyed and buried." This does not happen till "we are buried in the earth."[11] Why God has ordered it in this way, why He does not, as He could, bring the one who has been justified to immediate perfection, by an act of sheer power, remains a mystery whose answer has been reserved for the hidden counsels of His Majesty. Sin certainly remains as an element in our lives,[12] even though its domination has been broken by the Spirit and faith recognizing its fearful danger hates it accordingly.

---

[10] Exodus 20:2; Ez. 20:10; St. John 17:19; II Cor. 7:1; I Tim. 6:12; Phil. 1:27; 3:12; Col. 3:1; I Tim. 6:12; II Tim. 1:6; Rom. 6:12; 13:12 *seq.*; Gal. 5:25; I John 3:3; I Peter 2:11; I Thess. 6:6-8; 4:7; Eph. 4:1.

[11] Luther: "On the other hand we must understand the nature of Christ's office and work in His Church, that while He pours out His purity on us at once, through the Word and faith, and, in addition, renews our hearts through the Holy Ghost, He does this in such a way that this work of purification is not completed all at once, but He daily labors with us and purifies us so that we become continuously purer and purer." Er. Ed. 8:174 *seq.*; 52:90; 58:382.

[12] Form. Conc. 592,18; 603,64; 608,84. *Manet quidem etiam in renatis rebellio quaedam.*

"There is no one among us who does not possess a big, fat share of the flesh; a whole kneeding trough full" (Er. Ed. 48:65). What is true of the cosmos, in the time intervening between the resurrection and return of Jesus Christ, is also true of the little world of our personal existence. Since the triumph of Christ over the powers of darkness the new aeon has begun, its forces are at work, but it is still completely hidden behind this present, visible, temporal world. In the same way the regenerate man is a combination of two wholly different and conflicting worlds. He is always both flesh and spirit, sinful and righteous, dead and alive.[13] So as the two worlds, the fallen cosmos and the kingdom of Jesus Christ, are still in irreconcilable conflict with each other, so within us "the flesh lusteth against the Spirit and the Spirit against the flesh" (Gal. 5:17). As Satan tries to avert his defeat through Michael the archangel, so the natural will that has not yet been "swept out" contends stubbornly against the center of faith and seeks to withstand the impulses of the Spirit.

In view of this terrible dualism of flesh and Spirit the imperatives of the New Testament receive a second significance, wholly different from the one we have been considering. When St. Paul regards the Christian as a pneumatic personality, who is in living union with Jesus Christ, his commands are only a description of what has been given him in that relationship and which has consequently to do with actual possibilities. But when St. Paul considers the actual, natural, visible condition of the regenerate man his commands have another meaning and emphasis. It is not by accident that they are mostly negative: to flee, not to be deceived, not to despise the riches of His grace, not to harden the heart, not to cast aside our confidence, not to turn aside from the living God.[14] All these prohibitions are intended to tell us that the flesh can never by itself renew and quicken our will or understanding, but it can defy, reject, destroy, and for that reason needs continued warnings, threats, exhortations and coercion just as well as the man who is still under the Law.

[13] Cf. the keen observations on the blotting out of the guilt and power of sin in the theology of Augustine and Luther in R. Hermann's book, Luthers These "Gerecht und Sünder zugleich," Gütersloh, 1930.

[14] I Cor. 6:9,18; 10:14; I Tim. 6:11; II Tim. 2:22; II Thess. 2:3; Eph. 5;6; Rom. 2:4; Heb. 3:8; 10:35; 3:12.

So the dissension between the "spiritual, new and inner" man and the "old and outward man" brings about a double form of imperative. "And on account of this difference statements are made concerning him [man] in Scripture that are directly opposed to each other" (Luther).[15] All the directions of the New Testament only paraphrase and confirm this twofold truth that has been forcing itself on our attention. That the commandments become gifts to the spiritual man manifests the sole activity of God. That nevertheless the sinful, carnal will still receives and must receive warnings and commands shows clearly that it has the ability to hinder and corrupt the living work that God is carrying on within it. In the Gospels the contradictory relation is shown in unparalleled clearness when Jesus says to the impotent man at the pool of Bethesda *after* his cure: "Behold, thou art made whole, sin no more, lest a worse thing come unto thee" (St. John 5:14).

As a result of the fact that the believer is always "dead and alive at the same time," it follows that there is a *difference in the motives that drive him to holiness*. At first sight Scripture shows us a great number of such motives. On closer inspection, however, they can all be reduced to two great classes, which coincide with the dualism we have been discussing, namely, that of joyful liberty and that of bitter compulsion. We shall accordingly limit our consideration to these two. As far as a man lives according to the Spirit his actions will spring from thankful love and from the power of the example of Christ; but as the antagonistic will, that lusts after the world, still continues with him his life requires the compulsion of obedience and fear.

The difference between Evangelical and Roman Catholic morality has been reduced correctly to the formulas, "out of thankfulness" and "for the sake of thankfulness." If the will of God is done for the sake of a reward not only does the entire burden of legal obligation rest on sanctification but the entire pride of self-confidence that believes it can gain salvation by its own powers. When the will of God is done out of thankfulness the whole idea of becoming good through doing good is excluded. Then I no longer claim any reward for my works because God has already given me everything. Then the reckoning

[15] Er. Ed. 27:176.

of merits, according to St. Augustine's splendid phrase, is nothing but "a reckoning of God's gifts." The good works of Christians are no "accomplishments" that deserve meritorious distinction but they are "fruits" that have grown out of the creative power of the Word, out of a living union with Christ. *Omnia Dei facta sunt flores, omnia facta sunt Dei flores.* This fact of the sole activity of God in effecting good receives its fullest expression in the impulse of thankfulness. The one sanctifying himself because of thankfulness does not claim for himself any honor for the renewal of his life. His opportunity is his reward. He who gives thanks remains humble for he gives the glory to God alone. For this reason Luther has called thankfulness the Christian's "most excellent virtue and the highest form of serving God," "a virtue that no one else can display" except a Christian. Whoever would thank God "must acknowledge and confess in his heart that all he gives thanks for comes as God's gift and from God's grace." Whenever anyone can say from the heart *Deo gratias*, "you need not fear that he is proud, obdurate, unfruitful and wild, or that he will use his possessions against God." Therefore none sin more grievously in this respect in the Reformer's eyes than "the most glittering saints, who are satisfied with themselves and love to hear their praise, glory, laud and honor sung to the world."[16]

As gratitude makes the doer humble, so it also makes him ready to do his own tasks. On this subject Martin Luther could speak as no one before him had done. Because the inner man is one with God for Christ's sake it is a joy for him to serve God for naught, with willing love, gladly and eagerly and free from all compulsion. Out of thankfulness towards God, Who has shown such great grace, comes the love "that gushes forth from the heart like a fresh rivulet or brook, that flows continuously and is not hindered nor does it fail." The comparisons that Luther invariably uses in this connection are, like the discourses in St. John, always intentionally drawn from the natural organic world. For the believer, as one of whom the Spirit has really taken hold, is in a really living, organic union with the Head and so cannot help dispensing blessings from the stream that descends with its nourishment upon him. It is not a mere accident that almost all

[16] Er. Ed. 40:209 *seq.*; 16:145.

of the apostolic letters begin with a thanksgiving. In so doing the leader and those he guides enter together into the unseen field of force of their faith. Thus they are reminded that they are parts of a newly arising world, no longer under the Law but possessing the richest gifts of Christ, that they are to use with freedom and rejoicing, in all humility.

When we live for God "out of thankfulness" we have before our eyes His benefactions that He has bestowed on us: we think of forgiveness and redemption. But "to arouse us still more completely Scripture tells us that the Father has not only reconciled us with Himself in Christ, but that in Him He has also expressed His image, to which we are to be conformed" (Calvin). So we come to the second motive for sanctification, which as well as thankfulness springs from and is in accord with a real incorporation into the spiritual Body of Christ. It is the power of the example of Christ, operative in His members. (Rom. 8:29.)

The idea of a likeness to God, the *imagio Dei* is not—as we must affirm in opposition to the philosophers—applicable in the Christian religion apart from the historic basis of the atoning work of Jesus and the sending of the Holy Ghost on the day of Pentecost. For the fall destroyed the image of God in man. It is true that everywhere there is still a longing for the lost Paradise but this nostalgia does not bring with it the right of return nor the power of restoring what has been lost. In our state of alienation from God to "put on the new man" would only be possible when God Himself makes a fresh beginning with the "new man which after God is created in righteousness and true holiness."[17] Christ knows that He has been sent to the earth to restore the lost image of God in His person. As God gives His revelation to the sinner in Christ He proclaims the fact that He has, in His grace, forgiven the sin of the world. But at the same time He has made it clear that we shall also be conformed anew to this image. "The Holy Ghost works faith in us and through that faith we regain the image of God that was lost in Paradise." (Er. Ed. 46:269 *seq.*) Because the incarnation of Christ is both the condition and also the effective force in the renewal of God's image every believer, according

[17] Eph. 4:24; Col. 3:10; Rom. 13:14.

to Luther's beautiful statement in the commentary on the Epistle to the Galatians, should always wear two robes of Christ: "the robe of justification and redemption" and "the robe of imitation."

This imitation is not to be understood in either a casuistic or moralistic sense. "When we speak of a pattern for our personal life we do not think of a model that is to simply reproduce over and over again but it has the clear meaning of a fundamental outline in the mind that can be carried out independently and in very many different ways" (M. Kähler). We must not think of it as a model in the sense of Tolstoy or as a certain ascetic, monastic ideal that is to be slavishly copied. It is a part of the nature and power of the original model that it can produce copies in living variety just because "it is no copy itself but the living prototype." Man is not *deus*, he is *a deo*; he is not the Creator but a creature; a copy, he points to something higher than himself. But Christ is *deus*, not *a deo*, and so in the spiritual imprinting of His image on His members He has at His disposal the freedom and riches of the divine creative power.

As the legalistic trait is lacking in gaining conformity to the image of Christ so is the moralistic tendency. There is no stoic ethical teacher standing before us who by his precepts urges his disciples to gain moral self-perfection, nor a law giver after the pattern of Mohammed who threatens them with his severe demands, nor even a pattern of the virtues, according to the ideas of ethical rationalism. The living picture of Christ operates like light, like a seed or like salt, which imaged in faith, like a creative power, is implanted in the heart and becomes effective in a transforming renewal of the life. Where Christ is recognized, says Luther, as the Man "Who helps," through Whom we obtain the forgiveness of sins, "there His brightness is reflected in us, in the same way that the rays of the sun are reflected in the water or some other mirror, so Christ reflects Himself or bestows a ray of Himself in our heart, so that we are transformed from one glory to another, that we daily increase and recognize the Lord ever more clearly. . . . This does not take place as a result of our own exertion of powers, but God, Who is the Spirit, must effect it. For even if the Holy Ghost were to enkindle such light and illumination within us and then were to forsake us we would become as we were before."

(Er. Ed. 14:219.) Because the image of Caesar is stamped on the coin it is his property. Through the hidden operation of the Spirit the lost image of God has again been stamped on the believer by means of baptism and regeneration. Henceforth the motive that impels him to sanctification must be: "Render to God the things that are God's."

After the idea of the power of Christ's example has been purified from the danger of legalistic narrowness and of being considered a meritorious offering, it is necessary to remind ourselves most emphatically what a deep significance the concrete contemplation of the historic picture of the life of Jesus has for our sanctification. For us men who have daily to contend with flesh and blood it is of supreme importance to see how the Holy One of God conducted Himself amid the sinful, wretched, contentious realities of this earth and at the same time preserved His holiness. A picture of God presented, we will say, in the form of a hazy, painted doctrine of the attributes of God, would not only fail to provide us with clear conceptions but it would lack convincing certainty. Because as thinking, feeling, willing beings we find ourselves daily and hourly in the midst of the befouling, defiling, reality of the conflicts of this life; we strive after clearness of thought, purity of emotion and strength of will to meet the problems of *this earth*. For that reason only such an example has a liberating effect, which comes from a complete, real human life that was lived in this world and that has known and overcome the needs and trials of humanity. For the formation of the image of God within us, for the renewing of our minds (Rom. 12:2; Eph. 5:17), for the control of our emotions, for the determination of the manner and form of our conduct, the contemplation of the teaching, praying, healing, suffering Savior as He is portrayed in Scripture is indispensable.

Here we must recall how often the apostles consoled, admonished, and encouraged their congregations by reminding them of the concrete example and the clearly defined image of Christ in the flesh. Christians can subdue their angry emotions and feel no necessity for avenging slanders, abuse or threatenings because before their eyes is the image of Him "Who, when he was reviled, reviled not again; when he suffered he threatened not." The slaves who suffer scourgings from their masters are reminded by St. Peter that Christ has also suffered. The congregation at Philippi lacks somewhat in humility and therefore in unity. St. Paul recounts to them the humiliation of the Lord, Who took upon Him the form of a servant, and so shames them and incites them to holier ambitions. The great hymn of love would never have been written if the example of Jesus had not furnished its every detail. As in I Cor. 13 so the Apostle may have portrayed Jesus in like fashion to the Galatians. In obedience to Jesus' direction "Learn of me," St. Paul became a "follower of Christ," learned from the Lord Himself how to be gentle and meek of heart and admonished the conceited, easily offended Corinthians to a similar imitation. Our temptations can be overcome, says the writer of the Epistle to the Hebrews, because the Lord has overcome the tempter. And in another place he shows how the prayer of the disciples can support itself by the prayer of Jesus in Gethsemane, by Him Who "learned obedience by the things which He suffered."[18]

Luther, the preacher of the *theologia crucis*, was always especially strengthened in the many severe trials of his life by the "contemplation of the holy sufferings of Christ." In the well-known sermon of 1517, that bears this title, he writes: "When your heart has been confirmed in Christ and you have become a foe of sin through love, not through the fear of punishment, the sufferings of Christ shall henceforth be the example for your whole life, and now we shall recall it in another fashion, for till this time we have thought of it as a sort of sacrament that works in us and which we receive, now we recall it that we may do likewise. When an evil day or some sickness burdens you think of how trifling it is compared with the thorny crown and the nails of Christ. When you are compelled against your will to do something or to omit doing something remember how Christ was bound and made prisoner, how He was driven hither and yon. If pride assails you, see how your Lord was derided and scorned, in the company of the malefactors. If uncleanness and lust assail you, think how bitterly the tender flesh of Christ was scourged, pierced and smitten. If hatred or envy or the desire for revenge come upon you

[18] St. Matt. 10:24 *seq.*; 11:29; I Peter 2:20-23; 4:1; I Cor. 4:12 *seq.*; 11:1; Phil. 2; 3:10; I Thess. 1:6; II Cor. 4:10; 10:1; Heb. 2:18; 5:7; 4:15; I John 2:6; 2:3; 4:17; Rom. 15:3, 5-7.

think how Christ with many tears and complaints prayed for you and for all His enemies, when He might more rightly have avenged Himself on them. If tribulation or any bodily or spiritual evils burden you, strengthen your heart and say: Why should I not also suffer a little affliction when my Lord, in His anguish and affliction, sweated blood in the garden. . . . But this sort of contemplation has become unusual and rare though the Epistles of Sts. Paul and Peter are full of it. We have changed the substance into a mere appearance and only recall the sufferings of Christ as it is written in the letters and painted on the walls."

We have intentionally quoted at such length because in this meditation we have such a vivid description of the living experience of all who study Scripture seriously. Even the smallest traits of Scripture attain a more and more important significance for the reader and the praying believer who feels himself oppressed by the burdens of life and who is seeking strength. So long as any one has not been assailed by the naked despair of life and sin, in actual conflict, so long he can live in the delusion that it is enough to have a clear idea of the super-historical content of the message of Jesus concerning the supremacy of God. Helpless, sick, imprisoned men, all those who occupy difficult or deserted outposts in the education of their souls, have always found that the truth is the exact opposite. Such persons have never regarded it as unimportant or unessential whether or not it is true that "we can know as good as nothing concerning the life and personality of Jesus," whether the accounts written about Him are only "literary compositions"; "idealized and frequently overdrawn pictures of pious curiosity" that "fade away into the glimmerings of the legendary." The controversies between a Biblical and a modernistic regard of Scripture, that were waged twenty years ago, were more than a mere contention regarding a more or less conservative estimation of certain literary monuments. It is not a matter of indifference for the faith that desires to be renewed here on earth by the power of the living, personal image of Christ, as to whether, for example, the entire Passion history be only a legendary construction that grew out of the needs arising in the cultus of the Church, or whether words of prayer, spoken on the Cross, lack all historic certainty or were merely pious inventions patterned on Jewish piety as it was expressed in the Psalms. The mocking of the vinegar which was endured by the One suffering silently for His enemies, is attributed to the use of a popular, burlesque bit of mockery, often used in the drama and similarly employed here for the sake of a contrasting effect: "as means of attaining a short mental relaxation," like certain similar passages in Shakespeare's tragedies. The misunderstanding of Elohi and Elias is interpreted as a favorite, popular literary device. Any one is privileged to make such statements if his scientific convictions demand it, but he must likewise realize what is at stake; how poor the Church and the individual become in restraining the passions, in suffering and in action, when the colorful, historic lineaments of the image of Christ, are resolved into the deceptive triflings of a later pious, poetic fantasy; when the faith that is seeking the *truth*, and not mere emotions, in the midst of the terribly hard temptations and difficulties of its pilgrimage, is turned from the beautiful picture of a perfect life to the abstractions of a few sayings of Jesus that have been left it by the critics.

The ethical forces that proceed from a living association with the Christ portrait of Scripture are enormous. Because the picture is so true to life it throws light on all the situations of this aeon. "The devout use of the example" sharpens to a marked degree our appreciation" of all the roots and ramifications of evil in our own lives." The eyes become clear in perceiving the perversity of the world. We gain the proper proportion of helpful sympathy and of purifying rejection in our twofold attitude towards it. Above all "the conformity of our own life to the example of Christ influences our consideration of other imitators." We then judge every brother "by his indestructible likeness to God, believe in its possible purification and perfection, and recognize his duty and right to strive after brotherly fellowship." (Kähler.) All in all, to use the language of St. Paul (II Cor. 3:18) it will result in our being "changed into the same image, from glory to glory." Such a happening lacks all that is intentional, conscious, strained or that seeks approbation. This continuous sanctification can never be used for selfish side issues, for the One whose image is gaining clearer form in the believer is the humbled, crucified Lord, Who conforms us to His sufferings (Gal. 4:19) and Who wages a ceaseless war against the pride and lust of the flesh. "The deeper and more firmly you contemplate this image and impress it upon yourself, the more the image of death will fall away and disappear of itself, without any effort or conflict, and so your heart will have peace and you can die peacefully with Christ and in Christ."[19] But, as long as we are still on our road of pilgrimage sin is ever flaming up anew and never lets us come to a complete likeness with Christ, so our very experience of such sanctification urges onward to the revelation of the new world, where the scales will fall away and God will perfect the image that has been begun on the basis of the promise that He has given to the world in Christ, its eternal prototype.

So in the sanctification of one who has been justified by faith as it is worked out in thankfulness and through the power of the example of Christ, the truth that the Kingdom of God comes indeed of itself, without our efforts, again finds its realization. The light shines into the darkness, penetrates it and at last makes that luminous which by nature is and always would remain dark. The living activity of faith should be like the natural ripening of the fruits of the earth, not like a compulsory "shall" and "must" connected with the fulfilling of forcibly imposed religious prescriptions. *Justis non est posita lex, quatenus spiritu vivunt.* "Let the new man remain unentangled with laws." However to stop with such a naturalistic description of sanctification would mean anticipating the parousia. We do not yet live in the new aeon but are still in that peculiar, tense time of transition, when the new life is indeed present, and is growing secretly, and is making its way, but when at the same time the very real old man is also present with all the power of his opposition, dislike and slothfulness directed against the good will that God has worked in us. This contrary will of the old nature it behooves us "to drive out without ceasing" by the incentives of obedience and the fear of God. That we do not simply give thanks like children nor live only like the son who bears the father's image and lives in his father's house, but that we also have to hear and obey like servants in the presence of their master, reminds us, as nothing else can, of our guilt. When at the final judgment the old man has completely fallen away then the warning, goading obedi-

[19] Er. Ed. 21:261.

ence and the terrifying fear will no longer be needed. The new congregation, completely fashioned in the image of God, will henceforth sing nothing but hymns of praise: "I delight to do thy will, O my God." But a *theologia viatorum*, which is the only sort possible to us here on earth, cannot dispense with the admonition to obey and fear God.

When the sweet and willing motive, "the love of Christ constraineth us" has no compelling power over us, then the harsh, military order, "out of obedience" must compel the old nature and assist in its self-conquest. For periods of dead slothfulness, in times of fiery temptation, when the spontaneous desire to serve God has completely disappeared, there is only one help: it is the serious realization of the Holy, unconditional will of God that *must* be fulfilled if our souls are not to be grievously hurt. God *wills* our sanctification, God *desires* the act of obedience that we "flee evil lust and purify the soul."[20] God requires that we serve Him and if it be not done through the spontaneous power of thankful love, then it must be through the holy discipline of obedience. If faith in the contemplation of the example of Christ sees what it *can* accomplish, obedience tells it that it *must* be done.

Because sin prevents us from ever attaining the perfect image of Christ, faith never comes to its full perfection either in knowledge or in the fulfillment of the divine purposes or commandments. Therefore it must continually be subjected to the Word that gives the knowledge of the complete, unabridged demands of God, even where they do not please us. As a result of the cunning, underhanded nature of the old man that which is most important we would very gladly see suppressed if the Word did not ceaselessly emphasize the hard and clear necessity of obedience. Only thus will nature be reminded of those incentives it likes to disregard and which even the devout man, who is concerned about his own sanctification, would like to be spared, like the painful transition from inclination to action, the consideration of the weak, the willingness to engage in self-sacrifice, and the obligation of carrying on the work of missions. Without such honest obedience there will be neither the victory of faith nor its growth and continu-

[20] I Thess. 4:3; I Peter 1:4 and 22.

ance in this time of hardheartedness. Without the disturbing impulse of a holy necessity the terrible calamity might take place of the Church lapsing into the inertia of slothfulness, because it imagined that it was living by grace without works. In accepting the truth, stated in Scripture, that the branches live from the life of the vine, the other equally important truth is forgotten, that the fleshly nature of the justified and redeemed man needs the continuous watchfulness that comes with the following of Christ, and that he will die if this be neglected.

That the belittling of the duty of obedience is no small matter but of terribly serious importance becomes evident through the fact that there is nothing in the world that so completely destroys man as disobedience towards God. This is the place where theology has to treat of the wrath of God as His reply to the contempt shown to His commandments. Where this is earnestly done it at once becomes evident that the seriousness of our situation demands a harder, sharper warning: "We should therefore dread His displeasure and do nothing contrary to His commandments." That even the regenerate need this crude, hard compulsion of former days must humble us most deeply, and bring us to a merciless judgment concerning man's position before God.

How much space is occupied by the motive of fear not only in the Old but even in the New Testament, is easily overlooked. To escape the cowardice and desperation of human fear Jesus bids the disciples to remember Him Who can destroy both body and soul in hell. Beside it He places the retributive severity of many of the parables: the trees are burned, the salt that has lost its savor is trodden under foot, the bad fish are thrown away, the foolish virgins are excluded from the wedding feast, the unfaithful servant is cast into prison. St. Paul warns the branches that have been newly grafted into the vine: "Be not highminded but fear." He admonishes the slaves in Ephesus to be obedient to their masters "with fear and trembling, in singleness of your heart, as unto Christ," while the Corinthians are exhorted to continue "perfecting holiness in the fear of God."[21] Furthermore the two main reasons why the soldiers of Christ dare not cease from such anxiety

---

[21] St. Matt. 10:26,28,31; Rom. 11:20 *seq.*; II Cor. 7:1; Further, I Peter 2:17-18; 3:2, 16; Heb. 4:1; II Cor. 5:11; Rev. 14:7.

are clearly indicated in Scripture. The one, to use the language of St. Peter, is the contemplation of the fearful power of Satan, who goeth about like a roaring lion seeking whom he may devour. The other is the contemplation of the holy God, "Who without respect of persons judgeth according to every man's work." Even the strong man can fall, the watchful one be beguiled and those who have stripped off their armor in glad expectation be betrayed by folly. The unclean spirit can return; the man once set free by God can speedily become capable of descending to the basest vices.[22] And as sin separates us from God, behind it all is "the somber possibility of being lost" (Martensen), which even troubled St. Paul. No sin can be made nonexistent. Neither the length of time that has elapsed nor later attempts at making amends can relegate it into forgetfulness. "Doth not he see my ways, and count all my steps?" cries Job, and Paul is certain that God "will bring to light the hidden things of darkness and will make manifest the counsels of the hearts." Therefore it is a terrible thing to fall into the hands of the living God.[23] Such a fear of God is more than a mere "numinous trembling" before the incomprehensible, unspeakable depths of divine mysteries. It is entirely determined by a conscious, ethical seriousness in viewing a judgment according to works to which even the disciple, who is in a state of faith, must submit.

It is impossible to restrict the statements of the New Testament concerning the final judgment to the ungodly or to self-righteous zealots for the Law, to say nothing of trying to explain them as remnants of Jewish ideas in the theology of St. Paul. The Son of Man will require a special reckoning from those who have been engaged in His service and have been endowed with His gifts. That the returning Judge would reward every man according to his works was told to the *disciples.* Every idle word spoken by man must be accounted for at the last day. St. Paul regards every earthly tribunal and every earthly self-judgment as unimportant, whether it be approval or disapproval, for that day shall declare it; the day in which the Lord will judge. Then will man's work first be revealed, of what sort it is. Each one

[22] I Peter 5:8; 1:17; I Cor. 10:12; St. Matt. 25:1-13; St. Luke 11:24-26.
[23] I Cor. 9:27; 4:5; Job 31:4; Jer. 17:10; Psalm 139; Heb. 4:13, 10:31.

will reap what he has sowed. All must appear before the judgment seat of Christ to receive the final judgment on this earthly life. Whoever in the earthly congregation continues to serve evil shall not inherit the Kingdom.

All these declarations that could so easily be multiplied[24] are so unanimous and overwhelming that the evasion of the older orthodoxy, according to which all this is to be understood hypothetically and cannot be applied to the one who is justified, is no longer permissible. At the end of days the judgment will actually be passed on the works of the sinner and of the righteous, and so the fear of displeasing God must accompany even the life of the believer as a holy fear and as an aid in overcoming temptation. Insincere life, an unbridled tongue or body, impure passions, implacable enmity which faith that possessed the Spirit might have restrained or turned aside, will go with us and accuse us before God. But when the idea of judgment on the entire attitude of the one who is justified has been maintained, there will be no room for the ancient antinomian misunderstanding which has always accompanied Paulinism and Lutheranism like a dark shadow; the question whether the Christian cannot continue in sin because the working of grace would thus become so much more mightily evident (Rom. 6:1 seq.). If even the justified sinner must face the judgment it is no longer a matter of indifference as to the degree in which he has allowed himself to be purified by the Spirit from the "defilement and evil of the flesh."

But is not the nature of forgiveness completely destroyed by such an opinion? Do we not in this way find ourselves face to face with the Roman Catholic commendation of work-righteousness and the Anthroposophic views of life after death? The question must be answered in the negative because in the judgment only those works will be recognized that have been done in penitence and, through the grace of the Spirit, have been done in Christ. "He that soweth to the spirit shall of the Spirit reap life everlasting." There can be no question of any self-praise on our part. "God crowns in us the works

---

[24] St. Luke 19:11-26; St. Matt. 16:24-27; 25:32; 12:36; I Cor. 4:3; 3:13 seq.; 6:9 seq.; Gal. 6:7 seq.; 5:19-21; II Cor. 5:10; II Thess. 1:8-10; Rom. 2; I Peter 4:11. Cf. H. Braun, Gerichtsgedanke und Rechtfertigungslehre bei Paulus, Leipzig, 1930.

of His mercy" (Augustine). And, furthermore, while unbelief experiences the wrath of God in the judgment, the one who is justified experiences the loving kindness of God, Who by this last painful punishment would only purify, prepare and perfect His members for the unhindered communion that He has promised the believer and has mediated to him through His Word. So each retains its inalienable right; the holy majesty of God that judges according to works, without respect to persons, and is on that account to be contemplated with fear and trembling, and the perfect mercy of God, Who through unmerited grace saves the sinner and draws him to Himself.

What is to be said then, from this viewpoint, concerning the "theology of death"? It is evident that a very serious emphasis now falls on dying. Besides the bodily pains and the soul's anguish in its departure, there is present, even for those who "fall asleep in Jesus" the knowledge of an impending hour of judgment. "The modern theologians assert that death is no evil but a haven that we may enter into and be safe from the labors and sorrows to which this present life is subjected. It is the utmost blindness and an added misery that is heaped on top of original sin when we lightly regard sin, death and other miseries of the human race . . . and flatter ourselves with the most frivolous and vain imaginations."[25] We must learn to speak more seriously and severely of death. It is the wages of sin and the portal to judgment. It is the demand, "Give an account of thy stewardship!" Such a serious regard of death becomes a real "bridle to sin and spur to sanctification." "Whatsoever thou takest in hand remember the end, and thou shalt never do amiss" says the Wisdom of Jesus the Son of Sirach (Eccl. 7:36). Jesus counseled men to be reconciled with the enemy "whiles . . . yet in the way with him" before they come to the end in the presence of the Judge and it is too late. After the disciples' question: "Lord, are there few that be saved?" follows the admonition, strive to enter in that ye may be saved! Kierkegaard required of a Christian that he should always live in the "eleventh hour," in which everything is so different "from the days of youth or the busy times of manhood." To men like Wm. Löhe and H. Bezzel the thought of the dying hour was always present. Amid the shadows of

[25] Luther, *Op. Lat.* XVIII, 266.

the graveyard there came to them an anxious longing for the deliverance of eternal life; that holy discipline of body and soul that is so easily put aside today as a mere pietistic exaggeration. But even so, the fear of judgment is not the last word in the theology of death. In the life of faith the joy of expectation triumphs over all fear, because after the judgment comes complete communion with God. The Judgment on every evil deed does not destroy the acceptance that is promised to faith. The child comes to its Father, the injured one to healing, the one in the depths is exalted. So hope becomes stronger than the fear of death; the homesickness for the true home becomes a "strengthening and steeling aid" for the pilgrimage and conflict of life.

We have learned to know the four great fundamental motives in sanctification. They have grown out of the intense antagonism of spirit and flesh within us, that exists in the life of every believer, during this present age. For this reason the two phases had to be recognized together; the freedom of the new life without compulsion or fear, that is exercised through gratitude and the power of Christ's example, and the stern ethical rigor that wages its warfare with sin through obedience and fear. The contrasting statements of Scripture no longer contradict each other. The inner man who shares in Christ's resurrection no longer knows fear because fear has been driven out by love. The "spirit of love" is stronger than the "spirit of fear" (I John 4:18; II Tim. 1:7). But since evil is ever painfully active it is necessary to consider just as seriously the possibility of being lost and to sanctify ourselves in the fear of the Lord. From our previous discussion it is evident that there can be no dispute about the necessary combination of the two contrasting situations. Neither side dare be considered without the other. To attempt completely to deny a free activity in the Spirit would mean turning the New Testament into the Old. But to make ethics depend only "on the slender thread of thankfulness" (Schlatter) would be to underestimate the terrible power of sin, whose nature according to the fine description of the Second Article of the Augsburg Confession consists in the lack of a fear of God (*sine metu*), and so can be overcome only through the awakening of a holy fear.

As to which one of these motives shall have first place is an entirely different question. Shall it be thankfulness or obedience, the love of Christ or fear? The way the question is answered and precedence given to the one motive or the other determines the differences in the ethical viewpoints of the various confessions. It is evident that the order of pre-eminence here observed is not a mere matter of taste but that it has a far-reaching systematic background. Luther and Calvin have both said the same things but in different order and with a different emphasis. For Calvin's spirit, which was so closely akin to the Old Testament, the holy and terrible mystery of God stands out above His revealed love, even in the New Testament.[26] So his language became stern and cold. God's right to us is like that of a master to the obedience of his servants. The King calls His soldiers to His service that they may subdue the earth to His dominion. The Second Psalm became the expression of the Reformed view of the fundamental motive for sanctification: "Serve the Lord with fear and rejoice with trembling." Luther too could quote this statement of the Psalm in the exposition of Romans, and in the commentary on the Penitential Psalms in connection with the Sixth Psalm he says emphatically: "So in a just man there must always be the fear of the judgment of God, because of the old man within." But such words were not the fundamental notes of his faith. The true Heart of God and His deepest impulse he saw in "the love of the reconciled Majesty," that is no longer angry but overflows "with unspeakable, paternal, affectionate" lovingkindness. For this reason thankfulness for "the love of God and for His praise," was for him the first and strongest motive for sanctification, and the references to compulsion and punishment, though they are not lacking, occupy only a second place. As St. Paul begins his Epistles with thanksgiving and closes them with the call to obedience, so Luther's theology rests primarily on thankful certainty, and out of it flows the duty of keeping the commandments. The comparison of the servant that occupies the more important place in Reformed ethics, emphasizes more strongly the fact that man still lives in the old aeon and needs the goad. In the

[26] Cf. K. Barth, *Dogmatik*, I, p. 327. "The *Sola fide* of Luther is true but only in so far as the *Soli Deo gloria* remained *superior* to it in his estimation . . . !"

other comparison of the relation of a thankful child to God there is expressed the fact that the new world of God has already commenced; "that our resurrection and life in Christ has already begun," and that we possess in anticipation "its best portion and chief part." Both phases, trust in the present power of the Spirit that has been assured us and a strong mistrust of the continuing nature of the old man, must alike have place and consideration in the life of the individual and of the Church. "Nothing is more closely welded together than fear and confidence. . . . For they are so closely united that one is swallowed up by the other. So there is no mathematical relationship on earth similar to it."[27] A time like ours, "which fears everything except God and that dreads the numbers 13 or 7 more than the sins against the Ten Commandments," needs to have the fear of judgment and the duty of obedience, that mark Calvinistic zeal, hammered into its conscience with holy fervor. But in doing so we dare not forget to say that such "Draconian legislation for the servants of the house" (Schiller) is only a bitter emergency measure that ought not to be necessary and would not be necessary if we would allow ourselves as children to be supplied from the riches of the Father, which He has prepared for us.

The double series of motives that we find in the sanctification of the Christian, freedom and compulsion, privilege and obligation, has originated from the simultaneous presence of old and new man, and because God acts independently from us and yet will not act without our submission. The realization of the Kingdom of God is something that is only *given* us and yet at the same time it is a task that is assigned us; it is completely the fruit of the Spirit and yet cannot be realized without the spirit of fear. Neither, as we have seen, excludes the other, but each demands its opposite. The last task then of this chapter is to describe how the practical activity of sanctification takes place and what form it assumes under this paradoxical contrast of "gift and responsible fidelity," and this will have to be shown in connection with the three most central expressions of the life of a regenerate Christian—in prayer, discipline and service.

We have to consider prayer not in its edifying but in its theological

[27] Luther, *Comment. ad Gal.*, II, 113.

significance as that situation in which the paradox of divine grace and human responsibility finds its most intense expression. For the mystical spirit given to introspection no such duality arises in prayer. The inherent hidden prayer gift is there aroused and intensified and, as it arrives at its goal in a beatific dreamy state of ecstasy, it unites itself with the Brahma, the All, the essence of Divinity. Here the question of the possibility of access to God is not felt as a deepest need. It is different in the case of Biblical, "prophetic" prayer, where nothing so much troubles the suppliant as the question, Whence shall I, who am but dust and ashes, receive the παρρησία, the confidence to come into the consuming presence of God?[28] Who will open the closed door at whose threshold the Cherubim watch lest any should enter? The privilege of praying, of drawing near to God is one that according to Scripture no man can or may gain for himself. The condition that makes it possible is grace; that God Himself, through Christ, has opened the way of access to His presence. "Because the Lord has regarded the lowliness of His handmaiden," says Luther, in the exposition of the Magnificat, Mary can praise God in prayer. For the Christian the consideration of the benefactions of Christ is the only possible religious basis for prayer that has an assured promise connected with it. The liturgical conclusion of the formal prayers of the Church, "through Jesus Christ, our Lord," is something essential and indispensable for faith. If forgiveness is necessary for the beginning of prayer so much the more is it needed for its continuation and completion. For sin not only opposes us and needs to be purged out when we enter upon prayer but it clings to us even during prayer, in the form of unbelief, doubt, inattention and selfish desire, and so destroys anew the right of a hearing before God. So over the beginning, middle and end of every prayer are written the words of the Small Catechism: "for we neither merit nor deserve those things for which we pray, but [we ask] that He would grant us all things through grace." If God's pardon gives the *right* to pray, it is God's Spirit that gives the *strength* to pray. Not only for the permission to pray but for its continuous living activity is the continually renewed giving of God required. Without the gift of the Holy Ghost there

[28] Eph. 3:12; Heb. 4:12; I John 3:21; 5:14.

may be the most intense attempts at concentration, the strivings of ascetic exercise, the excited emotions of the soul but there will be no real, spiritual praying and supplication. God Himself must aid our weakness, must enkindle in us an unspeakable groaning, a great desire and longing that we may be drawn upwards toward God. If, however, true prayer be only possible when God's Spirit provides the impulse, and if again the gift of the Spirit can only be received by faith then these two inseparable consequences follow: Where there is unbelief the Spirit is lacking, there is a silence of God, a prayerless state that cannot be quickened by any artificial devices; but when there is faith then there is also a continuous living conversation with God, there is a joy of approach as well as the needed incentive and strength for prayer. No one who believes the Word remains without the presence of Him "Who teaches us how to pray aright" (Paul Gerhardt).

So here we again face the whole paradoxical riches and severity of Christian ethics that deduces the obligation from the possibility. "We know not what we should pray for as we ought" but the Spirit must make intercession for us. But because God never denies this Penecostal gift to faith but bestows it richly each day, no one should "grieve the Spirit" by withstanding this impulse toward prayer, that is bestowed upon him, instead of yielding to it. So it becomes a holy duty faithfully to use this privilege. Because God is continually ready to speak to us it is not only a privilege but also a duty for us to reply to Him in prayer continually (I Thess. 2:13; 5:17). As we have seen before the connection of justification and prayer, so now it becomes necessary to make clear the inseparable connection of sanctification and prayer. It would be false and in complete contradiction with all that has been said previously if we were to speak only of the right and possibility without mentioning the *necessity* and *duty* of prayer.

One of the most outstanding traits in the portrait of Jesus that is given us in the Scripture is that of His prayer life. He Who was nourished by the will of the Father continually gave back this will of God in prayer. "He went into a mountain alone to pray," was both the preparation for and the echo of the great events of His life. At His baptism, before the selection of the Apostles, before His miracles of healing, at the grave of Lazarus, after temptation and conflict with the powers of Satan, after days of trying exertion, in the death agony and at His final breath,—in the fullness of His labors as well as in the silence of suffering, at all times and in all places the Son of Man praises the Father and cries to Him in prayer.[29] As He continuously engaged in the holy exercise of communion with God, so He tirelessly exhorted His followers to do likewise. A chief part of the care of souls that Jesus exercised towards His disciples was their training in prayer. With many a clear direction He guided them into its practice, admonished them to quiet, concentration, watchfulness, purity and constancy, and instructed them concerning those things for which they ought to pray. In obedience to such directions of the Lord the apostolic Church sanctified itself "with prayer and supplication" both during the time of anticipation of the gift of Pentecost and afterwards in its preservation. After prayer and fasting the Church sends out her messengers for missionary preaching. The hidden source of strength for St. Paul in the edification of the Church is to continue in thanksgiving and intercession "without ceasing." The same Apostle, who understood so much more thoroughly than many others that everything that works salvation comes from "the supply of the Spirit of Jesus Christ" (Phil. 1:19), likewise exhorted them unweariedly to continue instant in prayer, to "strive" in prayer and to watch; to intercede with all the saints "day and night" that they might grow strong in the Lord and that His Word might not be hindered.[30]

The call to fidelity in prayer never became silent in the Church. We can state as a purely scientific judgment that all the fathers of the Church, her leaders and theologians, who in the course of her development have said anything of lasting value, were all likewise teachers of prayer. We will pass by the great number of valuable devotional works of the ancient and medieval Church, the writings of Origen, Tertullian, Cyprian, Augustine, Tauler, Bernhard and Thomas a Kempis, which the Church of the Reformation too often neglected because of an exaggerated antagonism to Romanism, and

---

[29] St. Matt. 14:23; St. Luke 6:12; 5:16; 9:28; 3:21; St. Mark 1:35; 7:34; 9:29; 14:36; St. John 11:42; Heb. 5:7.
[30] Acts 1:14; 2:42; 4:31; 6:6; 10:9; 9:11; 14:23; Col. 1:3-10; I Thess. 1:2; 2:13; II Thess. 1:11; Eph. 1:15-17; Phil. 1:3-6; 1:19; 4:6; Rom. 1:8-10; 12:12; 15:30.

we will recall only Luther's precious little treatise, *How we should pray* [*written*] *for Master Peter Balbierer* (1535), and the many directions to prayer in his letters, sermons and table talk. We remember John Gerhard's *Sacrae Meditationes*, Wm. Löhe's dissertation *Sabbat und Vorsabbat* and the twentieth chapter of the third book of the *Institutes,* where Calvin explains prayer as "the best exercise of faith and the hand that daily appropriates God's benefactions." In addition there is the still unexhausted treasury of evangelical ascetic literature, its devotional writings and prayer books, whose adequate consideration is one of the most urgent tasks of Protestant historical investigation. Lutheranism has always been an *ecclesia orans.* The justification of prayerlessness has never been derived from the article of justification. It was the age of the Illumination that first brought about that weakening of fervor and of discipline in prayer which our race has not yet succeeded in overcoming.

All those who have been mighty in prayer have realized that a true conversation with God can take place only when His Spirit has first touched the heart. That aid did not prevent them, however, from giving many practical suggestions and statements concerning the right exercise of prayer, both in connection with its form and its content. A return to these directions and their living revival is, in the face of the terrible prayerlessness and helplessness of the present day, one of the most important tasks that theology must undertake for the people of our own times. The full development of the various considerations that arise in this connection must be reserved for a new evangelical ethics and pastoral theology. We can refer only to a few of the chief viewpoints that seem particularly important in the development of our own problem.

Every prayer demands concentration, the exercise of will power and a firm resolution to really practise it. "Just as a good skillful barber must keep his thoughts, mind and eyes fixed exactly on the scissors and the hair and not forget where he is in his strokes and cuts; for if he wants to talk continuously and think of other things and look elsewhere, he would soon cut off the lips and nose and even slit the throat. So anything that is to be done well requires the whole attention of man, with all his faculties and members, . . . how much more must prayer possess the heart exclusively and completely if it is to be a good prayer" (Luther, Er. Ed. 23, 223). The outward physical attitude must conform to the inner purpose. Only one who approves the Platonic duality of body and soul will call the external attitudes like standing, kneeling, folding the hands, closing the eyes, mere worthless unimportant devices of liturgists, for when any one has once recognized the impossibility of such an "animistic" separation his body will assume an appropriate attitude. Either the *entire* man in his spiritual-corporeal unity is present before God in prayer or he is not there at all.

A second equally important rule says that prayer demands time and likewise fixed times that must be strictly and faithfully observed. The modern haste and unwillingness to take time has its roots chiefly in men's greed for money and honor. Where men calculate the riches of the earth they count the minutes they are willing to give God. Whoever remembers that God spared no pains to help the world will not be sparing with the time he devotes to thanking God for what He has done. Where the grudging of time has been overcome and there is a willingness to pray it is necessary that the time devoted to that purpose be carefully regulated and the regulations strictly adhered to. There is an observation true to life in the statement of Claus Harms: "Whoever does not pray at determined times does not pray at undetermined ones." It is fanaticism and a disregard of our situation as sinners to think that we can dispense with such a regulated custom, usage and rule of prayer. If the observance of such order be lacking, if prayer is left to inner impulse or fancy, it will practically end, as a result of the slothfulness and lukewarmness of our nature, in omission. "Therefore it is well," Master Peter is advised (in Luther's little treatise of 1535, that was referred to before), "that early in the morning prayer be the first work and at evening the last and that we guard against the false, treacherous thought: wait a little, in an hour I will pray, there is this or that I must finish first, for with such a thought we come from prayer into business that will hold us and absorb us till the prayer of the day comes to naught."

The third important regulation for the guidance of a life of prayer is included in the statement, also found in Luther, that prayer is an art that just like every other art must be *learned* by lifelong exercise, regularity and patience. The fundamental principle of all art, *Qui enim non proficit in via Dei, defecit,* applies here as well. If we omit prayer for one day, we have lost, at least such was Luther's experience, "a great measure of zeal and faith." And H. Bezzel says, as a result of his rich pastoral experience, "The less we want to pray, the less are we able to do so, and finally the art of praying is unlearned." Evangelical faith may simply reject the spiritual gymnastics and prayer technique of the Yogi, and the artificial ascending stages of mysticism, but it dare not on that account or through a mere fear of monasticism omit every *agricultura sui ipsius* in prayer. The "exercising oneself unto godliness" (I Tim. 4:7 *seq.*) in prayer may be done in evangelical liberty but it must also take place in holy fidelity and constancy. The training in prayer both of our pastors and congregations has been very much neglected by our Church during the past four decades. A comparison drawn between our zeal and joy in prayer and that which was shown at the time of the confessional revival of the nineteenth century puts us to shame. That the attempt has occasionally been made to make a virtue out of this need can be an occasion for real anxiety concerning the further development of theology in the Church. If the Apostles, the fathers and teachers of our faith have unweariedly exhorted men to concentration, order and exercise in prayer, so that they should not lose their faith through restlessness and slothfulness, through vacillating emotions and desires, how much more (to use Löhe's words) "does a poor late comer of our days, like our soul, have need of meditation" and preparation for prayer!

The spirit that reaches God in prayer is the "spirit of a sound mind" (II Tim. 1:7). The one who resists it can never experience the real blessing of prayer. No matter how important such a directive rule may be it can be useless and even dangerous to the sanctification of life if it is not applied to the true *content* of prayer. The exercises of devotion may then only serve as a pious pleasure and as a form of self-enjoyment, thus becoming a kind of self-deception when their matter is not determined and purified by the guidance of God's will. Prayer escapes the danger of disorder and confusion only when it is enkindled by the words of Scripture. From the Word proceeds its inner justification, as well as its life-giving power and the clearness of its petitions. A prayer life that does not stick to Scripture will soon become poor in ideas, poor in faith, poor in love, and will finally die. Free prayer and silent prayer require years of faithful association and training with the spirit of Scripture. No one can begin with it, but even the Christian who has attained the age of spiritual manhood will not cease, ὡς ἀρτιγέννητα βρέφη (I Peter 2:2) to desire anew the uncorrupted, pure food of the Word that he may satisfy himself therewith. Christ Himself furnished the example for His Church as He used the words of the Psalter when He wrestled in His death agony. How Luther loved the Psalms and used them continuously is well known. The more the *oratio* arises from the *meditatio* of Scripture the more moving and pure will the prayer be. That Rosicrucians, Yogis and Anthroposophists have externalized this idea into a playful dalliance must not lead us to esteem meditation on the words of Scripture lightly. Luther at all events laid the greatest stress upon it. Because God will not give His spirit apart from the external Word we should "read it and reread it with studious attention and consideration of what the Holy Ghost means by it." (Luther, Er. Ed. 1,70). Only where the Word of God dwells richly in the heart can the prayer of the heart continue without decreasing or pining away.

The natural, unregenerate thinking and willing hastens past the prayers of penitence and overlooks in false security what God alone, in His freedom, can overlook. But where the Word is quick and powerful no one tries to avoid the exposure of sin and there prayer for its covering arises to God. As the man who rests securely in himself does not think of his guilt, so he does not think of the need of its remission. Scripture, however, leads to ceaseless praise and it is especially true of the prayer of thanksgiving, more than of any other form that it "instills humility into the character." In the same way the proper proportion of adoration and of personal petition will be maintained only where the Word is used. A glance into the history of religions shows us the contrast of either a primitive begging for pleasure and earthly good, or else super-spiritual speculation that despises every supplication as spiritually worthless. In the teachings and example of Jesus these antitheses have been overcome. In a marvellous unity we find here both offering and surrender; the adoring praise of God, that loses itself in the contemplation of His great purposes of redemption in the world, so that personal affairs become small and insignificant, and beside it the utterly practical requests for the needs of the body, for protection against and victory over the evil one, that are made because God is not "the static All" but a living will, Whom we may trust and Whom we are to importune.

But since the native selfishness of man can still misuse prayer for mere self-satisfaction Scripture continually admonishes to _intercession_. That such an admonition is necessary shows how easy it is to deceive oneself. Intercession is the strongest weapon of the Holy Ghost against egotism. So the last dangerous nucleus in man; the fundamentally evil root of self-love is attacked, and it becomes clear that prayer is not concerned with private religious needs but that it is a preparation for the service of our neighbor and for the battle for God's glory. Where there is prayer for each other the desire for prayer with each other will be awakened. The one who withdraws from common prayer discloses the fact that his piety still suffers from a calculating desire for enjoyment. The use of the "our" determines whether the _orare_ is healthy or unwholesome. In the "Our Father" the Lord overcomes the isolation of His members, edifies the life of the Church and awakens the desire for the fellowship of the Eucharist, where each one is present in the "corporealness of his complete personal life" (Kähler § 651) and all are nourished together. The sight of the brethren strengthens faith. What the weakness of the one cannot attain becomes possible when many "combine their efforts" and bring their prayer to God.[31] But for the soul that through faith has grown into communion with all true believers on _earth, heaven_ will also be opened

---

[31] Luther: "Oh, if God would . . . that a universal heartfelt cry should ascend to God from the entire nation, what immeasurable strength and help would result from such prayer! What could happen that would be more terrifying to all evil spirits? What greater work could be done on earth? By it so many of the devout are supported and so many sinners would be converted. For the Christian Church on earth has no greater power nor strength than such common prayer against all that may assail her. The evil spirit knows this very well, therefore he does all he can to hinder this prayer . . . for where prayer is neglected no one will deprive him of anything, nor will any one withstand him." Er. Ed. 16, 171. Johannes Seitz, _Erinnerungen und Erfahrungen_, p. 153: "We must learn that there are victories that cannot be won by the individual but are only gained by a larger company."

in spirit, and he will through faith attain participation in the *Communio sanctorum*, in the great and blessed multitude of perfected witnesses, who in song and prayer unite with the pilgrims of earth in adoration and praise before the throne of God.

But since all the words of penitence and thanksgiving, of supplication and intercession remain nothing but an empty river bed as long as the Spirit of God does not flow through them with His power, the chief object of prayer remains the petition for the gift of the Holy Ghost. In the life of the Christian this must become in a very special sense the prayer without ceasing that ascends in words and hymns and ejaculations. If this be omitted it is because of our guilt and not according to God's plan. If we permit it to become a living thing it is "the gift of God, not of works, lest any man should boast" (Eph. 2:8). Martin Kähler remarks on the statement of the 90th Psalm: "We pass our years as a tale that is told," that we might and we could pass them as a conversation with God, as a prayer. Then we would not have to spend them "with sighing."

We have seen that the ability and readiness to pray comes from justification; that sanctification through Word and Spirit brings the right preparation for prayer and its true content. We have still to inquire what *effects* prayer has on faith and life. As prayer leads us into the immediate and holy presence of God it produces, as nothing else does, a thorough knowledge of self. The γνῶθι σεαυτόν of philosophy and naturalistic pedagogy does not penetrate nearly so deeply into the "virgin soil of character" as the language of the Psalms: "Lord, thou has searched me and known me, thou understandest my thought afar off." Formal self-examination has never been able to uncover the presumptuous pride that in secret accompanies our words, thoughts and works; only as we come into the terrifying presence of God will our self-deceptions vanish. Unrecognized sins, hidden failings, forgotten vices of the past God reveals "in the light of his countenance" (Ps. 90:8). In prayer the conscience sees even more clearly the relation of the law in which the sins of all men are united in a common guilt. The senses become keener and more widely awake to the treacherous game that the deceiver Satan is playing with the world. Only by prayer can the effort "to always have a conscience void of offense toward God, and toward men" be realized (Acts 24:16). "So we can always tell by a man's character whether he lives under God's discipline or under his own" (Hirsch). At the same time we can see why so many fight shy of prayer and prefer self-laudation. They are afraid of the beggarly poverty, they hate the utter nakedness that no one can escape in connection with it.

As the conscience is awakened so it is also guided by prayer. Only through the *oratio* does the Spirit of God impart clearness concerning the bounds and the content of moral actions. For the greatest and most important thing is not that we speak to God but that God speaks to us, as He gives particular commands, and bestows fresh understanding, as He directs us into certain paths and bars others. Only by prayer can the problem of what is permissible (*adiaphora*) be solved. When the conscience has been wavering, perhaps because of its selfishness and unwillingness to sacrifice, God points out to it where freedom is to be surrendered and where it is to be exercised.[32] Only with such an attitude dare any one venture to write a theodicy or a philosophy of history. For God permits the recognition of His ways on earth only to the *hearer*; only he can understand God's ways in the history of his own personal life or in His larger dealings with the nations. Understanding and prayer are most closely related. As soon as we comprehend that the limits and defects of our understanding (just as in the case of the will and the emotions) are ultimately rooted in the moral and religious extremity and guilt of the world, we will gain a clearer understanding of the very close relation between *cogitare* and *mediatare*. Not only can there be no true theological culture without prayer, but even in all of the "profane" sciences prayer can become the key to the understanding of undreamed-of riches and unsuspected new possibilities. If according to St. Paul's statement (I Tim. 4:4) the use of all things "is sanctified by the Word of God and prayer," that statement will also apply to all our understanding of creation. If prayer be communion with the all-pervading Spirit, Who proceeds from the Creator and the Redeemer of the world, then the hidden secrets of God's creative wisdom will be revealed

[32] James 1:5: "If any of you lack wisdom, let him ask of God, that giveth to all men liberally and upbraideth not, and it shall be given him."

much sooner to reverent, adoring thought than to mocking questionings. Only through prayer will the spirit that is striving after understanding be put in a position *"in nulla creatura haerere, sed omnia in deum referre."* There was a time when artists and physicians, teachers of astronomy and botany labored and studied with a devotion like that of the service of God. Today men simply smile at the thought of prayer outside the Church or the secret closet, and in their laboratories they simply worship reason, which is neither the Creator nor an end in itself, but a creation and an instrument that has been given by One, Who is greater than all His creatures, for His service.

Recently, in connection with the question of the possibility of a "pneumatic exegesis," there has been considerable discussion about the specifically theological connection and the understanding of Scripture. Aside from that we have two valuable investigations of the subject by Rudolf Hermann and Martin Riemer, to which we would here call special attention. As we have seen above, Scripture will always remain the mother of prayer. "On the other hand, however, the explanation of Scripture is essentially conditioned by the prayer life of the Christian." No linguistic symbolism or philosophy of language causes the words of the Bible to become the Word. No verbal inspiration, no extraction of the historic nucleus, no dialectic teaching concerning Scripture can escape the danger of a purely theoretical consideration, if the prayer for the guidance of the Holy Ghost, the prayer that asks that He may give the right words for the interpretation of God's Word, be lacking. For this reason Luther so closely united prayer and the study of Scripture and, at the same time, proved that edification and scientific exposition do not have to come into the irreconcilable antagonism that exists almost universally today between the "inspired exegesis of the laity" and academic investigation.

Prayer arouses the conscience, refines its perceptions, guides and illuminates the understanding and strengthens the will in its conflict with sin. By nature man is a chaos of wild desires and opposing wishes unless they are united, as though bound together by a ring, purified and ordered through prayer. When this exercise is neglected it is Luther's opinion that "no one can rescue anything from Satan nor can anyone withstand him." Any one who does not arm himself for the time of temptation with the "bright, clear, mighty" words of Scripture "the devil will whirl away as the wind whirls away a withered leaf." "Where the Word has been allowed to slip away there is no support nor foundation and man sinks so deeply and so utterly that he must despair."[33] By the "evil imaginations and desires" of man's heart we may measure the significance of prayerless days, prayerless years, prayerless generations. The destroying forces of disintegration, uncleanness, worldliness, wrath and hatred keep entering ceaselessly through all the gates of sense, and there is no one able to overcome them. Man is never independent. He is ever dependent either on the powers above or on those below. Either God or Satan dwells with him.[34] The less there is of the bread of life the more there will be of the meat of death; the less of the light of the world, the more of the darkness of sin.

Yet that is only the dark, negative, reverse side of a very tremendous positive fact. "The more we deal with God's Word the clearer and newer it becomes and it can truly be said: the more we possess it the more we love it." The more supplication and importunity, the more strength will there be for the conflict. The more we wrestle in prayer, the more the evil spirit suffers and the more profitable it is for all men. (Cf. Er. Ed. 16,166.) Even a small company engaged in prayer can be of tremendous significance for the Church, the school and the family, for city, vocation and nation. Speaking with God gives more power to human speech than any rhetorical gifts.[35] Here the hidden decision is made concerning the success of preaching, instruction and pastoral care. Whether we may effect something for the glory of God or not; whether we are real witnesses of the message or only messengers bearing letters, finds its ultimate answer here. Likewise all natural understanding, esteem and love receive their secret power and depth from this source. Here we learn to understand the

---

[33] Cf. Er. Ed. 28,223; 48,379 seq.

[34] Luther, Er. Ed. 33,55: Man must either bear the image of God or that of the devil, for he is bound to be like the one toward whom he inclines.

[35] A. Bengel: "If a soul has really engaged in prayer it will find that it then for the first time possesses real power over others. . . . As we can perceive when any one has been in a quarrel so we can also perceive when anyone has come from communing with God." Württembergische Väter, I, 55, Stuttgart, 1887.

experiences and sufferings of others *sub specie aeternitatis*. "How different is our approach to those for whom we pray."[36] As the neglect of prayer first produces awkwardness in its exercise, then inability and finally an unwillingness to pray, so its use produces joy and a growing desire for its exercise. Devotion becomes a "characteristic trait" that shows itself in the ability and resolution always to pass over from temporal relations into explicit prayer (Kähler). Man is unable to exist without it. If he falls into sin the fall only drives him with still greater yearning into the presence of God, just as one who is sick longs for light and air much more intensely than any one else.

So prayer remains "the best exercise of faith and the hand that daily grasps God's benefits." It is true that it is not the basis of faith but depends on it as the prerequisite of its free exercise. And yet, as we have seen, it exercises a significant influence on faith. Upon the basis of this mysterious reciprocal influence Luther, on occasion, placed the two on an equality. "A true faith will turn into a simulated faith if we do not live in the fear of God, watch and pray." (*Cf.* Er. Ed. 58,392.) Whether skepticism becomes repentance, whether reflection about sin turns into the fear of sin, whether we merely declaim or really bear witness, whether we talk about man's end or really are men at the end, whether we chatter in eschatological figures of speech or have a longing for the consummation, whether we simply desire good or actually do it, in all of these situations, so closely associated and yet so infinitely far removed from each other, which must be daily faced anew and where the transition from one to the other is often so puzzling, it is prayer that is the determining factor. Of course we are again faced by the same paradox that God would have us seek and labor for that which He alone can actually give.

Prayer is "the chief work of the Christian." Because it comes from God it has the transforming power of goodness, which is always so much stronger than the mere repelling of evil. While the preservation and willing appropriation of what is good remains the chief means for expelling evil, and therefore prayer always retains the foremost place in the life of the Christian, yet the deliberate attack on sin that plans its destruction of sin also has an unmistakable place in over-

[36] P. Althaus, *Das Heil Gottes,* p. 205, Gütersloh, 1926.

coming evil and in strengthening faith. As in sanctification the spiritual motive of thankfulness must have added to it the scourge of obedience and fear, so besides the constructive blessings of prayer there must also be the defensive efforts of ascetic discipline. If prayer in the last analysis be nothing but the manifestation of the life and activity of the new man God has created within us, who will not be restricted in his activity, so fasting (understood as self-discipline in the widest sense of the word) is the exercise that is continually demanded by the presence of the old man, whose activities still continue even in those who are in a state of justification and sanctification. The neglect of such necessary efforts means the denial of the presence of the ungodly opposition that still clings to us. It would be a veiling of the true situation and a presumptuous deception, an unallowable anticipation of the final perfection of the parousia, an attempt to be what we are not, and a refusal to admit being what we are. Because we are men and not angels, sinners and not perfected saints; because we are daily assailed by flesh and blood, we need to use the keen-edged sword of discipline against our old nature.

The "Protestant" fear of work-righteousness has looked with disfavor on asceticism. What Löhe said in 1857 in his *Proposal for the Union of Lutheran Christians in an Apostolic Form of Life* still applies to the present situation: "When today we hear talk about asceticism there is the immediate objection that it is 'priestly domination over the people.'"[37] But properly understood the use of such discipline can never endanger the nature of the Gospel but, on the contrary, will only demonstrate and strengthen it. To assert the necessity of asceticism is only to proclaim the fact that we do not perform what is good out of free, spontaneous love to God, but that we have to force our will to such activity by dire compulsion. But this "is certainly calculated to keep the Christian in a state of humility, rather than to establish a feeling of high moral attainments." That the suppression of our self-love requires unrelenting self-discipline certainly

---

[37] Stuttgart, 1857, §21. Further, p. 40 *seq.*: "So we regard it as a necessary duty for all true members of the Church to pray for the spirit of holiness and discipline, and by word and deed to bring about, as far as possible, the recognition of the command of discipline in the widest circles." Also, *Drei Bücher von der Kirche*, p. 108, Stuttgart, 1845.

deprives us of every basis for self-satisfaction, every idea of meritorious action, and sternly directs the one who is fasting to seek the forgiveness of sins. In the evangelical conception of faith the necessity of discipline preaches to us with special emphasis the magnitude of sin and the necessity of justification. The more we are admonished to self-restraint and temperance the more our poverty, weakness and helplessness become apparent. The admonition of Scripture to the disciples and the congregations to crucify the flesh with the affections and lusts thereof, to mortify our members, to strive to enter in through the strait gate, to fight a good fight, to strive to attain the goal—all these admonitions after all only testify how easily the believer may still be lost and what full measure of grace is needed if any one is to be saved.

Though the Church that has justification as her fundamental article of faith was especially well protected against a self-righteous misunderstanding and misuse of asceticism, Lutheranism nevertheless interposed an additional bar and explained that the needed crucifixion of the old nature was not to be effected by particular "disciplinary inventions" of human origin or tradition, but through the genuine and willing fulfilling of the duties of one's calling and in the humble patient endurance of the sufferings sent by God. Before we choose for ourselves "childish, unnecessary works," we should demonstrate our fasting by fidelity in our God-ordered station, when the "father of the family labors to support his wife and children, and bring them up in the fear of God, the mother bears children and cares for them, a prince and government rules over land and people, etc." Idleness has been rejected by Lutheran theology, and out of this conception of an asceticism that is exercised within the life of the world the tremendous cultural achievements of Protestantism have come forth as a sort of matter of course. Alongside it there is a second sort of *vera mortificatio*, which takes place *per crucem et afflictiones, quibus Deus exercet nos.* No one is to seek the cross or impose it on himself but to whom it comes, in marriage, in the discharge of his duties, in sickness (and no one is spared his share, at least in some form); let him bear it willingly and obediently as his God-ordained lesson in humility. As the ancient Church in conformity with the words of Jesus united "prayer and fasting," as a weapon for overcoming the satanic fortifications, so Luther united *oratio* and *tentatio*; "prayer and temptation through the cross and sufferings of our vocation" and saw in this the real university of God, for the preservation of faith. How diverse the tribulations are which God sends to the individual, how loving the purposes He thus furthers and how He brings them to fruition, were topics on which Luther, so observant of the realities of life, could speak at great length and in our own pastoral care they have never yet been exhausted.

If asceticism be practiced in the form of the patient endurance of temptation, it will be preserved from any trace of forcible, self-chosen, legalistically meritorious character. We may quietly wait till God imposes the burden. We do not have to trouble ourselves about its artificial creation nor should we seek a special spiritual credit through it. Nevertheless it will not do to limit the wholesome chastising of the Christian to the spheres just mentioned. Neither did the Reformers attempt to do so. *Verum praeter hanc mortificationem, quae fit per crucem, est et voluntarium quoddam exercitii genus necessarium* (*Apology*, 214, 46). The chief enemies of man are not so much his evil as his prosperous days, when the purifying fires of affliction are not burning and the unbridled impulses of nature spread more easily than at other times. It is necessary to wage war on this army of desires "not only at certain times but at all times," in fullest freedom, it is true, but also with the most intense zeal. The same emphasis must be laid on both sides.

Christian freedom forbids a purely legalistic regulation of the ascetic ideals. What is allowable for one may ruin another. What confuses and injures the one may edify the other. Here a spiritually minded ethics is demanded which by personal communion with God in His Word and through prayer receives immediate guidance concerning the attitude required by the circumstances. Pietism, that at other times was all too inclined to rely in a fanatical way on an immediate guidance of the Spirit, was here entangled by a legalistic viewpoint, and its invariable accompaniment came with it, namely intolerance and a Pharisaic judgment concerning those who acted differently. Whoever used tobacco, that "abominable smoke from the abyss of hell" was (and still is) esteemed a "hireling and an enemy of the Cross of Christ." In opposition to such a placing of confidence in the use or disuse of certain things, Lutheranism has again and again appealed to the example of the Reformer, who could give to over-anxious, punctilious souls the cheerful advice "in defiance and con-tempt of the devil" occasionally to eat and drink, to sleep or to jest more than usual, so as not to let ethical discipline become ossified into trivial, narrow, bigoted prescriptions. There can be circumstances under which the "drink no longer water, but use a little wine" (I Tim. 5:23) can be just as good evangelical care of the body as the opposite may be under other circumstances.

The individual conditions modifying the practice of asceticism dare never be overlooked. But these considerations dare not limit its funda-mental and inexorable use. If Pietism was too much inclined to neglect the element of freedom, neo-Protestantism is indifferent to the need of discipline. Kierkegaard in his day called attention to this defect very emphatically. He missed in the Christianity of his times the trait of heroic renunciation that was so characteristic of the message of Jesus. For the sake of belonging to the Kingdom of God it is necessary to be ready to make any sacrifice, even though it would involve the cutting off or tearing out of members of the body. Everything that would prevent us from being good warriors of Christ, according to St. Paul, is to be put aside relentlessly.[38] However inapplicable specific counsels may be for certain individuals the exercise of hardness to-wards ourselves is an absolute necessity. A thankful enjoyment of the world is only possible when it is united with a strict discipline.

Because the vices that tempt individuals are so varied, different in different lives and even different in various periods of the same life, the proportion of freedom and discipline will have to vary and change continually. Scripture repeatedly mentions four spheres of temptation in which every one alike must exercise a special and unrelenting watchfulness because the roots of those particular evils of fallen nature have everywhere struck very deep and will multiply very quickly un-less they are properly pruned. They are the sins of the tongue, avarice,

[38] I Cor. 9:25-27; II Cor. 6:7; Eph. 6:10 seq.; St. Matt. 17:27; 19:21; 8:21; 10:38 seq.; 16:24.

impure thoughts and the corruption of the body. If anyone regards these as unimportant and does not guard against their dangers on every hand he is in imminent danger of suffering the shipwreck of his faith.

As a wonderful power to establish fellowship among men inheres in words, so they likewise possess a terrible ability to destroy that fellowship. Most serious of all is the destruction they can produce in our own heart. According to Scripture[39] an unbridled tongue can defile man's whole life and is, as it were, itself set on fire by hell. All divine service is only vain self-deception for the one who does not bridle his tongue. Because the slandering of one's neighbor serves the purpose of self-exaltation the self-humiliation which listens to God alone is lost more and more through such gossip. It was quite Biblical therefore when a preacher discoursing on the Advent pericope taken from the 13th chapter of Romans, said: "Many Christians make no progress in sanctification because they are continually giving way to their garrulousness and gossiping. There must be a discipline in silence when our danger lies in talking, a discipline of renunciation, of hard labor without intermission."[40]

As the thoughtless, unprincipled use of words destroys the best in our lives and in the lives of others, so the unrestrained desire for money has a similar effect. Watchfulness and an ordered discipline are therefore as necessary here as in our conversation with our neighbors. Because the source of the evil is not in the thing itself but in the evil thoughts of the heart Jesus did not declare that the mere possession of riches was sin. But He was very clearly conscious of the "deceitfulness of riches" and warned men against it with uncanny keenness, because it makes men anxious, hard, satisfied, proud, unwilling to sacrifice; because it chokes out the new life as the thorns choke out the good seed.[41] This is not the place to discuss the problem of social ethics, of capitalism and socialism. In his individual ethical existence the Christian overcomes the power of Mammon, that threatens him, as well as others, through the unwillingness to help others, by his

---

[39] St. James 3:1 seq.
[40] P. Althaus, Der Lebendige, p. 112, Gütersloh, 1924.
[41] St. Matt. 13:22 seq.; 19:22; St. Luke 12:19; 16:19 seq.

sacrifices. As he gives he demonstrates and likewise exercises his inner freedom from the yoke of temporal good. In such almsgiving there can be no thought of a meritorious action, for the willingness and the ability to surrender visible treasures spring from the faith that possesses greater treasures in heaven. Therefore the right hand does not know what the left hand has done either now or at the last judgment (St. Matt. 25:37-39). But if the benevolent impulse that has been given by faith is not exercised the destructive powers of selfishness will gain ground and divert the attention from the coming Lord to the uncertain illusions of that which is temporal (I Tim. 6:17). The freedom of surrendering our possessions that is given to us by the Spirit, is turned into the bondage of avarice. In connection with this money question we can see clearly the "modest" character of asceticism. God is no shopkeeper from Whom it is possible "to buy His favor as if He were an idler or a day laborer, who would not give His grace and favor for naught" (Er. Ed. 16:132), and anyone who uses the good entrusted to him like a stingy peddler himself loses the eternal good of divine adoption. Simon Magus is unable to buy the saving grace of the Spirit from the Apostles, but is directed to the way of repentance and faith. Ananias and Sapphira, on the other hand, who wanted to avoid the surrender of all their possessions, perish through the lie that originated in their greediness.

A third decisive sphere for the activity of Christian asceticism is the training of our thoughts to purity, to chastity in the wider sense of the word, by cleansing the whole mental life from wrath, envy, malice and immorality. Here particularly our previous statement, that uncleanness is best overcome by the believing and prayerful contemplation of divine holiness, becomes very evident, and yet, because of our twofold posture in sanctification we still need the negative attitude of avoidance. To bring the matter immediately into the practical life of our day we can say that the avoidance of the modern dance and questionable films, of the excessive frequenting of theaters and the intemperate reading of fiction (particularly during the years of adolescence, and for that matter during all later times of special temptation or of lowered powers of resistance) is as important as the attendance at divine service and the practice of prayer. Because sin has such a mysterious influence and ensnaring power, those places where it is glorified in sensuous and wild revelry are to be absolutely avoided. At the present time there are many things about which previous generations might have had differences of opinion but which today are no longer permissible for a Christian. In a time as morally lax as ours it is necessary in considering the Pauline assertion, "All things are lawful unto me, but all things are not expedient" to lay the greatest emphasis on the second part of that statement, "all things are not expedient." But it is not enough to exclude the gross, sensuous, defiling lusts, there must be a continuous readiness to surrender all secular good, no matter how exalted it may be, when it threatens to master us. "It can be a part of the care of souls to take the newspaper out of some one's hand—even out of our own."[42] The study of music may lead to a soft sensuous sentimentalism that manifestly weakens the power of resistance against evil. Indeed every form of quantitative intemperance in collecting, in sport or reading, can become a dangerous passion and an enslaving of the whole intellectual life. That all these things are by no means unimportant can be seen in the severe disturbances and disasters that afflict the life of faith where men imagine that they are superior to the need of "fleeing fleshly lusts that war against the soul."

The place, however, where asceticism has to perform its main task, is in the sphere of corporeal life. Here, of course, we come at once to fundamentally different conceptions concerning the significance of the body. According to Plato's and Philo's doctrine of the soul, which was continued in the mediaeval mysticism and in Schleiermacher's *Glaubenslehre*, sin is to be explained as that which is sensuous. Because a relation to God is not expressed by the corporeal existence of man, that existence is therefore worthless and contemptible. It can be destroyed by excess but better yet by fasting and castigation. The body has no part in the life after death. As a result asceticism is described as *mortificatio carnalis*, as the dulling, weakening mortification of the flesh for the liberation of the soul that is imprisoned in the material. In the domain of Biblical ideas we find a very different conception. Here the body is regarded as something that possesses a value of its

[42] Althaus, *op. cit.*, p. 131.

own and that together with the soul forms one indivisible, living organism. The motive for bodily discipline is no longer the mortification
of nature because of contempt for it, but it becomes a disciplinary
culture that springs from reverence for that body, which God has
prepared to be a temple for His Spirit and which shall have a share
in the resurrection. Because the *complete* man must undergo the
judgment and will be transformed in his entirety it is proper that he
be sanctified wholly and that the "whole spirit, soul and body be
preserved blameless unto the coming of our Lord Jesus Christ." (I
Thess. 5:23.) Evangelical ethics grounds the right and duty of asceticism not on the final repudiation of the body but on its recognition
as the end of all things. What God Himself has created and sanctified
dare not be despised, either through frivolity or by a "pious" spiritistic
conception of man's nature. It is impossible to serve God with the
soul "as such," and at the same time exercise no restraint in bodily
affairs (*caveant pastores!*), as the reverse is also true, an undisciplined
soul destroys the body (*caveant medici!*). Both parts, the external as
well as the internal, will avenge themselves on each other, until the
indissoluble unity of our corporeal-spiritual is recognized and our discipline unites the two.

Because chastity is something that affects both soul *and* body, it
requires not only a discipline of the thoughts but also a *disciplina
corporalis*. If the body is not the source of sin it can nevertheless become the place in which its tempting, corrupting work is particularly
carried out. It is a part of sin's devilish power of delusion that what
seems especially glorious to the body (κῶμοι καὶ μέθαι)[43] ruins it most
quickly. As in fallen man intemperance in spiritual things is the chief
characteristic of his·fall so it is the same in corporeal matters. A man
who has become "decadent" can devise a luxury of feasting so utterly
senseless in its extent and character that it brings its own judgment
with it, and the one who enjoys it perishes through it in body and
soul. It is impossible to tell how much spiritual life has been choked
through the unrestricted emphasis that has been placed on the question,
"What shall we eat, what shall we drink, and wherewithal shall we
be clothed?" "Where the body is filled it serves neither for preaching

[43] Rom. 13:13; Gal. 5:21; I Peter 4:3.

nor for prayer, or study or any other good undertaking; so there is no room left for God's Word" (Er. Ed. 65, 128). How much sickness, brutality, indecency, lack of resolution and laziness arises yearly from the misuse of alcohol in enormous quantities by our people, is something that is recognized by all theologians. Where hearts are "overcharged with surfeiting and drunkenness" (St. Luke 21:34) there has always been an entering door for sin. But even an uninterrupted career of easy-going enjoyment can in the course of a lifetime dull the ability to concentrate on the Word of God and prayer, or to remain aware of the spiritual and physical needs of the brethren and our duty of providing for them. If the willingness and strength needed for voluntary sacrifice is never practiced the ability to deny oneself and to govern oneself is more and more completely lost, in every direction, just as the reverse is true that the strength gained by physical discipline prepares one to enter at some other part of the battle. You can easily see in any man whether he is prepared to sacrifice or whether he is afraid to suffer pain. The fear of suffering, the demand for an unruffled existence on the part of our nation (to say nothing of the far-reaching, insatiable desire for pleasure) stand in marked and shameful contrast to the attitude of responsibility towards the corporeal that marked both the Bible and the age of the Reformation. In both of the latter we see the deep-seated connection between prayer and fasting, between the readiness to sacrifice for duty and bodily discipline, clearly expressed and realized.

Luther, who was not so poverty-stricken mentally that he could not grasp more than one idea at a time, could poke fun at the people who proudly thought that "it was much more excellent if they did not eat flesh, eggs, or butter" (Er. Ed. 16, 180), but he also knew that "gourmandizing, intemperance, excessive sleeping, loafing and idleness are weapons of unchastity by which purity is speedily overturned" and therefore he did not cease, by invoking the authority of the "holy Apostle Paul" to warn men against gluttony and drunkenness (Er. Ed. 16, 211). In the same way Calvin—that "no superstition might creep in"—reminded his readers, on the one hand that the statement of Joel (2:13) "rend your hearts and not your garments" must be decisive, but, referring to the great mass of Old and New Testament pas-

sages, he also strongly commended fasting as an aid in the performance of difficult tasks, as well as an encouragement to prayer, "as a
holy exercise, profitable at all times," which has been in use in the
Church since apostolic times, as these, in turn, had followed "the
example of the Law and the prophets."

Our times need both statements; the emphasis on the freedom of
faith as well as the exhortation to maintain a watchful discipline. In
the new life program of the Youth Movement in the linking of the
reform of life and natural hygiene, a situation that demands the
careful consideration even of Christians, has again come to its fitting
expression; it is the recognition of the multitude of sinful temptations
that arise ceaselessly from the great morass of improper nourishment,
clothing and neglect of the body. It is the awakening consciousness
that our responsibility toward God is for our physical welfare as well
as for that of our souls and that the whole previous separation of the
two (Greek and Roman Catholic) has been a mistake that was
fraught with serious consequences. But unfortunately all these efforts,
so excellent in their intention, have again degenerated into a pedagogi-
cal moralism, and seek to find their justification before God under
the cloak of reform, abstinence and vegetarianism. So out of what
was in itself a wholesome thing, that was occasioned by the "necessi-
ties of this life and the care for the control of the body," and which
might have served to produce humility, became a tower of Babel constructed with all the pride of human self-salvation. Contrasted with
such legalistic regulation of conduct and its frequent evidence of vain
presumption the Christian who does not base his salvation on such
futile regulations but lives his life in "confident helplessness" possesses
a distinct advantage. Luther even held it to be "salutary" in the presence of such "stiffnecked, hardened, ceremonialists," who "exalt, emphasize and command their usages as a means of justification without
faith," "to eat meat, to break fasts and to do other things, that they
regard as the great sins, for the defense of the faith," in short "to
give them decided offense," by doing the opposite of what they demand.

But we must give just as serious consideration to the other words of
Luther that he was in immediate connection with these. "As we are
not righteous because we are slavishly devoted to works and cere-

monies, neither can we be accounted righteous because we omit and despise such observances." "Many when they hear of this freedom of faith take it to mean a freedom to do anything they please, and want to appear free and Christian only through the contempt and disapproval of human ceremonies, usages, regulations and laws, as though they were Christians because they did not fast on a particular day, or ate meat when others fasted or omitted the customary prayers, with a supercilious mocking of human commands, while they completely shove into the background the remaining requirements of the Christian religion. The danger to the Church that came from libertine, antinomian fanatics in Corinth, Rome and Muenster was faced by Paul and Luther all through their lives just as much as the mischief that came from teachers of work-righteousness in Galatia or in the ranks of medieval religious orders. Today, in view of the crass weakness and unbridled license in nation and Church, at home and in heathen lands, the danger of luxury and debauchery must appear much greater than its legalistic opposite. The number of those destroyed by the mad zeal of monastic methods of seeking sanctification is small compared with the millions who are the victims of the lowest defilements of the flesh. A one-sided opposition that is directed exclusively against work-righteousness cannot for the time being be the task of theology. At all events even asceticism can be described by the paradoxical statement: Its exercise can give salvation to no one but its neglect can corrupt anyone.

Prayer and asceticism are the two powerful weapons of faith for the preservation of the life of the new man and for the mortification of the old. Their neglect inevitably strengthens the yoke of sin and endangers the existence of faith, just as their use increases our strength against sin and establishes the faith we have received. But even though prayer and discipline are commanded and great promises have been given in connection with their use, there still remains a last mysterious danger, namely that all this can in the end be made to serve our own pious enjoyment and personal glorification. If the ability and talent necessary to become knights, orators or artists and to gain the fame that goes with those positions be lacking can we not perhaps become virtuosos of holiness, on whom the multitude will gape as on some acrobat? If we have traveled the paths of purification does not the sweet intoxication of religious virtuosity beckon us? The purifying corrective to an egoistic sanctification that is otherwise always given by a belief in justification is not present in this case. For the one who is wrapt up in himself can even find a sentimental consolation for his conscience in the teaching of the cross as he applies it only to his own person. We need only to think of the negligence of the Church as it is revealed in the history of missions. Faith is only sound when it understands that all the statements concerning God and all that has been received from God are a reality that applies just as truly to our neighbor as to us, and that it must be imparted to him. Whoever is satisfied because he has escaped the evil floods of this world by his cultivation of holiness and thinks that he at least sits secure in the lifeboat, is in truth already shipwrecked.

While Luther was pursuing the monastic way of salvation in the convent he learned by his own experience and by that of others what a terrible danger is inherent in all exercises in holiness if men become absorbed in the selfish care of their own souls and as a consequence arrive at utterly false standards of faith. For neither visions nor merciless castigations nor ecstatic feelings at the reception of the Sacrament are the true signs that we are in a proper state of faith, but the test is whether we feel constrained to assist our neighbor and to help him "bear his sorrows and sufferings." In the place of the wealth of mystical experiences of God has come the "certainty of experience" described in the First Epistle of St. John: "We know that we have passed from death into life because we love the brethren." Even the need for prayer and fasting Luther derived from the obligation of being prepared at all times for the service of our neighbor. "For at the last day Christ will not ask how you have prayed, fasted, gone on pilgrimages or done this or that *for yourself*, but how much good you have done to others, even to the very least" (Luther). If the idea of service be lacking in devotion, or benevolent offerings, or these become only a secondary appendage to sanctification, their exercise becomes more dangerous than their omission. Only when service has become the central motive, when the very "subjugation of body and soul" is only for the accomplishment of this purpose, is the sanctifying process of a Christian's life honest and profitable, otherwise it remains selfish and worthless. We no longer then simply guard against sin because it is a hindrance to our own internal progress but because through it we sin against our neighbor and so against God. We fear God because disobedience might make us unqualified for parenthood, for service, for leadership in Church, community or nation. Because one can fall on account of another (Lev. 26:37) and one can lead another astray, each one will pray God that He will let him stand securely. Because my lawlessness would offend those about me I will strive after purity. Because my timid silence would lead others to cowardice, while my confession will help to strengthen the witness of the Church I will speak and not refrain timidly from utterance. If according to Luther's beautiful expression "Each one shall be the other's daily bread" then the bread of life must first become my food. Shall "one become the other's Christ" (*Cf.* Er. Ed. 27, 196), then the Pharisee within me that does not want Zachaeus to come along, must first be suppressed by prayer. If any one is even called to be a leader, on whose life and conversation the attention of many is centered, how ought he not to gird himself in eternal vigilance.

So the idea that I exist for others and not simply for myself will on the one hand give to my actions a more exalted responsibility and on the other hand will remove all false importance and the secret tendency to fall into a self-satisfied striving after personal perfection for its own sake. As intercession purifies devotion from the destroying deception of selfishness, so deeds of love done for our neighbor are even more effectual. For only as we no longer stop at friendly thoughts and speeches but actually do something, really sacrifice time, money and effort, will we really cease to mean only ourselves. Because it regularly requires a special decision to pass from a merely benevolent disposition to the actual accomplishment of the work, "a new willing that all too often is missing" (Schlatter, *op. cit.,* p. 408), so it is not a matter of indifference as to whether we merely write and preach about service, even though it be with the very best intention, or whether we actually engage in it. Because the disposition of faith to do good is again tempted and halted by the sinful will at the very threshold of action and the "priest and levite of Jericho" within us must be coerced once more, everything depends on our not merely issuing information on social questions, attending congresses in the interests of practical Christianity or belonging to charitable committees but that each one, without exception, really serves somewhere.[44] For "the final step out of the trenches into the line of fire is the hardest" (K. Heim). The feeding of the hungry, visiting the sick and imprisoned, and the clothing of the naked can never be relegated to a group of professionally active agents, who are paid for doing it. For as closely as knowledge and prayer are connected, so closely knowledge and service are also knit together (I Cor. 13:2). No one can excuse himself from the common workday obligations towards servants, the sick and the aged without being punished. It is a part of the scientific consideration of the whole matter that we discuss it in a practical, unscientific way. Learned scientific discussion without the actual service of the Church is therefore, even theologically, a serious defect. *Theologia est disciplina eminens practica.*

Lutheran ethics has maintained the principle that love for one's neighbor must be exercised in what "lies close at hand," nor is that direction superfluous. For just as asceticism, regarded as a protection against temptation, is prevented from using all arbitrarily chosen, exaggerated forms of mortification, so by the same rule, love is prevented from becoming an ineffective and voluble sentimentality about needs afar off. Just as the artificial penitent often fails with amazing suddenness in the face of real trials and sufferings so the love of what is far removed does not function in daily intercourse with those close at hand because the burdens and the sacrifices we have selected for ourselves are always lighter and easier to bear than the obedient carrying of a cross that has been laid on us by a higher power that did not consult us in the matter. To remain faithful under the needs and trials of family life or of our vocation we need to be reminded that the love required of us begins at home. That Lutheranism has succeeded better than others in this particular is due in large measure to its recognition of the ethical principle we have been discussing. But while this rule is valuable in training us for the hard sacrifice that is often involved in faithfulness in little things, yet it fails to see the

---

[44] A. Schlatter: "So long as we issue proclamations the conscience is not yet on fire."

many more distant tasks, because they "do not lie close at home." Our evil nature shows itself not simply in the evasion of what lies close at hand by offering a "kiss to the whole world," it also shows its perversion in thinking that its obligation of service has been fulfilled by attending to the duties connected with the smallest circle of our lives and forgetting the needs of the millions who do not happen to live on our street. Even when the Christian is ready to serve others he still has to meet the temptation of only loving those who love him, of only being kindly disposed towards his brethren, and so is no different from the publicans (St. Matt. 5:46 *seq.*). Beside the willingness to be my brother's keeper there must be the deepest compassion for the millions at home and abroad who still "dwell in the shadow of death." Only where there has been prayer, service, sacrifice and a sympathy that reaches farther than what lies just before our eyes and is included in the narrow circle of our personal vocation, is there a real and complete separation from egoism; only then do we have true love. Any one who does not want to soil his hands with the wretchedness of the masses nor is willing to help in healing the wounds in the body of the nation, any one who feels a responsibility for the world's suffering and guilt only as it is found in Berlin and not as it exists in Madras or Kapstadt has a faith that is sadly deficient, no matter how holy his life may seem to be. A Church that does not engage in works of love becomes a mere theory and perishes.

Any one whose conscience has recognized his duty towards the multitudes and has striven to serve them will always be confronted by four different situations, by four different tasks. The first is the realization of the terrible connection between the external and the inner need. Wichern talked about a "Gordian knot of physical and moral corruption." Miserable housing conditions and prayerlessness, lack of proper sleeping quarters and sexual catastrophes, a lack of employment on the one hand and drunkenness and seduction on the other, are only the physical and ethical halves of one and the same evil that cannot be remedied either by the economic endeavors of the social reformer alone, or by the mere preaching and pastoral care of the pastor, but only by the combination of the two, even if, at first, it is only in the study of the situation and the approach to the problem.

The official social worker is just as helpless in the face of such terrible distress as the preaching theologian. The one is deceived by the American dogma that favorable social conditions will bring about a realization of the Kingdom of God on earth, the other lives in the illusion, so contrary to all actual experience, that the Word alone will do everything. It is terrifying to see how unrealistically, vaguely and untruthfully theologians frequently talk at the present time about the Word of God and its power. In reality almost nothing is realized in actual fact of what is so magnificently proclaimed on paper. The founder of the Salvation Army is reported to have said: "They must all at least have warm feet if they are to understand the Word of God." This statement expresses in somewhat crude fashion the quite essential truth that the preached Word without the "silent word" of ministering love, without the serving ministrations of living men remains ineffective. A preaching Church that lacks the Samaritan's love remains dead in spite of all its proclamation of the Word. It has become like the "salt that has lost its savor and is henceforth fit for nothing but to be cast out and trodden under the foot of man." So we must be cautious and restrained in accepting the attacks on Inner Missions that have become fashionable in some quarters. As long as congregations do not attempt to realize the rich heritage that is theirs in the Lutheran conception of the Church, and fail to help carry the burdens of their suffering brethren, so long a little band of voluntary workers must step into the breach, and we must be "slow to speak, slow to wrath" when the greatness of the wretchedness and distress they see brings about an exaggerated and over-hasty activity in the prosecution of their work.

Because the distress of external circumstances, as well as the evils within, can obstruct the way to God, a faith that is prepared to help must address itself to the whole man in his actual condition and must offer to help with both hands; the Word with the right hand and love with the left. It must bring forgiveness *and* fellowship, the physician *and* the remedy, the bread of life *and* daily bread. The second precept of social ministration says that we must always be ready to give up what is allowable in itself for the sake of the weaker brethren when it would become a snare to them. This is the other side of the question concerning the adiaphora to which we have already alluded in its individual significance in connection with the practice of asceticism. The decision as to how I shall exercise my freedom must be determined not merely by its effect on myself but just as much by its effect on my immediate or more distant surroundings. It is the nature of sin to regard others as existing for our personal benefit, so the regenerate man realizes that he exists for the benefit of others. The question of personal enjoyment and our own strength in dealing with pleasures and possessions plays no part here when our conduct involves the question as to what the weaker brother will do with what I can use freely and without danger. St. Paul with all his inner superiority to legal requirements was always ready to surrender his rights unconditionally when the use of his freedom would have led others to abuse them or would have caused them to fall. (I Cor. 8; Rom. 14 and 15.) The more unbridled the times become the more the freedom of the Christian must consist in surrendering his freedom and in abstinence rather than in the right of possessing and enjoying. By refraining from luxuries others must be shown that the riches of God do not require the riches of this world, so that to the man whose will is undisciplined and bound, the ability to escape his apparently inescapable fetters may be demonstrated, by the lifting example of a man of faith. This is one of the most important ways in which the Church of Jesus can today serve its members and its fellow countrymen. Not every one, just to cite one example, may feel equally strongly the need of becoming an abstainer for the sake of some person of his parish who is intemperate, but no one should smile at the efforts of those brethren who unite in voluntary associations of abstainers for that reason, and who strive thus to offer their aid to the great numbers who have become intemperate.

The sacrifices of abstinence for the sake of one's neighbor are however not enough. If the Church is to protect effectively those who are endangered she has to advance an attack against the array of evil forces which, banded together, continually seek their victims. The systematic hostile attacks of mammon, uncleanness and untruth drive the Christian from his defensive attitude of patient silent endurance to a holy wrath, and thrust into his hands the weapons of truth and purity that are to be used in active conflict. It is surely senseless to be striving to save a little band by painstaking efforts while thousands are plunging anew into destruction because no one attempts to attack the evil, morbid conditions by which great numbers must be poisoned. No preacher dare depend on the Word's accomplishing everything if he does not at the same time engage in a bloody conflict against the devilish forces that are sowing the tares that will choke the good seed almost as soon as it has begun to grow. We cannot pray God to protect our children from "unbelief, doubt and other great and shameful sins" and at the same time never raise a hand to correct the conditions that inevitably will lead our youth into the severest temptations. If we do not comprehend the solidarity of service we will have to experience the solidarity of the curse. If the world, laden with temptations, is not emptied of its dangers by an offensive attack by the Church the dark powers will empty their fury like a thunderstorm over our heads. Abstinence and attack are reactions against the dissemination of evil and so are only negative forms in which faith maintains its duty of service. It is not enough however to erect dams against the flood, to clear the weeds out of the fields; the protected land must be cultivated and built upon. The seed and the building materials are both the Word; the Word of Jesus Christ that covers guilt and liberates from sin. But if a congregation does not want to come under the suspicion of possessing nothing but a verbal possession it will not only speak, it will also be concerned about the way in which this Word is imparted in the public services, in picture and song, in festivals and in diversions, in education and in common customs. This particularly applies to children who are not to be preached at nor "converted" but who are decisively formed and fashioned by the visible and tangible influences of the Church in which they grow up. We cannot here discuss more in detail the individual forms of "the raiment of the Word" but will only refer more particularly to one of the points mentioned because it has such extraordinary significance both for the personal progress in sanctification as well as for the congregation and therefore should be used both in the service of others as well as in our personal development; this is the education into churchly usages. Its importance is best measured by observing the terrible power of moral laxity. When, as at the present time, the desecration of Sunday is regarded as unblameworthy and a matter of course, when the proprieties in the relations of the sexes have ceased to exist and the fashions have become boundlessly indecent, such degeneration cannot be overcome by a single outburst of moral indignation. For custom whether it be noble, dead or repulsive always exerts a compelling influence over the collective consciousness of men; it has the power of producing an atmosphere by which thousands are consciously or unconsciously affected. It is always more powerful than a passing changing word. And, as Bruno Gutmann has correctly stated, "only evil customs grow by themselves," while good customs need continual fidelity and renewed inculcation.

Because customs always possess such an overmastering and formative influence, that is so much stronger than mere admonition, it remains as an essential task of the Church to use the power of custom in her constructive work that it may here serve to overcome the evil spirits and bring a blessing, as there it serves to destroy. Of course the matter is not so simple as Romano Guardini, for example, would have it in his book on *Liturgical Culture*, namely just quietly to create and use pious forms and holy symbols, because after a sufficiently long use the spirit will be naturally conformed to them. This proposal is entirely too convenient to be true. Just the opposite is true. Where "the Word of God is preached in its truth and purity and we, as the children of God, live holy lives in accordance with it" there the Spirit of God in ever new incarnation, creates new corporeal forms in his redeemed creation, and fashions holy times, holy symbols, pious customs, because God's working is always of a corporeal-spiritual nature. Such clothing of the Gospel, produced by the Word itself, it is proper reverently to receive, cultivate and preserve, so that they may become defensive, productive, edifying forces for the Church. The power of the Word to create such customs has always been highly regarded and valued by Lutheranism. From Luther to Löhe the value and the blessing of a churchly attitude in public and private has been recognized, loved and carefully observed, as, for example, in the use of the Church year, liturgical colors, the adornment of the building, morning and evening prayers, table prayers, the ringing of the prayer bell, correct observance of Sunday and Holy Days and birthdays (Matthias Claudius), appropriate music, and art that encourages devotion. It was first the Illumination, with its fleshless, bloodless, "pure" spirituality and the pietism that was so closely related to it in such things, and that wanted to consider nothing but inner experiences, that robbed the Church of her true treasure of pious living customs. The preservation of the small treasure of pious observances we still possess and the conscientious cultivation of all the new additions that are bound to arise under the influence of the Word as it is purely preached and lived, is one of the most important tasks in the service of our congregations today. Without customs and usages the gathering of the congregation becomes merely a sermon audience. If the Holy Ghost no longer finds a starting point in churchly customs that He can use as His instruments, no true substantial growth can take place in a congregation that is nothing but a group of personal followers gathered around a pulpit orator. Where the disregard of custom has become rampant there the danger of demoralization is close at hand, which in turn produces a loss of faith in the individual and an unchurchly attitude in the great mass of the people.

The presupposition of all faith is that "we do not present our supplications before Thee for our righteousness, but for Thy great mercies" (Daniel 9:18). Asceticism, as the circumcision of nature, through labor, suffering and discipline has a meaning only if a new life has been given, a life in which the contrast to the old evil nature is manifest, so that we gain encouragement in our warfare against the flesh. If prayer and fasting depend completely on the prevenient grace of God it is still truer of all service. God Himself must first liberate us before we are free to help our brethren. No one is able to exercise the faculty of loving others until "the love of God is shed abroad in our hearts by the Holy Ghost which is given unto us" (Rom. 5:5). The wreath of ninefold love that St. Paul weaves in the Fifth Chapter of Galatians (v. 22), is called the fruit of the Spirit. The servants trade with the talents of their Lord. It is not only the fact that in our serving we continue to receive that prevents us from claiming any credit but also our failure in serving with what has been given us as we could and should. The amount of service remains far short of the amount of ability God has given us. There is a great deal of neglect and unwillingness mingled with all our benevolence. Consequently there is no divine commandment that produces such deep penitence in our self-judgment as the one that says, "Thou shalt love thy neighbor as thyself." On every side we are accounted "unprofitable servants" who have no claim on God through what they have done. (St. Luke 17:10.)

But if our ever incomplete service of God can never give us a claim to His fellowship, if those who are most willing to work feel their need of forgiveness most keenly, the same paradox we encountered before applies here, that service can gain salvation for no one, but that its omission inevitably destroys everyone. St. James and First John are not accidental portions of Scripture. They bring the "necessary corrective" to the Pauline teaching of the righteousness of faith, the other side of the paradoxical relation that exists between grace and human responsibility in the one who has been justified by faith. Who hates his brother walks in darkness. If one sees him in need and shuts up his bowels of compassion against him, the love of God is not in him, for how can he love God whom he has not seen if he love not his brother whom he hath seen. Thus the Apostle of Jesus wrote to the Asiatic world that was so set on attaining deification, when he wanted to point them to the One Whose blood cleanseth from all sin (1:7).

In all questions concerning sanctification, in those relating to its motives and in those dealing with its activities we meet with the same rigid dualism: God the only source of salvation and man the only source of his own destruction. The reason lies in that paradoxical antithesis of flesh and spirit which is produced by faith and which will continue till the parousia brings its perfect vision. Because the new life is wholly God's work it brings with it the willingness to return thanks and to love. Because the "husks and fragments" of fallen nature still cleave to us, we carry on our conversation in obedient fear. Because the sons of God are led by the Spirit of God (Rom. 8:14) we are able to serve, to pray and to purify ourselves. Because men know the weakness and evil of their hearts they seek to serve others, for this reason they arm themselves prayerfully with the power of the Word, and for this cause they hate and shun all license. So the sanctification of the Christian is always expressed by two statements by the *"Confiteor"* and by the *"Gloria in excelsis"*; by the confession, "By the grace of God I am that I am," and by the words of the prayer, "that His grace may not be given me in vain."

CHAPTER VI

The Significance of Sanctification in the Preservation or Loss
of the State of Faith

IN THE course of our previous investigations we have seen that no
attempts to attain sanctification by ourselves, whether of moral,
mystical or speculative sort, are able to establish a communion with
God, because all our human powers have been crippled through the
enslaving and condemning power of sin (Chapters I and II). What
no efforts at deification were able to attain God freely gave the world
in Christ Jesus (Chapter III). In Him He promises and assures us of
the two facts: "Thy sins are forgiven thee," and "Arise and walk!"
This renewal applies to the whole man and reaches to all the spheres
of life; to body, soul and spirit; to understanding, emotion, will and
deed (Chapter IV). So no creative part, nor cooperation, which might
carry some merit with it, can be attributed to the one who yields to
the offer of salvation as it is proclaimed in reconciliation and redemption. On the other hand man possesses the fearful ability to cast away
the salvation that has been offered, and perhaps even attested to him
personally, and so to destroy himself. Faith because of thankfulness
and obedience, because of fear and love drives man to ceaseless exercise in prayer, self-discipline and service, but the natural man does
not cease to despise, to hinder and destroy the "drawing to the Father
by the Son" (Chapter V). This conflict in which faith and unbelief
strive for the mastery continues till the hour of death. But this conflict has not been sufficiently described if it is simply considered as a
general conflict that is bound to come between flesh and spirit because
of their divergent principles. It has an animated history that is as full
of incident, as difficult and as trying as any warfare between two
nations. Here there are great battles and small skirmishes, the gain or
loss of territories, displays of courageousness and of weakness, and

finally the certainty that its termination must be one of two things, either a final decisive victory or a final and utter defeat. As a general must be vitally concerned in gaining information concerning the position, resources and tactics of the enemy, and as the utilization of all that might bring failure or success in a battle calls for his most strenuous exertions, so it is of vital importance for the *miles christianus* to know the concealed moral laws governing sin and grace that can either imperil his state of faith, or strengthen and preserve him in the conflict he must face. It is this *concrete* "history of the warfare of the heart" that we would discuss in the following pages.

Whosoever wants to describe the doctrine of justification must first possess a doctrine of *sin*. This we tried to furnish in the second chapter. Whoever wishes to provide a doctrine of sanctification must also furnish a doctrine of *sins*. But is not one sin like another sin, of equal seriousness and with similar consequences, or should we and must we classify them? The Reformation theology in opposition to the Roman Catholic distinction of mortal and venial sins, and the frivolous use often made of that distinction in the practice of the Confessional, always emphasized the fact that sin is an "absolute category" in which there can be no differentiation. Before God every sin, the most trifling as well as the most serious, is a *complete* rupture of the proper relation of trust and obedience that we owe to God, which in every case makes the offender unconditionally guilty. The theology of the 51st Psalm excludes all "puppet sins." Before the Holy One the insidious entrance of a presumptuous thought is as grievous as the act of adultery. The degree of guilt is *always* infinite and requires infinite mercy for its erasure and remission. But so far we have seen only the one side. Every sin involves something more than its accusing or condemning status before the holiness of God. It likewise exerts a fettering and mastering power over man and it is this aspect we have to consider as we inquire whether every sin has an equal power in enslaving our moral intentions, in dulling and confusing our ability to understand and perceive. It is evident that the answer to this question is of the greatest importance for the preservation or the loss of our state of faith.

A survey of the history of theology shows that this very essential problem has received very little consideration. We find the most attention given it in the casuistic literature of Roman Catholic moral theology and in the confessional manuals, the third volume of Albrecht Ritschl's great work on *Justification and Reconciliation*, the writings of Johannes Müller and the latest literature of Anthroposophism and of the Christengemeinschaft. True, all these tendencies have shoved the doctrine of sin to a place behind their teaching concerning sins. They think of it more lightly and less seriously than the Second Article of the Augsburg Confession and consequently have always severely criticized this article of the Confession. Here we once more receive the painful impression that theological perception is apparently unable to apprehend or express more than one statement in its entirety. The other side, which in this case is the more important one, is not stated clearly and emphatically, just as the churchly dogmatics has neglected this phase of the question.

However there have always been some evangelical theologians who saw the fact very clearly and who maintained that every sin established the same infinite gulf between God and man but who did not, on that account, fail to furnish a detailed history and psychology of sin, a satanology and a demonology. The old Lutheran dogmatics, besides their fundamental definitions of sin, provided a classification of "actual sins." During the past century Culmann, Martensen, Julius Müller, Harless and Vilmar particularly felt this problem and applied themselves to its solution. The last named deserves especial commendation because with all his painstaking discussion of particular sins he always distinguished them from original sin and subordinated them to it, while the two first named, as a result of their theosophical affinity to Jacob Böhme and Franz von Baader, often neglected this essential difference in relative importance. Recently men like Schlatter, Althaus, Elert, Piper and Heim have again called attention to the twofold character of this question. Nevertheless evangelical theology still lacks a hamartiology which adequately describes the fearful possibilities of sin both in its accusing and its enslaving character, and which is not afraid to learn from the unquestionably able Roman Catholic moral theologians, from Ritschl, R. Rothe and Steiner, without losing Luther's fundamental view of the enslaving burden of guilt that pervades all sin. For our own presentation, as well as for pastoral care and for training in the service of our neighbor, it is necessary to realize both; how sin invariably destroys communion with God and how it works to accomplish this end. To the dogmatician this second question may appear entirely secondary, but as soon as we begin to reflect more deeply on the moral problem of sanctification we can no longer pass it by as unimportant psychologizing. We have to pause and consider because of what is involved. The one who dodges the question will not get very far.

In his vigorous polemic, *Die Theologie der Tatsachen wider die Theologie der Rhetorik*, Vilmar called for a "teaching concerning temptation." It is indeed a prerequisite for successful warfare against any foe that we know the way in which he gives battle. The diabolical, uncanny way in which sin operates shows itself through a double manifestation. The one is its apparent insignificance and apparent harmlessness on first sight. It is never suggested that the spark may become a fire, the snowball an avalanche, idle thoughts turn into terrible passions and a voluntary yielding (once does not mean anything!) result in a terrible bondage. Only with the passing of time do the fetters become evident which had been fastened by the commission of the first sin. The first slip seems voluntary and easily retraced.[1]

But the enemy has a still more dangerous weapon at hand. When enlisting men in his service he not only disregards all reference to future obligations but with the very first handclasp bestows intoxicating pleasure, apparently boundless liberty, and promises still more for the future. The Bible tirelessly paints pictures of the enemy and his manifold deceits, with great clearness and unmistakable warnings; on occasion compares the cozenage of sin to the harlot "who sitteth at the door of her house, on a seat in the high places of the city, to call passengers who go right on their ways." Whoever follows her "knoweth not that the dead are there" (Prov. 9:14-18). Out of the appreciation of the tricky wiles of the beginnings of sin, from an

[1] Culmann, p. 79 *seq.* "Because we do not immediately fall dead after the commission of a sin we think it is not dangerous. A man feels his physical burns but the seared conscience causes him no trouble. The burden of unrecognised and unforgiven sins he can drag along from one year to another without suspecting what he is heaping up for himself." *Cf.* Eccl. 8:11: "Because sentence against an evil work is not executed speedily, therefore the heart of the sons of men is fully set in them to do evil."

understanding of the deceptive inversion of all values in the first temptation (*eritis secut Deus*), faith will acquire a holy fear and vigilance and will understand how the deceiver is the most tricky, and therefore the most dangerous, at the time of his first approach. Once men are pledged to him he soon drops the mask. The one to whom the Spirit has given a "renewed mind" sees the end of the road from the very beginning; sees the ripe poisonous fruit in its seed—and smiles at the efforts of the tempter.[2]

A second bit of understanding that is quite essential for the conflict of sanctification is an insight into the difference in the enslaving power of different sins. The old Protestant division of sins, which is quite in accord with Scripture,[3] into those working internally and those acting externally; into sins of the heart, the tongue and the deed (*peccata interna et externa, peccata cordis, oris et operis*) is anything but irrelevant trifling. It is true that Jesus in the words of the sermon on the mount used the very expressions that dogmatics employed to designate distinctions in acts, in the opposite way, expressly to remove every distinction. The angry thought in God's sight is on an equality with the act of murder, the lustful glance is as evil as the adultery. But because we know ourselves equally guilty in God's sight in the commission of every sin it does not follow that the effect of evil thoughts, words and deeds is equally significant for myself or my neighbor in every case, and that therefore there is no difference occasioned by the instrument used in its commission, whether it be the heart, the tongue or the hand.

In the first place we cannot take the influence exerted by either a morbid or a wholesome mental life seriously enough. The worst delusion of the materialistic thinking of the past decade is its almost complete loss of reverence or fear of the mighty, invisible power of "mere" ideas. Even a morbid imagination that remains limited to fancies and desires is a terrifying, living power, that can torment and enslave

---

[2] *Cf.* Bezzel, Ruprecht. "There is a possibility of smiling at satanic temptations, because they are too trivial. And I do not know whether the devil is not driven away more by contempt than by serious consideration." P. 49 and p. 355, note 2, with references to similar statements by Luther and Hamann.

[3] St. Matt. 15:19; 5:21 *seq.*

its victims to a fearful degree,[4] creates an atmosphere around itself and infects and poisons others, as it tremendously increases the power of evil in the world, while in a blessed way, all pure, wholesome thinking and feeling, even when it happens in the most obscure places, spreads irresistibly and bears its certain fruit. The unbridled fecundity of morbid and evil imaginations must therefore be mercilessly combated and avoided because, under any circumstances, it is sufficient by itself alone to corrupt man utterly. But the most uncanny thing about such a play of desires is something else. It is the fact that the unrestrained roving thoughts never remain confined to the hidden chambers of the soul, but they crowd out into the open and display themselves in words and actions, that enslave, burden and shape the future of their author still more certainly than the morbid thoughts. We might say that as in the transition from the friendly disposition to the helpful deed there is always a demon present who would prevent its realization, so in the progress from the wrathful unclean desire to the hurtful work and destructive act, there is a guardian angel on the watch, seeking to hinder us from crossing the threshold. The very hesitation that restrains an evil thought from becoming an external act is proof that here again there is a fresh realization that it would involve a renewed, conscious, deeper descent into evil than that of the previous slavery, and one that would consequently still further weaken the soul.

An evil word is like a sped arrow that cannot be recalled. Its results are immeasurable and beyond all human control. The word has stronger formative power, it multiplies itself more rapidly and quickly than the originating thought. It produces lasting history, enmity and contention; inconspicuously and without effort it moulds the opinions and views of many, thus involving all the more responsibility, and so there is special justification for another distinction of the old dogmatics; the one it made between *peccata propria*, sins that involve only the individual, and *peccata aliena*, sins that involve others, either by awakening in them the slumbering passions or by inciting and

---

[4] M. Kähler, *Theologie und Christ*, p. 43. "Often, till the latter days of manhood, unconquerable bitterness rose in my soul when I had to wrestle with the after effects of the poison which had been injected into K. by the imagination of the boy."

strengthening those already active. Because a malicious statement not only weakens the one who utters it in his own powers of moral resistance but involves at least two others, the one spoken to and the one spoken about, it becomes of great importance as to whether the evil intention realizes its purposes or whether it is repressed by the fear of God and the might of the Spirit.

"The word is worse than the thought, the deed worse than the word" (Vilmar, *op. cit.*, p. 224). For it is the deed that finally involves the *whole* man, binds him closer and closer with the fetters of sin and "makes return harder, the growth of sin easier." Deeds leave a deeper impression on the character than thoughts. Deeds produce terrible situations that cannot be recalled nor changed and whose bonds the entangled wretch tries in vain to sever by still more serious wrongdoing. It was not the covetous thought, the lustful glance nor the storm in his soul but the actual deed that drove David into such humiliating shamelessness that he caused the rightful husband of the stolen wife to become drunken, so that he could not enter his own house and that finally led to his murder. Scripture is especially severe in dealing with the sins of the flesh, not only because of the terrible consequences for the companion in sin but above all because they invariably destroy the spiritual gifts of the believer. Adultery and whoredom are therefore always associated with the sins that exclude men from salvation.[5] The other items of the catalogues of vices include a striking number of sins of action. Perjury injures life much more seriously, and ruins it more terribly both within and without than the mere dalliance with the thought of its possibility, even though such an evil thought is just as bad in God's sight as the false oath itself. The power of murder to darken and becloud the soul is far greater than the hateful thought. An accomplished swindle enslaves and torments a man's life in an entirely different way from the "mere" desire for gold. Erotic stimulation is destroyed and vanishes again where the spirit of discipline prevails, but man loses forever his moral integrity and honor by *one* act of transgression. The recourse to magic, the "charming" of children produces a deeper depravity and a greater

[5] I Cor. 6:9 *seq.*; Gal. 5:19 *seq.*; St. James 4:4.

immersion in satanic power than the tempting suggestions of ungodly superstitious thoughts.

Any one who would foolishly permit himself to be drawn on and stumbles down step after step because thought and deed, inclination and progress towards evil are alike sinful in God's sight and because God can easily rescue us from every deep, would be subject to a fearful delusion. The surrender to evil deeds shows a much greater loss of the divine spirit of faith and prayer and a far greater obsession by satanic powers than the subjection to evil thoughts. When theology regards all sins alike or when even it declares that only hidden pride is destructive, it comes into complete contradiction with the colorful utterances of Scripture and at the same time neglects one of the weightiest tasks in the care of souls. It is true that pious pride is the pre-eminent sin of theologians and of those who have been regenerated. But God does not only resist the proud, He also repels the lecher, the mammon worshipper, the political tyrant, murderers, sorcerers and despisers of parents. The sins of thought doubtless weigh as heavily before God as those of word and deed. $\Phi\theta\acute{o}\nu os$ and $\phi\acute{o}\nu os$ accuse the sinner alike before Him and require the same forgiveness. But as God's justice does not remove the consequences of sin, even where He forgives and overcomes sin, so in the revival of faith in the soul it is by no means an indifferent matter as to how deeply the furrows of sin have been ploughed into the soul, or as to how many unchangeable, disfiguring branding marks of sin we carry in our bodies and souls. Evil thoughts can poison days and weeks, false words can destroy fellowship for years, but evil deeds can ruin a life irretrievably. Even a whoremonger may be received and may exalt the mercies of God by his faith, but his body broken in health can no longer render the service which his faith would gladly undertake; wasted years that should have been given to labor can no longer be redeemed. The melancholy regret continues to overshadow the renewed life of faith because by the testimony of facts it is daily reminded, with renewed sorrow, of the depths of its fall, and so meets with renewed trials of its faith. As faith perceives the persuasive deception and corrupting purposes of sin when it first approaches, so it particularly sees its abysmal devilishness in the lying suggestion that the step from thoughts to words and deeds is more or less unimportant. This secret danger will be overcome when the Christian meditates not only on sin in general but considers his own concrete sins, repents and guards against them with renewed watchfulness. "A general repentance is the death of repentance," Hermann Bezzel, with his solid background of Lutheran theology, said quite rightly. The recognition of the particularly enslaving burden and the special shame connected with certain sins demands a special repentance and aversion, a special resolution never again to permit it to go so far, not even once.

A further and very important ground for differentiation in our judgment on sins lies in the fact that evil works far more mischief in a life that has been enlightened concerning the nature of sin through the Word, than when it comes into the life of the unregenerate. Any one who possesses full knowledge of the greatness of his guilt and of the servitude of disobedience, who has tasted the heavenly gift of reconciliation, who has been a partaker of the renewing power of the Holy Ghost (Heb. 6:4; 10:26-29), sins much more seriously, and his fall is much more tragic than in the case of one who walks in darkness because the "Light of the world" with its radiant brightness has not yet appeared to him. The servant who knows his master's will and yet does not do it is specially punished. Judas who betrayed his Master, Who had ceaselessly sought him and had tirelessly wrestled for his soul, committed a "greater sin" than Pilate. The cities that beheld the most of the works of the Messiah were to be punished above all other ungodly cities.[6] Guilt increases in proportion to the knowledge of God that has been bestowed on the transgressor. "The more spiritual life becomes, the deeper is the fall that comes with evil intention."[7] The one who knows that the enemy stands before the gate and straightway lets him enter the city; the one who has been warned of the descending steps of sin but does not heed the warning; the one who knows what is the armor of faith and has been clothed with it but does not use it to repel the evil spirits, mocks and despises the good gifts of the Kingdom of God more than the heathen. The violent conflict with shame, dread and hesitation that always rages in his

---

[6] St. Luke 12:47; St. John 19:11; St. Matt. 11:20 *seq.*

[7] Schlatter, *Dogma*, 235.

heart before a Christian consents to sin, in contrast to the easy course of a "child of the world," "does not lessen the grievousness of that sin but makes it worse."[8] It is the Spirit of God contending against the evil powers that makes the contest so violent. If we are obedient to the warnings, urgings and promptings of the Spirit the adversary will retreat and the one who has "fought a good fight" will receive new ability to "be strong in the Lord and in the power of His might" (Eph. 6:10). But if we yield to the foe and admit him to the house that has been swept and garnished, "he goeth and taketh seven other spirits worse than himself," enters, dwells there and "the last state is worse than the first." Above all we must consider the *number* of lost battles. Repeated sins in the life of the Christian are worse than single transgressions, and are far worse than those in the life of the unbaptized. Backsliding is an evil guest. "After every fall we return to the duel weaker than before" (K. Heim). Finally the courage and readiness to return to the conflict are completely lost.

There is a third law that must be considered in relation to the distinction in the weakening and coercive power of certain sins. Scholastic dogmatics correctly distinguished between *peccata regnantia et non regnantia, omissionis et commissionis,* between *peccata involuntaria (infirmitatis, ignorantiae, praecipitantiae)* and *peccata voluntaria s. habitualia.* The sins of weakness, of an outburst of temper, of an access of anger, of rash words, of omission because of fear or violence accuse us severely before God. Their consequences may often be immeasurably sad, but they do not darken and destroy the life of faith with such fearful permanence; they do not so hopelessly hinder retracing steps and the return to God as does the intentional dalliance with pet sins or carrying out to their conclusion evil deeds that have been long considered. The flesh may be weak but if only the spirit be willing the heart will be softened to bitter tears of repentance; there will be confession and restoration. But when one goes on his way and says: "What will ye give me that I may betray him unto you?" it has become completely night, and Satan has entered into his heart. "If a man be overtaken in a fault" the congregation is able and is expected to set him right in the spirit of meekness. But if one of their number

---

[8] Cf. Vilmar, *op. cit.,* p. 245.

persists in intentional and open vice he is lost and should be excluded and the congregation is "to deliver such an one unto Satan for the destruction of the flesh."

It is a long way, with many intermediate stops, from the moment that "Satan desires to have the heart that he may sift it as wheat" till that dark termination when he possesses it (St. Luke 22:31 and 33). Many steps are taken on the road of vice before the heart is hardened. Many warnings of the Spirit must first have been rejected and overcome, much of the beginnings of eternal life must have been destroyed before sin has free course. Between the poisoning of the thoughts by the will of the world and the devil and a permanently morbid sexual imagination, between desire and the consent to the evil deed, between "the ignoring of God and the avoidance of God," between a slight indulgence and the shameless glorification of sin (hatred of God) lie very many resolutions that lead to ever new, voluntary falls.

But why does man permit himself to be driven on by sin, step by step, and why does he not stop in time before the danger is too overwhelming and deadly? The question leads us to a last fundamental law of sin, at which we have frequently hinted in our previous discussions. Sin has its own hidden law of gravitation that, at every stage, compels its victim, with ceaseless automatic power, to proceed downwards a little farther, and at the same time operates with a geometrical progression that, of its own accord, continuously widens its extent in every direction. Its power of growth and propagation appears as unbounded and the law of its development as rigid as the very laws of nature. "A little leaven leaveneth the whole lump."

The Epistle to the Hebrews states that sin besets man and weighs him down (12:1). It clings to him and goes with him. When the foe makes his second assault the past is there like an enemy approaching from behind. The will no longer possesses its full ability to meet the frontal attack of temptation. It is divided and consequently weakened. After frequent defeats temptation finds a helpless will whose power to say no, to escape, to resist is gone. The sentries of conscience that stand at the dividing lines between the sins of thought, word and deed have been slain and the most dangerous trenches are passed over unhindered. But with the increasing growth of sin the rule of

God's Spirit in the heart grows ever less. The sanctifying motives of
the fear and love of God become continually weaker. The spirit of
prayer becomes visibly less and man, forsaken by all "good spirits,"
finds himself defenseless against the increasingly violent and frequent
attacks for whose repelling he needs the help from above more than
ever before.

Sin could not carry on this degrading, enslaving activity, it could
not bring the will into such a terribly crippled condition, if it did not
simultaneously exercise a dulling and darkening influence on the man's
powers of understanding. It displaces all his standards, makes "what is
visible become a terribly imposing power," gives to empty worthless
things a magic glamor and distorts and divides the moral coordinates
that the Word of God has given to conscience.[9] Where there would
be good ground for fear of conscience, for zeal and discipline, it
awakens false confidence and security. And where there is no reason
for anxiety it causes a great commotion and fills men with foolish
unrest, care and ambition. The case of the disobedient will has an
exact parallel in the increasing darkening of the understanding, which
is accompanied by a progressive confusion of all spiritual powers
(Saul). So the pride of knowledge, a lascivious heart and slothfulness
—excesses, mental disturbances and melancholia—skepticism, despair
and vice are only variations marking the same stages of the fall.

If sin only destroyed portions of man's life, or if it only, with proper
retribution, ruined the life of the one who served it, its judgment, no
matter how terrible, would still be tolerable. The curse would only
lie on certain portions of our being or would at least be limited to our
own personal existence, it could be borne by each one, with its judgment and punishment, in repentance and faith, it could even be removed according to the measure of a man's faith or unbelief. But sin
is not thus limited. It is forever contagious. It penetrates not only to
the depths of our own personal existence but it reaches out on every
hand and drags the lives of other men into the same painful connection. A single lie compels the use of other lies and so frequently compels others to join in the lying. One betrayal usually necessitates a whole

---

[9] Luther. *Hoc enim diabolus in omnibus tentationibus solet, ut, quanto homo a verbo
discedit longius, tanto videatur sibi doctior et sapientior.* Er. Ed., *Op. Lat.,* I, 203.

series of dishonorable transactions which can hardly be carried on without the assistance of accomplices (I Kings 21:8 *seq.*). A vain person is always envious, an over-ambitious man is brutal and full of proud contempt for all his equals or those beneath him. The miser is tormented by the vice of care. Where there is revelry men's substance is also wasted on harlots (St. Luke 15:13 and 30). It is impossible to keep the field free of weeds as long as they are consciously and willingly allowed to flourish on one part of it. They will spread from one end to the other and ruin its whole extent. One diseased member will infect the whole body. But sin reaches its bitterest climax as its consequences reach beyond the life of the one who commits it into an immeasurable future. "The sins of the fathers grow if the children do not repent."[10] Men have to see the evil sowing for which they have perhaps long since repented (Ps. 51), springing up in the lives of those whom they would have protected from it at any price. In Ammon and Absalom David had to recognize the reflection of his own incontinence and his own deep fall crippled his ability to exercise paternal discipline. The wrongdoing of one to whom far-reaching power has been given may become an avalanche that will bury families, generations, yea, whole periods of time with its destruction. Sometimes a curse may come from a single happening (Joshua 7, II Sam. 21 and 24) that will involve a wide range of humanity and may even include posterity. In the public transactions of whole movements, parties and tendencies in the larger outlines of the history of nations or of the Church, we can often fix the point in time when "God withdrew His hand" and the blessing on the work ceased. The curse reaches to the "third and fourth generation," no longer, because no flesh can withstand God any longer. Either it then surrenders and returns to Him or it is destroyed and vanishes from the earth.

We have only been able to furnish a few fragmentary contributions towards the history and characteristics of sin. A complete hamartiology would have to develop a number of other sides of the question: the laws of forgiveness, the distinctions between sins of the body and of the soul, and their mutual influence on each other; the little sins of

[10] Vilmar, *Collegium Biblicum A.T.*, II, p. 174, Gütersloh, 1882.

habit,[11] of neglect and procrastination, the temptations of sorrow and of dejection, which are so utterly different from those of good fortune and power. From modern psychology as it deals with mechanical skill, money, sports, dance and the fashions we might derive important contributions towards an understanding of the psychology of sin and the laws controlling it. Each stage of life,[12] every period of history has its peculiar sins affecting the special time, calling or station in life. Even the progress of each day and year, with its attending conditions, brings changing dangers and temptations with it, to say nothing of the times of extraordinary temptation. Even the "vengeance of sin" needs particular study, as it destroys fellowship and seeks to make us solitary, as it uses exactly the same instruments that we have used to intensify our own pleasures and with which we have wounded others in doing so, to intensify our plagues by permitting those things which at first were perhaps only desired playfully to reach their ultimate consequences.

A theology that is really concerned with the miseries of life and that is not merely interested in playing with ideas but really understands the *concrete* wretchedness of human temptations will never fail to present a doctrine concerning sin, without, however, in any way weakening the fact of the infinite guilt of every sin before God. Any one to whom the fact that "deep guile and great might are his dread arms in fight" has once become actually visible, will fear and guard against "committing so great a sin against God" much more easily than one who is only threatened by an abstract doctrine. Any one

[11] *Cf.* Augustine-Harnack, pp. 15 and 154. "Little sins often repeated become deadly if they are disregarded. Small are the drops that form the great rivers, small are grains of sand but when they are heaped up they become great crushing weights. Seeping water that is not checked becomes at last like an onrushing wave. It seeps in gradually but if it continues to do so for a long time and is not bailed out it will sink the ship." Further S. Kierkegaard, *Reinheit des Herzens,* p. 78 *seq.*

[12] *Cf.* Large Catechism 482 (which is at the same time a contribution towards the distinction between *peccata regnantia et non regnantia*): "To feel temptation is therefore a far different thing from consenting or yielding to it. We must all feel it although not all in the same manner, but some in a greater degree and more severely than others; as youth suffer especially from the flesh, afterwards they that attain to middle life and old age, from the world, but others who are occupied with spiritual matters—that is strong Christians—from the devil. But such feeling, as long as it is against our will and we prefer to be rid of it, can harm no one. . . . But to consent thereto is when we give it loose reins and do not resist or pray against it."

who knows the particularly fatal consequences of certain sins will not compare them so lightly with some others nor console himself with the unquestionable fact that "we are all sinners." Christian preaching is guilty of serious neglect when it does not explain these matters nor mention them by name. Here, as far as is possible, no one should "collect personal experiences in order to understand the matter clearly." The matter is too serious for that. The language of the Old and New Testaments speaks clearly enough of the curse-laden history of sin and so it is not necessary for us presumptuously to find out by experiment as to whether things actually turn out in this way. Only in the light of such a satanology do we clearly understand that in every temptation we wrestle not only with flesh and blood but also "with evil spirits, the prince and power of darkness." What grace is, what salvation is and how we would perish hopelessly without them; what significance is possessed by prayer, the hearing of the Word, discipline and fellowship; how utterly and absolutely we need salvation cannot be rightly understood except by one who has actually seen the wiles of the devil, with their mysterious power, revealed both in Scripture and in life (Eph. 6:11 seq.).

As soon as sin enters and we yield to it the certainty of faith begins to waver. What we could never gain by ourselves, what God alone has given and maintains by Word and Sacrament, we throw aside. Even the unclean thought and look have the result that God is further removed from us, that love grows colder, and we are increasingly tempted to think that all the statements of faith may be only delusions. If we do not seek the forgiveness of sin at once and turn from it, the guilt remains as an unpardoned burden on life, and gives the demons new cause and new opportunity to forge our fetters. The more grievous the sin, the greater is the measure of guilt that is accumulated, the severer are the shocks to the life of faith. The less the old lusts are put aside the more peace disappears and the certainty of His supporting grace. To use the vivid expressions that are common in revival literature: If only one key be intentionally withheld at the surrender of the fortress, God cannot be the conqueror. A little grain of sand in the eye can injure the sight. A little stone in the shoe of the wayfarer can make every step painful. The wagon with a broken wheel, the boat that is not bailed out will progress but poorly. A soldier burdened with a heavy pack is hindered in his fighting. A broken screw may endanger the operation of the whole machine. A little leak in the ship may sink it. A little bolt or a rusty lock can prevent the door from being opened. The most strenuous efforts for God's cause when accompanied by the non-surrender of one perverse path are like "rowing an anchored boat."

According to both Scripture and the Confessions, faith and the continuance in sin are irreconcilable. It is impossible to do as the rich young man wanted to do, serve God and Mammon at the same time. With all his honest desire for holiness he lost Jesus completely for the sake of one thing that bound him. God the Lord will not tolerate our service of any idol alongside Himself. To have fellowship with Him and at the same time to walk in darkness is an unbearable lie. Certain sins (Gal. 5:19-21!) must cease or else faith will cease. Christ shall not be found a servant of sin, even in the person of His servants. We cannot keep the Easter Feast with "the old leaven of malice and wickedness." Christ and Belial have no fellowship. To sin willfully after having received the knowledge of the truth is to blaspheme the Spirit of grace and destroy one's self forever.[13]

The great Confession of the Reformation has taken over this "either —or" of Scripture in all its severity without any abbreviation. The claim on pardon and the simultaneous, secret resolution to hold fast to some sin absolutely exclude each other. *Nova vita non stat cum peccato mortali. Nec fidem nec justitiam retinent illi qui ambulant secundum carnem.*[14] The *conversio Dei* demands, on the other hand, the *aversio* from the flesh; allegiance to God demands separation from sin. "For faith and an evil sinful life cannot endure each other's company." "God's honor and our honor cannot be bedfellows." Therefore the desire for honor "is always an immeasurably great vice but it is never more dangerous than when it appears among the preachers . . . for God has not given His Word that we should turn it into an honor, an industry or a business, and if a preacher seeks honor

---

[13] St. Mark 10:17-25; St. Luke 14:33; I John 1:6; 3:20 *seq.*; Rom. 8:12 *seq.*; 12:2; Eph. 4:22 *seq.*; Heb. 10:29; 12:14 *seq.*; I Cor. 5:8; II Cor. 6:14-16.

[14] *Cf. Apology*, 146,227 *seq.*, 222,90; 98,64; 112,22; Smalkald Arts. 319,42; F. C. 533, 19; 627, 15; 630, 31.

and riches it is impossible for him to preach or believe rightly, as the Lord Christ states in the Fifth Chapter of St. John, when He says: 'How can ye believe which receive honor one of another?' Whoever seeks honor in the ministry and desires to be great in the world or would be accounted learned and wise is unbelieving and if he be unbelieving himself how can he preach rightly?"[15]

It is true Christ gathers sinners to build up His Church. Ethics is not essential to the call. The amount of already acquired ethical strength and maturity is not the ground nor the condition for acceptance. God calls publicans, fanatical supporters of the Law, proselytes and depraved heathen, calls Levi, Saul, Cornelius and the profligate Corinthian. But as soon as any one has become incorporated into the Body of Christ by faith and desires to remain a part of it, the attitude of that sinner becomes a matter of anything but indifference. His very entrance is possible only through true repentance, sorrow and a horror of sin (Augs. Conf. XII) and demands a break with evil intentions.[16] And that is especially true regarding perseverance in his calling, for the *non amittere dona vocationis: Qui contritione carent, et propositum in peccatis pergendi et perseverandi habent, vera et salvans fides in iis non manet.*[17]

The irreconcilable antagonism between communion with God and every conscious evil plan comes most clearly to light in prayer. Even in the Old Testament this is most keenly felt. Whoever cries to God in the midst of shameless adulteries cannot expect to be heard. God hides His face from the one who without conscience oppresses and bleeds the poor. The arm may be stretched aloft to heaven and the prayers may be many but there will be no answer if there be blood on the hands. As long as the guilt is not confessed and put away, so long God remains invisible.[18] If the Old Testament particularly shows how the *coarse* satanic bonds rob prayer of its promises, Jesus lays His

[15] Er. Ed. 35,45; 38,230; 44, 266.

[16] *Oportet enim praecedere veram et non simulatum contritionem.* Form. Conc. 614,23; 619,41.

[17] *Cf.* F. C. 615,26; and Apol. 222,90; and further 614,22; 618,36; 624,64.

[18] Jer. 3:3-5; Micah 3:1-4; Is. 1:15; Hosea 5:15; Psalm 66:18; Ecclesiasticus 34:18-26; Prov. 28:9. Of Saul the disobedient and implacable it is said: "Saul enquired of the Lord, the Lord answered him not, neither by dreams, nor by Urim nor by prophets" (I Sam. 28:6).

hand with great emphasis on the subtle hypocrisy that can make prayer equally ineffective. Its side glance, that watches the effect on the observer, robs the holiest action of its efficacy. An implacable spirit defiles and cripples devotion. Adoring doxologies are fruitless if the simultaneous surrender of the will be lacking. Paul reminds us that even in marriage erotic impulses time and again require watching and limitation if prayer is not to suffer as a result. James warns us against envy and wrath, for where these forces burn in our members we may ask much and yet obtain nothing.[19]

Luther on frequent occasions pointed out the subtle, unseen connection that exists between sin and the barred gate of heaven on the one hand and between purity of heart and a glad assurance of being heard on the other. Faith and the invocation of God are for him "tender things and it may easily be a very small wounding of conscience that expels faith and prayer, as every experienced Christian has often had to discover."[20] Spiritual as well as physical distractions and annoyances the Reformer felt were equal hindrances in the way of the undistracted ascent of faith to God. *Ego sane si vel minimae offensae aut livoris mihi conscius essem, non possem orare. Oportet igitur cor ab omni malevolentia, odio et invidia erga proximum liberum esse, quod nemini male velit, sed omnibus optime cupiat et ignoscat.* (Op. Lat. IX, 146.) "If you want to pray, don't come with a full belly but bring out some care or need that will drive you to prayer, or else put it off." (Er. Ed. 34, 199.) The history of missions furnishes many examples of the close connection between a lapsing into old sins and the simultaneous extinction of the spirit of prayer. We need only to recall the unanimous testimony of all observers in Africa, who tell how during the riotous weeks of the festivals of circumcision even baptized Christians, under the spell of that wild insane excite-

---

[19] St. Matt. 6:5 and 15;5:23; St. Mark 11:25; St. Luke 6:46; St. John 9:31; I Cor. 7:5; St. James 4:1-3. We must especially remember the Fifth Petition of the Lord's Prayer. We cannot gain God's forgiveness by our peaceableness but by our irreconcilable spirit we can forfeit it.

[20] "But here we must know that we cannot rightly invoke God or pray to Him when we do not refrain from intentional sins and have no desire for amendment. Therefore a sincere repentance must be a part of true prayer, and likewise a guarding against sins that are committed against conscience, that is that we do not consciously and intentionally follow evil inclinations contrary to God's laws." Er. Ed. 1, 125.

ment, are overcome by old lusts, and how devotion and the public services of the Church are utterly upset. All these examples from the days of the prophets down to the pastoral experiences of the mission fields of our own time confirm the statement that "faith and supplication are tender things," and show how serious it is for both when in giving ourselves to God we attempt to except certain things instead of offering them to God and surrendering everything to Him.

Because sin and the Spirit of God are at irreconcilable enmity with each other and because sin destroys God's holiest works, faith, prayer and renewal, Scripture demands that we break with it unconditionally. Because sin develops with such mysterious rapidity and continuously weakens the powers of resistance in its victims, Scripture also demands that we break with it immediately, not only in the beginning but also in the further maintenance of faith. Both demands, that of a radical and that of an immediate severance from sin are made by Scripture with such emphasis that it is well not to criticise too unconditionally the importance of Pietism attached to conversion. The psychological form it assumed in many revivals was and perhaps still is exaggerated but the fact of a call to conversion has the weight of Scripture behind it. The antagonism between Methodistic and churchly teaching does not involve the question as to the necessity of conversion. In this there should be complete unanimity. The difference in spirit appears when some come to regard the first, possibly sudden conversion, that can sometimes be fixed as taking place at some definite time, as something of unique significance that, like baptism, cannot be repeated, instead of recognizing the fact that daily renewal, the daily journey to the Cross is extolled by Scripture as the only possible expression of a living state of faith and that it holds good even for the one who has been justified and is progressing in sanctification; that it is necessary if we do not want to fall into a dead legalism or a false freedom.

Whenever regeneration and renewal are mentioned in the New Testament (whether as a statement of fact or as an admonition) the recollection of the dark background of the life that preceded it and from which the life of the believer has been separated, and is to remain separated, is never lacking. It would seem as though the Apostles wanted all the discords of sin to be heard once more so

that the canticle of praise to Christ for the deliverance from darkness which He had brought might resound all the louder; so that the
realization of the need of a lasting separation, and the resulting fear
that accompanies sanctification, might remain quick and active. On
the one side is sin in its coarser or more subtle forms, the "works of
righteousness which we have done," the idols, the veil, the desires of
the flesh, with all the lusts of a perishing world; on the other side,
communion with the true and living God, the holy conversation in
the Spirit, the members that have been mortified, and these two are
separated like darkness and light by an obedient "conversion, renewing of the mind, putting away, washing away," that has been effected by the Spirit. It is to result in a complete change of scene
(μὴ συσχηματιζόμενοι, I Peter 1:14), in a complete revaluation of all
values, in a "conscious and definite separation of the sinner and his
sin" (Kähler), and in a daily crucifying of the old nature. Sin is to
lose its supremacy and shall surrender it to the Spirit, Who makes
His abode in a humble and broken heart. Just as faith says daily,
"Lord I believe, help thou mine unbelief," so it also cries continually.
I will not sin, dear Lord, help mine infirmity![21]

If a man ever comes to that state when he no longer hears the call
of the living God to repentance, a call which his conscience must
accept and which urges him to break with sin, it is because sin fearful of losing its power resorts to a last desperate deception by which
all too often it succeeds in regaining its lost conquest. It can no longer
persuade the conscience that a reformation is not absolutely necessary,
God has become too powerful for that, so now it whispers the most
deadly suggestion of the old nature that we can imagine. It is the
counsel of inertia. It says, wait a little, there is no hurry. The classic
example of this conflict is found in St. Augustine's *Confessions*. "The
new will that had begun within me was not yet able to overcome
the former will that had the strength of maturity. I now had two wills
and the two tore my soul asunder! . . . On every side Thou hadst
shown me that Thy Word is the truth, but though I was convinced

---

[21] Luther: It is the glory of the grace of God that it makes us enemies of ourselves
(*Atque haec est gloria gratiae Dei, quod nos fecit nobis ipsis hostes*) W. ed., II, 586,
18 *seq.*

of it, I did not know what answer to give Thee, except the reluctant, dreamy words, Soon, Soon. Only let me dream a little longer! But the 'Soon, Soon' had no end and the 'Yet a little while' was ever prolonged" (Harnack, *op. cit.*, p. 9 *seq.*).

As the autobiography shows very clearly the underlying cause for such dilatory waiting is always some last, strong bond that we do not want to break. "My erstwhile female friends, all the baseness and vanities of the past held me back; they stealthily touched the garment of my flesh, they plucked at me from behind and whispered softly, Will you really send us away, Shall we from this moment really never again be with Thee?" (12). Sin is tireless in the invention and suggestion of such spirit voices that keep urging the postponement of the whole undertaking.[22] On occasion it is thus expressed: "We will hear thee again concerning this matter" (Acts 17:32), again we keep on listening, listening repeatedly simply to avoid the necessity of coming to a decision, while the call of grace, which has its time in every life, passes by; it comes and goes again like the passing showers that water the earth. "The longer we try to delay the worse our conscience becomes, the further is it removed from God" (Er. Ed. 18; 55). Because of the great danger of such delay, which threatens every one, even when he is close to the goal, Scripture demands not only a complete surrender but explicitly requires an immediate surrender to the saving message. In almost all accounts of decisive calls to God's service there is also a statement of a preceding indecision and resistance. The destroyer seeks once more to restrain the elect instrument of God. But the decision follows it immediately. For this reason Scripture places such great emphasis on the "today." The final discourses of Jesus are a great warning concerning the impossibility of delaying discipleship. The sermons of Peter and Stephen before the people and the council in Jerusalem through which the exalted Lord once more offered grace and eternal life to His murderers, beseech and urge them to repentance and faith, "while it is yet called today" before it is too late and judgment overtakes a city that would not heed the things which made for its peace at the time that God offered them.

---

[22] Kierkegaard: In Christianity or in becoming Christians we have the same experience as with every radical cure, we put it off as long as possible.

If the break with sin is not complete, nor rightly timed, nor constant, faith will at last be lost. If sin be not cut off it will grow and finally triumph. It is true that God's faithfulness that was pledged in baptism remains but there is no longer any desire for forgiveness, no hunger to seek His face in prayer. God's saving, purifying power is even still ready to act but there is no longer any willingness to be judged and renewed by His Spirit. We would recall what was said at the beginning of the fifth chapter that grace is full of strength and power but it is not irresistible. The human spirit, even in the one who has been regenerated, possesses a fearful freedom of choosing what is beneath when it will not accept the gift of the freedom of choosing what is above. He can oppose the impatience and stubbornness of his disobedience to the long-suffering and patience of divine love, and, as we have seen, the communion with God is lost not only by gross sins but incompleteness of surrender, delay, and the self-satisfaction that lacks daily repentance can likewise destroy the new life. Like a tree, it can be frozen overnight, or it can slowly wither and die.

In contrast to the idea of a double predestination, in the dialectic sense, which because it speaks an impartial message of judgment and grace to all flesh alike, because it condemns all and transforms all, and finally becomes "harmless," we have unconditionally to hold fast to a twofold termination of man's life on earth which establishes an eternal separation between men. We will guard against attempting to determine this separation exactly by eye or ear, and we have no business to speculate about the ultimate fate of "the branches that have been cut off" (Rom. 11:20 *seq.*) but must leave all that to the freedom of God's will. Yet the whole terrible activity of sin, the urgent warnings of Scripture, the surging conflicts with temptation lose all their intense seriousness if they merely become historical illustrations that disclose the two fundamental truths of a universal fall and the rising up beside it of a universal salvation through Christ.

Likewise the Reformed teaching of the perseverance of the saints, in connection with the doctrine of predestination, does not do justice to the fact of the conflict of faith. It is true there is a clear distinction here between the one who will receive salvation in the final judgment and the one who loses it, but this twofold result must be referred back either to an actual or an only apparent call from God, and a similar distinction between appearance and reality has to be made in illumination, sanctification and preservation, then the unique power of Scripture is lost as well as the significance of the struggle of faith through the power of the Spirit, "as a repelling of ungodly temptations and as the preservation from a fall and desertion" (Harless).

St. Paul (I Cor. 9:27) and Luther have understood much more profoundly this paradox of God's sole activity in working salvation and of human responsibility for its loss, which is so incomprehensible to reason. It is not God's will that we should fall in our temptations (I Cor. 10:13) but He "strengthens and preserves us steadfast in His Word and the faith until our end." The reality of grace and the will to save the whole world remain facts as far as He is concerned. But this certainty of redemption is not yet a certainty of predestination. God supports me with unwearied fidelity if I permit myself to be supported. He stoops to me (*condescendit*) if only I do not presume (Gal. 5:4; I Cor. 10:12). He raises me up if I do not cast myself down through slackness. "Besides, although we have received forgiveness and a good conscience and are entirely acquitted, yet our life is of such a nature that one stands today and tomorrow falls. Therefore, even though we be godly and stand before God with a good conscience, yet we must ever pray that He would not suffer us to relapse and yield to trials and temptations" (Large Catechism, Sixth Petition).

But Luther's certainty of salvation stands not only in contrast to the Reformed doctrine of election, but also to the average Protestant idea of the possession of grace. For him grace is no such passive, fixed quantity, devoid of struggle and conflict, as it has so often been represented. Luther possessed the most concrete satanology it is possible to imagine. Out of it grew his anxious, holy arming against the foe, "who never rests nor grows weary, so that when one temptation ceases, a new one always comes to take its place."[23] This feeling of

---

[23] *Ibid.* 482, 110 *seq. Sermon on Ephesians 6:10-17*: "For we do not sit at rest like a peasant, burgher or craftsman in the city, who lives in peace and has nothing to fear, but we are in a dangerous situation, in the midst of enemies and murderers, who mean

world fear and world loneliness in the face of these powers that creep about in the darkness, has come into Luther's Church and has fashioned her hymns and her litany; the art of a Bach and a Dürer. This "Lutheran consciousness of life" can hardly be expressed adequately in words and cannot be rightly described to one who has not experienced it for himself. Faith does not doubt that the salvation of God is eternally valid and available for him, therefore it rejoices and is immovably sure "in the Spirit." But because it knows from experience the daily diabolical temptations of the flesh it does not cease praying the verses of the hymn in which Luther himself most powerfully expressed that which in itself can hardly be told in words: "Holy Lord God, holy, mighty God, most merciful Savior. Thou eternal God, suffer us not to fall away from the true consolation of faith. Kyrie eleison!" It is only with such a background that it is possible completely to understand the jubilant note of the words of the dying Apostle, who could not easily be accused of claiming moral perfection, and whom every advocate of a Biblical teaching of sanctification must follow: "I have fought a good fight, I have finished my course, I have kept the faith!"

The gift of faith we have received may be lost (*amissibilis*). "Wherefore let him that thinketh he standeth take heed lest he fall." But the gift that has been lost may also be again recovered (*reiterabilis*) by virtue of the faithfulness of God, that is always seeking anew what has been lost, as the shepherd seeks the straying sheep of his flock. "Though at times some one may be overcome Christ is still there and raises him up and says, Rise Brother, rise, the case is not desperate, always renew the attempt for you must fight it through and that cannot be done without falls, only see to it that you do not remain prostrate" (Er. Ed. 41, 199). It is true, Scripture itself places a limitation to the access to the Father that has been made possible and is continually being made possible by Christ. "All manner of sin and blasphemy shall be forgiven unto men; but the blasphemy against the Holy Ghost shall not be forgiven unto men . . . Neither in this world nor in the world to come" (St. Matt. 12:31 *seq.*). Whosoever replies to Jesus'

---

business, who will rob us of our treasure if we do not guard it and from whom we are not safe for one moment." Er. Ed. 18, 22 *seq.*

repeated invitation: Let Thy spirit ever remain far from me, will receive what he desires: whosoever "declines the Spirit and calls God's gift diabolical and His grace evil shall likewise have what he desires."[24] God will not be mocked. It was not only Spener's opinion but also Luther's that "A time may come in His righteousness when there is no further grace nor urging to repentance."

It is a well-known fact that in the period of Pietism the question concerning the extent of the time of grace was discussed, with great violence on both sides, in the so-called "terministic" controversy, without, however, arriving at any agreement. What our previous discussion has shown must always be considered together was here divided into two opposing positions. The Lutherans feared that the objective character and the lasting validity of grace would be discredited by the significance for salvation of a single period of possible conversion, that might even be quite limited in duration, and so they asserted that the reclaiming grace of God was just as unlimited as the grace He manifested in calling men and that God assured a period of grace lasting till death. Their opponents, Spener, his son-in-law Rechenberg and the Diakon Böse, were not in complete agreement in the theological demonstration of their theses, as some particularly emphasized man's moral responsibility in his hardening, the others laid more stress on the divine decree of election. But they were agreed on one point, that there was a limited time of grace, longer for some and shorter for others, beyond which "no further opportunity would be given by God." The churchly theologians were contending for the lasting efficacy of the offering of the Cross; the leaders of the Pietistic movement for the Scriptural insistence on an immediate and complete decision on the part of the one who had been called to faith. The one side feared the pragmatic, the other the quietistic misuse of grace. The one opposed false despair, the other a false security in the presence of sin. The one brought the consolations, the other the warnings of Scripture. But the true Biblical teaching will always have to combine the two; the tremendous urgency of every invitation that comes from Jesus and the eternal, certain, continuing assurance of God to the sinner. The true answer to the question at issue in the terministic

---

[24] Schlatter, *Erläuterungen zum. N.T.*, I, 145.

controversy must always be a paradox. It must always contain both statements; the call to repentance; hearken, decide, believe, obey, pray, serve, as though today were the last day and the final call of God, and the message of grace; no matter how far you have wandered from God, hold fast to your baptism, which even in the hour of death, even after a completely wasted life, always points out the door to the Father's house. It is never early enough to grasp and preserve the gift of God, and it is never so late that any one because of his sins must die in despair.

Because sin is a *peccatum cordis, oris et operis,* the break with it must be made in all three spheres and so in a certain sense as *contritio cordis, confessio oris* and *satisfactio operis.* It is evident that the terms are here used in a different sense than in the Roman sacrament of penance. We do not require either a "perfect" contrition or a partial attrition as a necessary condition for the reception of grace (*meritum de congruo*), neither do we regard the enumeration of all remembered mortal sins, in auricular confession, as a necessary condition for forgiveness, nor yet do we teach that the satisfaction of works is the efficient cause for the remission of the penalties of sin (Council of Trent, sessio XIV, cap. 3-5).[25] But to this we must hold fast that the Word of God, wherever it is heard, arouses this threefold repentance and requires that it shall not be resisted. Where the Law and the Gospel have rightly accomplished their mission there sorrow and a "great fear" of God's wrath will be awakened in the heart,[26] there men will pass through the experiences described in the 32nd Psalm, learning how the hand of God lies heavily, day and night, upon the conscience, till the iniquity is no longer concealed, the transgression is confessed to God and forgiveness has been found for it. With the impulse to an inner confession to God in the secrecy and solitude of the heart, comes also the desire "to confess and pardon our sins one to another"[27] in a double way, as a confession of guilt in private confession for the humbling and relief of the tormented con-

---

[25] Augs. Conf. XI, *Apol.* 102,83; 151,276; 164,58 *seq.*; 168,8; 170,18, 20 and 23; 184,95; 187,14; 315,19; 321; Sm. Art. 3,III.

[26] *Apol.* 171,29; 173,44; 174,46; 186,10; 98,62; 112,21.

[27] Luther, *Eine kurze Vermahnung zu der Beicht* (Müller 774 *seq.*) *Appendix I ad Kat. Majorem.*

science, and as the admission of guilt, for the reconciliation of brethren to each other. (Apol. 186, 12).

Whenever in the history of Christianity the Spirit of God, through the Gospel has awakened true repentance and a living faith in individuals or congregations, we meet with an irresistible impulse towards the revealing of sins to a confessor. When John the Baptist aroused the entire Jewish people with his call to repentance, the multitudes came to him at the Jordan to be baptized "confessing their sins" (St. Matt. 3; 6). The same thing took place as a result of St. Paul's activity at Ephesus (Acts 19:18); with Blumhardt in Möttlingen, during the "great repentance on the Island of Nias"; with Hofacker and with Hans Nielsen Hauge. While the untouched man tries in every way possible to conceal his depravity, the penitent gives up "the false, hypocritical honor" and "willingly suffers the disgrace that clings to his guilt."[28] While the man whose pride is unbroken is prouder of nothing than his independent condition, that requires no help from his neighbor, the one who rues his sin desires absolution, counsel and aid against his sin from the mouth of his brother. The form of such confession to which we are already admonished in the Epistle of St. James (5:16), cannot consist in a "shameless pouring out of the degradation of our souls in broad daylight"[29] on an anxious bench or in an after-meeting. The seriousness of the matter and the rightful feeling of shame demands as the only possible form for its exercise the private confession that our Church has so wrongly neglected till it has been almost completely lost. Luther, as is well known, employed it all his life and highly valued its spiritual blessing and profitableness.[30] Löhe always regarded it as one of the greatest defects of his beloved Church that she permits us to grow up "without having it occur to us, that there was anything wrong in our silence concerning our sins."[31]

Because sin always serves to promote self-exaltation before men it is essential for its destruction that its humiliation shall also take place

[28] Schlatter, *Dogma*, 257.
[29] Schlatter, *Erläuterungen*, III, 215.
[30] Holl, 403 *seq.*
[31] W. Löhe, *Der ev. Geistliche* II, 263-285. Also *Einfältiger Beichtunterricht für Christen ev.-luth. Bekenntnisses*, Nürnberg, 1836.

before men by an oral admission in confession. Our nature that is
in love with itself will in this way be far more deeply touched, it will
be cut to the core far more effectively than by a mere reference to our
sinfulness in the course of our spiritual reflections. But because sin
always wounds the lives of others and works much evident as well as
hidden bitterness and injury in them, the "active repentance" of
reconciliation and reparation towards our neighbor must be added to
the shame of admission before God and the pastor. So it holds good
for the sins of the tongue that "when one has angered another he
shall seek his pardon." Zacchaeus returns the unjustly acquired goods
to the poor, and recompenses fourfold any one whom he may have
treated unjustly. The people in Ephesus bring to the Apostles the
instruments of sorcery to be burned.[32] As word and deed lead us
deeper into the bondage of sin than the evil thought, so confessing
and acting repentance lead the self-sacrifice that seeks for reconciliation and restoration, out of bondage and frees its burdened conscience
more efficiently than a mere prayer of confession. Indeed, we must put
it still more forcibly, without an honest purpose and intention to seek
reconciliation with an embittered enemy, without the readiness actually to surrender sinful possessions or acts the absolution remains
ineffective. *Ubi enim nihil horum fit, ibi procul dubio non est vera
ad Deum conversio.*[33]

The severest disturbances of faith, even its complete loss can result
from guilt that is not admitted nor reparation made for its evil results.
What psychoanalysis in its profane language designates as the sickness
of suppressed complexes, a psychology of faith recognizes as the curs-
ing effects of unconfessed, unforgiven sin, that has burdened the conscience to the point of despair and, as a result, involves the body in
its destruction. As long as the mighty, accusing enemy is close behind
us, so long all plans for the future, all forward progress remains only
a feeble approach with its continual failures and falls. The will that
is not in the clear with God lacks both the power of defense against
evil and the ability to attain what is good. But where there is a confession of guilt before God and man, against both of whom we have

---

[32] *Eine kurze Vermahnung zu der Beicht,* Müller, 774,11. St. Luke 19:8; Acts 19:19.
[33] F.C. 605, 70; 529,11; 627,15.

sinned, where reconciliation is sought with God and our neighbor, wherever our spirits do not resist the admonitions to humility and repentance, there God bestows a peace that passeth understanding, an unspeakable liberty, a strength that we had never known before. Where the message of judgment and grace has prevailed and has led men to break with sin, something of the resurrection and of eternal life is experienced even in this present life. Whoever hears and obeys the message recognizes with a certainty that is above all doubt that the teaching of Jesus is of God and not the self-made moralism of a religious hero (St. John 7:17). Any one who knows the working of the New Testament only through a traditional, devout piety, that has developed without severe catastrophes, will find it difficult to comprehend the unspeakable joy that overwhelms a hard-pressed man who has obtained forgiveness through Christ and so has gained the power to break with the sin that until then had held him bound.

God forsakes no one in the conflict with sin. He speaks on the basis of the reconciling Word, the life-giving Word, and offers the believer powers of the Holy Ghost, that he may courageously fight and overcome every recognized sin of his life. If the offered weapons are not used, if the battle of sanctification be not faithfully carried on, both faith and life will be lost. For what has been given together can only be maintained together or betrayed together. Where the disciplinary work of sanctification dies, there the faith of justification also dies. But that raises the grave question which these negative statements compel us to face. If faith without sanctification will be lost does that mean, when we state it positively, that sanctification is necessary for preservation? Can we say that the *sanctificatio ad conservandam, exercendam, augendam fidem, ad consequendam beatudinem finalem* is a necessity?[34] That good works do not bring about the attainment of salvation but because of the self-righteous ideals of holiness often associated with them more frequently obstruct rather than open the way to faith, has been made clear in the first chapters. We have just maintained that sin as *ad non amittendam fidem*, is to be eliminated under all circumstances, both in inclination and deed. But to reverse this last relationship by stating it in positive form and to speak of the

---

[34] *Cf.* F.C. 630, 30 *seq.*; *Apol.* 120, 68 *seq.*; 222,90.

"significance of sanctification for the preservation of a state of faith" is something more and is closer to synergism and so must by all means be formulated more carefully than in the consideration of the mutual antagonism between sanctification and a continuance in sin.

How this question was debated between the Philippists and the Gnesio Lutherans in the so-called Majoristic and Antinomistic controversies is a well-known incident of history. We cannot read the history of these controversies without being deeply moved. Here all the modern debates concerning the problems of ethics have already been met with great care and with great theological acumen. Major and Menius never intended to defend the Roman Catholic doctrine of merits. As far as the attainment of salvation was concerned they taught the forensic view. Only "to retain salvation and not to lose it again" they required the new life and new obedience as a necessity. Their opponents disputed the *necessitas praesentiae bonorum operum in articulo justificationis*. They feared a revival of the fatal Osiandrian mingling of justification and sanctification, of divine and human activity if not in the inception, yet in the continuation of faith. Menius, on his part, wanted only "to meet the papistic calumnies that accused the Lutherans of despising all good works and teaching that a man could be saved even though he lived in all kinds of shame." With his theses he combated the Antinomians, who removed all law and he wanted to meet the Osiandrians who complained that "the doctrine was taught in too cold-blooded a fashion," while he further opposed "the common rabble who sadly abused the freedom of faith."[35]

The Philippists acted as their master before them had done, in trying to protect the Church from the anarchy and indifference of the lazy multitude. The opposite party wanted to preserve the Gospel from the proud imaginings of synergism. The extreme statements that "Good works are necessary to salvation" and that they are "dangerous to salvation" (Amsdorf) when taken in connection with the opposite danger against which they were directed, are in *each* case correct. As soon, however, as they appeared alone, both became dangerous to the last degree and both worked offense, in the one case by furthering the Romish idea of meritoriousness of works, in the other by lowering

[35] H. Schmidt, *Lehrbuch der Dogmengeschichte,* p. 141 *seq.*

moral standards. For this reason the Formula of Concord rejected both statements as capable of misinterpretation (IV *De bonis operibus*), Amsdorf's statement because thereby "discipline and decency are impaired and a barbarous, savage, secure, Epicurean life is introduced and strengthened," and Major's *quod bona nostra opera salutem conservent*, because the reception as well as the preservation of faith are God's work alone.[36]

The rejection of both extremes in the Confession was anything but a weak compromising of the problem. It rather shows a much deeper insight into the paradoxical character of divine freedom and human responsibility, than the opinions of those who sit in deprecating judgment on the "mediating" attempts of the Formula of Concord. We will attempt to follow out the two lines of thought. Because sanctification is the work of God in the justified sinner; because it is not the creative cause but the consequence of grace it can neither bestow nor maintain grace in the sinner. What is always first given in and with faith cannot produce faith. Nor can the certainty of being received by God and being preserved by Him be grounded on a certain degree of experience or of progress in sanctification, though there certainly is such a progress produced by God, but always on the Word alone, the Word in which God, Who is never unfaithful to Himself, has assured us forgiveness and renewal. Fruitfulness, growth and the preservation of faith the Christian consequently does not recognize, and is not assured of, through a *syllogismus practicus*, that is by a deduction made from the height of his ethical attainments, but through the recollection of the Cross, which God's faithfulness makes certain. As sanctification is enkindled by faith and not the reverse, faith can preserve the Christian in sanctification but sanctification cannot preserve him in faith. In this way the last moral misunderstanding is avoided, the idea that in the course of the Christian life a second life-giving energy is inserted alongside of faith, that operating by its own impulse, cooperates in producing the completion of salvation.

If in the union with Christ we had had restored to us the childlike innocence of the original state of man, if we were in a position "to

[36] 632, 38 *seq.*; 533, 17; 533, 16; 631, 35.

render a perfectly voluntary obedience like the dear angels" (641, 6), we could confine ourselves to the above given single, unqualified manner of speaking about justification and sanctification. As the fruit ripens on the tree, so faith would unfold itself in sanctification by a natural growth till it came to the perfection of maturity. But here it is necessary again to remind ourselves of the duality of light and darkness in the life of the regenerate, which is never completely removed. The new life is never perfected on earth but is still in its beginnings. Even those who are being led by God still sigh because of their bonds. Because of the old man the believer continues in a lasting conflict with the flesh, which at any time can overcome him if he yields to it. As we have seen no one can acquire or retain the Pneuma nor retain it through his ethical attainments; from beginning to end it remains a gift of God, but salvation can be lost by our own fault, through the "weak, lazy flesh," through a *securitas epicurea* that thinks it possible that a correct faith and "the evil intention to continue in sin can exist together at the same time in one heart" (627,15). If man can neither save nor preserve himself, but can always destroy himself, the most important task of the Christian is to cut down and overcome the power of the old nature that continually threatens faith.

Here the positive significance of sanctification as well as of the Law again becomes apparent. For it is clear that such a spiritual circumcision can never be accomplished by a purely negative ethics, which "stops with the rejection of what is evil" (Schlatter), but only by a real fulfilling of God's will through obedience and discipline. Because the enmity of the two opponents, "the flesh and the spirit," is irreconcilable there can be no lasting neutrality in this warfare, but only the alternative of victory or defeat. Here there is only progress in the spirit and the breaking of the supremacy of sin, or the victory of sin and with it the defeat of faith; there is never a truce. We only have the choice between growing in faith through sanctification or dying; of being "fruitful in all good works" or "dead in trespasses and sins," always "becoming more perfect" or perishing.[37] *Non elevari est labi.*

---

[37] II Peter 3:18; II Cor. 10:15; II Thess. 1:3; Eph. 4:15; Col. 1:10; Eph. 2:5; I Thess. 4:1.

Whoever is not willing to separate himself from sin in God's service is separated by sin from the service of God. Whoever will not let himself be illuminated by God's Word is beclouded by evil. Whosoever does not receive the Body and Blood of the Lord to his salvation, eats and drinks to his own damnation. The one who does not trade with the talents given by the Spirit loses them altogether. If the conscience is not refined it does not simply remain as it was before but is hardened through the lack of progress. "Whoever begins to believe but does not always increase and grow finally loses his grace" (Luther).

What Lutheranism has always said concerning the *tertius usus legis*[38] is especially true of the sanctification that shall take the place of the Torah in the life of the believer. As the Law by its bridling and judging prepares the heathen for conversion to God, so sanctification in the life of the baptized Christian drives him ceaselessly to a return to God. Neither the Law nor sanctification in themselves possess a saving or preserving power, "but the Holy Ghost, who is given and received, not through the Law, but through the preaching of the Gospel (Gal. 3:14), renews the heart." (Form. Conc. 642:11.) But afterwards the Spirit uses the office of the Law and its disciplinary application against the "lazy, careless, antagonistic" flesh, so that faith may not become "lazy, dull and weary." Where the exertions of sanctification do not daily impel, threaten and coerce the natural desires, there sin, which persistently strives to regain its lost territory in the life of the regenerate, soon regains the mastery, and man loses his faith because he has not used the powers given with his faith to repulse evil or to protect and strengthen the precious treasures he has received. What was given as an undeserved gift is deservedly lost.

The Antinomianism that denies the necessity of sanctification for the preservation of faith would presuppose an ideal of perfection among the regenerate such as we find taught among the Darbyites and in the English and American revivals. There they dream of a "higher life" in those who are converted, a life of "lasting rest," of

---

[38] *Cf.* L. Ihmels: "It is my conviction as it was Luther's that the Gospel can only be understood where the Law has done its work in men. And I am equally convinced that just the humble Christian, however much he desires to live in enlarging measure in the spirit, would never wish to do without the holy discipline of the *tertius usus legis*." *Die Religionswissenschaft der Gegenwart in Selbstdarstellungen*, I, 82, Leipzig, 1925.

"continual victory" in which men are "holy, righteous and blameless" and "so live day by day with a completely purified heart."[39] For any one who can talk in this fashion obedience to the Law and exercise in holiness have, of course, been laid aside. For faith does the will of God spontaneously, *liberrimo spiritu, sine omni doctrina, admonitione, cohortatione aut impulsu legis* (*Cf.* 641,6). But any one who has understood St. Paul's statements in Romans seven as a description of our condition *after* conversion, will dismiss the delusion of a complete conquest of the old nature, and will always regard sanctification as the most serious business, because without it the never failing tares of evil will again choke out the growing seed of the Word in man's heart.

So here theology is again forced to the paradoxical statement that the activity of sanctification, because it is a fruit of the tree of faith, does not give us any claim on God, nor any occasion for self-praise (I Cor. 3:6 *seq.*), but that its omission destroys both the fruit *and* the root. The tree that cannot grow dies. When the strength given the body is not exercised it is lost and health is lost with it. Sanctification as a merit, as *causa efficiens* is "harmful to salvation," but sanctification that springs from obedience is "necessary to salvation," on account of the flesh. For the manifold gifts of the Spirit dare not be dishonored by self-praise, nor be misused by lawlessness.

In his theological ethics Vilmar has described the doctrine of sin, sanctification and preservation as "sickness, healing and health." These expressions can produce the most serious misunderstandings, for they suggest the idea of natural processes, either that original sin corrodes like a physical corruption or that grace works automatically like an inoculated serum, that purifies and heals the whole man. The fact is that in neither case has it to do with an organic "physiological" growth but with continually repeated decisions between faith and unbelief. Only their repetition and continual addition has the appearance to the outsider of a connected chain and produces the impression of a curve that is bending either upwards or downwards. The one who sees what takes place from within knows that every form of

---

[39] *Cf.* Fleisch, *Die Heiligungs lehre der Oxforder Bewegung. N. K. Zt.* 35,58; p. 61, notes 1 and 2.

"growth" here takes place only in the form of a conflict, be it continually new, definite conscious acts of thankfulness and obedience towards God or as a willful decision against God. The complete hardening of the heart is no iron necessity that has been involved in the very inception of temptation; it is not a product of direct causality and therefore of inescapable circumstances, but it is the sum of countless transgressions, continual disregard of the admonitions of conscience and a turning aside that the will has repeated day after day.

Furthermore progress in sanctification and the preservation of faith is no upward development in the sense of Greek theology, as though a certain mystical-magical process of salvation took place in faith which finally ended in a static possession. The external picture may give the impression that we have to do here with a natural, gradual growth and progress, with a holding fast and a continuance in faith, but the inside view shows nothing else than a *semper recurrere ad principium et a novo incipere.* For it is only by such a continual return to the beginning, that is, to the appropriation of the atoning work of Christ, which both judges us and sustains us, that we come to an increasing renovation. For the Christian, progress means to remain standing beneath the Cross. Growing in the Spirit means a continual growing less before the bar of justifying faith. To be preserved in faith is the same as a continually new judging of self. What seems like the natural completion of a straightforward development is in fact a continually new hearing and obeying of God's call. *Multi enim incipiunt, pauci proficiunt, paucissimi perveniunt. . . . Perseverantia antem quid est, nisi continua inchoatio et indefessa resistentis tum diaboli tum peccatis gravatae naturae tolerantia?*[40] Whoever would be provided with a special blessing by God must be ready to endure multiplied sorrows and temptations. Onlookers may wonder at the perfection of a "Christian character" but they do not know out of what great tribulation it has come.[41] Particular strength in prayer, in discipline and in love is not a special gift that has just happened of its own accord in the course of a Christian's life; it is no special station at which every one of necessity arrives on the way of salvation. It is possible to remain sta-

[40] Luther, *Op. Lat.*, XVI, 17.
[41] II Tim. 3:12; Rev. 7:13 *seq.*; Acts 9:16.

tionary, to retrograde, or to fail to attain that capability of rendering service that God's creative act would give us, because we have regarded growth as exaltation instead of recognizing it as humiliation. If a Christian possessed at once, in its full extent, the spiritual-corporeal life of Easter, which has been imparted as the first fruits of his faith in Christ and that by the power of its growth drives men to an outward manifestation of its presence, just as a new era strives to express itself, then we could describe the unfolding of the new life as a process like that which takes place when "the tender flowers willingly unfold." But since believers are never completely renewed in this world, because "the old Adam clings to them till the grave," the beauty, regularity and inevitableness of natural growth is lacking in renovation, and it is rather like the restless, changing history of warfare, where through many defeats and recoveries we come at last to the final victory. That God, in spite of so much resistance, still permits the completion of the course makes grace superlatively great and completely humbles man in his inmost being.

We have criticized the description of sanctification and preservation as a "history of sanctification and health." Nevertheless a man like Vilmar, who was schooled in Scripture to such a unique degree and who represented a positive theology of faith, would never have used these expressions if there were not a certain element of truth behind them. And such is really the fact. In our discussion of the doctrine of sin we saw how the play of evil (not mechanically but in an ethically progressive way) produces various degrees of limitation, hardening and restriction up to a final bondage of slavery. All the terrible things that had to be said about that were only a horrible echo, from out the depths, to the glorious message and working of the Holy Ghost that comes from on high and leads to the heights. According to the same laws that lead disobedience downward to destruction, Christ would lead upward those of His members who permit Him to hold them fast, and who are true to Him.

As each sin manifestly weakens the powers of resistance, so the resisting of sin strengthens steadfastness. As after each fall we come to the next duel so much weaker than before, so after each victory we encounter the adversary with a stronger, more joyous and more eager spirit. If the surrender to gross sin has darkened the mental life in increasing measure and estranged it more and more from God, so the enlightening power bestowed by faith, when rightly used for resistance and attack, has the power to assure us of the certainty of God's favor. As soon as the tiniest drops of faith have trickled into our spirits we begin to see God's kindly and gracious countenance, perhaps at a great distance, but with such certainty that all self-deception is excluded. And with every step forward we come into close and more intimate intercourse with Him. Our knowledge of God penetrates further and further through the previous fog." (Calvin, *op. cit.*, 294 *seq.*) The bewitched condition disappears. The growing Christian perception brings everything more clearly into the light of the truth and so gains new clearness and certainty in opposing "Satan's guile." Just as the willful continuation of a pet sin soon brings companions with it, so in the resolute rejection of one sin others will gradually perish with it. Breaking with one hidden vice weakens the entire fortification of the old bondage. When one salient fort has been taken the foe is forced in time to surrender others.

The more faith increases the more its accompanying love will grow. In the same degree that selfish desire which fills us so completely in our natural estate, is broken, the will becomes free to engage in the service of others. As a lack of readiness to serve God results in poverty of God's gifts, so the accumulation of treasures in God's service brings us wealth in God. The cheerful giver has his gift returned a hundred fold in his own spirit. The Church that does not neglect to provide the service of the Word to those who sit in darkness and in the shadow of death, experiences the "returning tide of blessings from foreign missions" (Gustav Werner). Every branch that brings forth fruit is purged that it may bring forth more fruit. The "milk faith" can develop into "a firm faith that will withstand Belial and all his evil devices" (Luther). It dare not continue indefinitely in the lowest sloughs, in unbridled imaginations, in helpless refusal.[42] The glorifica-

---

[42] Calvin, *op. cit.* 346. "No one's course will be so unfortunate that he cannot cover at least a little of it each day. Therefore we will never cease to make at least a few serious forward steps on the way of the Lord and will not despair if the results are only very small. Even the one who falls short of his intentions has not lost his efforts as today brings larger victories than yesterday. In undisturbed simplicity we will fix our eyes on

tion and perpetuation of sin has not been made a part of the Christian message. Of course it is to tell unreservedly of all the beggarly poverty that inheres in our own sanctification and it cannot allow any one to find in it the basis of his justification before God. The minister of God's Word has still to proclaim God's love for the sinner, even to the one who has fallen the lowest, even up to the hour of his death, but he has also to tell how it is God's purpose to call the Church not to uncleanness but to holiness, and that the neglect of the striving after holiness is an unpardonable contempt of the Spirit of God, Who has been bestowed by grace. Christ desires to be exalted in His Church not merely as the sin-bearer but also as the conqueror of sin. That God should "cleanse him from every defect of the flesh and spirit" more and more should be something that each one desires as ardently as the remission of guilt. Faith not only prays to be delivered from the accusing weight of sin but it is just as much concerned in having the painful bondage of the power of sin taken from it more and more. Because it suffers as much through the separation from God as by the restricting weight of evil it desires to possess Christ, Who has promised both that He will plead for us and that He will abide in us with His resurrection life.

The progressive sanctification of the Christian dare not under any conditions be confused with a belief in moral development, for it shares neither its ethical optimism nor its confidence regarding the attainment of its purposes. A humanistic perfectionist, as well as the religious one, engages in anxious self-examination and tries to demonstrate his approach to God by the number of stages through which he has passed. The Christian likewise knows that he must press forward if he is not to fall back but because his active renewal in Christ is always inadequate he does not find in it the ground nor even the confirmation of his fellowship with God; that he finds in the promises of the Gospel. For this reason the teaching of Christian perfection has been transferred from the realm of ethics to that of dogmatics (Augs. Conf. 16 and 27). According to the measure of time and

---

the goal and follow Him . . . until we finally attain to complete purity. This we seek and strive after all our life, but we will first attain it when we lay aside the weakness of our flesh and are permitted to enter into complete fellowship with God."

ability that God has given him the Christian will faithfully exercise himself in holiness, but he will never look to that for his consolation in the hour of death. Whether the stage of moral attainment that has been reached is larger or smaller makes no difference for he can in no case base his salvation upon it. His certainty is grounded on the perfection of the work of Christ, on the basis of which he may expect to receive complete acceptance and complete sanctification before God's throne.

The moral perfectionists not only have an unbounded confidence in the religious and ethical value of good works, but they are also possessed of an unshakable certainty that nothing can ever remove them from this course. How different from this self-confident certainty of the sectarian and the Stoic philosopher is the Christian concern about preservation in the faith! Here, even on the heights of holiness, the fact is never forgotten that our life is a journey over unfathomable depths. "Not until eternity has passed its judgment on our life have we arrived at the goal and left the danger behind. Before that time we may be exalted to heaven but we may also be cast down into hell."[43] And yet, though the awful possibility of a fall hangs over each one till the hour of death, the Christian nevertheless ventures to speak of his preservation in faith and holiness until his end, not because he is aware of an increasing measure of strength in his renewal or because he establishes his confidence on its power to support him, but he rests on the vicarious intercession of Christ, Who prays to God for the sanctification and preservation of all those whom the Father has given Him, and Who has sent the Paraclete to lead them into all perfection. Only because of this intercession the Christian believes in a "continuing steadfast in faith and in love and in holiness."[44] Through the power of the divine promises and not because of the strength of his own exalted ethical idealism, is it possible for him in the midst of great struggles and conflicts, because of a faith that sees with the eyes of God, to be certain of the final victory. Though still engaged in the struggle he knows that he has attained the end. While yet wrestling hourly for the decision of obedience he already possesses the end he is striving for.

[43] K. Heim, *Stille im Sturm, Predigten*, p. 77, on St. Matt. 16-24, Tübingen, 1925.
[44] St. John 17:11; Rom. 8:34; I Tim. 2:15.

CHAPTER VII

The Relation of Justification and Sanctification

MARTIN LUTHER described the ability to distinguish rightly between the Law and the Gospel, and to relate them correctly to each other, as a "very high," indeed as the highest art in Christianity. But if the correct relation of these two is one of the major questions in theology the relation of justification and sanctification is no less so. It is easier to distinguish the Law as a "word of death," as a "doctrine of wrath," as an alien expression, apart from Christ, of the holy and righteous will of God, from the Gospel than it is to distinguish the liberating work of sanctification from the redeeming work of justification. Moses and Christ are as far apart as heaven and earth. The one demands and accuses, the other absolves and liberates. But the completed work of redemption and the work of sanctification which has been begun in us but has not been brought to completion, do not proceed from two different masters but from one and the same Christ; they do not originate from a hidden, wrathful will of God, apart from Christ, and a loving will in Christ, but are both the product and operation of the same God of revelation. Therefore it is even more important in the case of justification and sanctification than in the other case not "to mingle and brew together" the two, and yet to keep them in true relation to each other.

Though sanctification because it springs from the power of the Holy Ghost, is essentially different from the obedience of the Law and the fear of the Law, that come from without, yet there are far-reaching points of resemblance between the two. Neither the Christian's practice of holiness nor the Jew's zeal for the Law could ever make a man just before God. All those who would depend on either way would remain work-righteous Absaloms, who remain suspended between heaven and earth. Of the righteousness of such we "have to speak most contemptuously, just as St. Paul does" of the Law (Luther).

But the other relationship also holds good, for the Law, as the school-master to lead us to Christ, as the expression of the good and holy will of God, is quite indispensable for faith, and so the Christian cannot regard sanctification "too precious or too highly" because it is the working of the Spirit of Christ. What the Reformers said concerning the preaching of the Law and of the grace of Christ and demanded for their preservation must apply, *mutatis mutandis,* as well to justification and sanctification. Therefore we take them together and say, using an expression of Luther's: These two, the word of reconciliation and the word of sanctification must both remain a part of Christian preaching, "for if one should be destroyed it would carry the other with it, and again where the one continues and is rightly taught it brings the other with it." (Er. Ed. 14, 151.)

The absolutely indispensable significance of sanctification for Christian faith can be described in these statements: (1) Faith that does not heed nor use this divinely given gift of renewal perishes through its self-imposed poverty. (2) Faith that proves its vitality in sanctification grows thereby in strength and constancy. (3) Faith that exercises itself in holiness is just the faith that turns men to repentance and teaches the one who is doing good works to seek after the promises of forgiveness.

1. When men are unequivocally taught that the saving faith that has been given through Word and Sacrament will be lost if it be without the actual following of Christ in obedience and love, then the antinomian misunderstanding that has followed in the steps of the Gospel like some dark shadow, even to our own day, will finally be overcome. The *Pecca fortiter* that was once written for the consolation of an over-anxious, timidly conscientious man can then never again be misunderstood, as though it meant that the greater or lesser amount of sinning in the life of a Christian made no particular difference. "The liberty of faith does not give a license to sin, nor does it gloss it over, but it gives a license to do all kinds of good works and to suffer all things, as they happen to come to hand, so that no one is bound exclusively to one sort or to several kinds of work."[1] The danger of ethical indifference or of the actual "glorification of

[1] Er. Ed. 16, 136.

the ungodly" is thus avoided. Because we bring labor on God with our sins; new labor and more labor with every transgression (Is. 43:24), because Christ suffered not only from the sneers of proud priests but likewise through the mockery and barbarity of ruffianly soldiers, it is not a matter of indifference whether we permit sin to reign in our members or whether we battle against it. A "carousing on Christ's reckoning" cannot be considered by one who has been baptized. The defense of a *Theologia irregenitorum* can be made only with the most careful reservations. But little is to be expected either from the minister or from his congregation when there is orthodoxy and pure teaching without a zealous, moral life; when there is busy ministerial activity without a faithful care of souls or the practice of prayer. Churches that "only believe and do not want to act" will become ineffective in their preaching of the Word. Congregations that no longer rejoice in proclaiming to all the world the salvation of God that has been entrusted to them will lose the ambition, the right and the claim of bringing true help to those at home.

2. Where, however, a Christian does not withstand the working of the Spirit of God but obediently submits to His will a *magis et magis crescere* results in faith and life. The Word of God commissions to service and gives the ability to serve. Whoever is ready to serve God sincerely in his peculiar vocation is aware, quite as a matter of course, of his need of physical and spiritual chastity. Where hard tasks are obediently undertaken hands will be folded in prayer and a desire will be awakened that nothing can still for daily inspiration for the conflict, for guidance and strength from the Scripture. Each impels and needs the other at the same time. Works proceed from love, and by way of prayer and moral discipline return to faith, only again to flow forth in spiritual joy and power. But if the impulse to action that has been given by faith is not realized there will be no exercise in prayer. If the readiness to act that has been given is wrecked by the unbridled desires of evil lusts the work itself will remain unfinished because of the lack of discipline. Instead of flowing back to faith, to be renewed and confirmed and again to stream forth in activity, it is weakened through its disuse. Again a congregation that is deeply concerned about the miseries of the heathen, the

future of the Church, its responsibilities for the young and for the poor, will be found not only ready to sacrifice but also eager for prayer and personal purification in thoughts and words.

3. But the greatest blessing of a progressive sanctification growing out of faith lies in the fact that it leads men into ever deeper repentance. The more regularly and clearly the Spirit of God enlightens the heart in prayer, the more clearly it recognizes its wickedness and perversity. Through it conscience learns to know its own hypocrisy ever more clearly. We "seem to ourselves to be continually more helpless, learn to know ourselves better, become more terrified by our estate and perceive how weak our faith is and how stammering our speech."[2] The more any one strives to realize the purity promised him the more he realizes the corrupt character of his nature and its inability to secure salvation by its own efforts because of the recurring opposition of the flesh and the continual need for its suppression. The working congregation that has not accomplished a clearly recognized task, that has failed in its efforts because of a lack of the courage of sacrifice, will sing the "Lord have mercy upon us" of its Sunday services with an entirely different sort of penitent heart from the congregation that rests serenely on its body of orthodox faith and that through fear of a false valuation of merits omits all meritorious service. Where sanctification is missing the knowledge of sin is also missing. "It is hard to discuss the feeling of guilt with one who does not pray" (E. Hirsch, op. cit., p. 25). It is impossible to make any one who does not labor for his own moral improvement understand his vicarious responsibility and common accountability with the nation and all humanity. A lazy man is never able to comprehend the mysterious judgments of time that passes on and never returns again.

If sanctification fails ceaselessly to carry on in a Christian's life that "alien work" of reproving and convicting, just like the Law, man will not attain to a knowledge of his needs and consequently will never come to a hunger for forgiveness or to an understanding of the central message of free grace. Tillich has called it the tragedy of Protestantism that it requires the actual realization of positive religious and cultural values before it is able to speak an intelligible no to them.

[2] Karl Barth, *Vom christlichen Leben*, p. 19, Munich, 1926.

Holl has emphasized the fact that between Paul and Luther lay monasticism, Augustine, the practice of confession and mysticism, and that it was only on the basis of this specially developed training of conscience that the rich, profound Reformation teaching of justification was possible. Both statements have their basis in the fact that justification, as the crisis of ethics, presupposes the existence of ethical actions. Where the holy zeal that seeks to attain fellowship with God and to preserve it in spite of all failures is lacking, where responsible service of men and of the Church is avoided, there a really living understanding of the gift of free forgiveness can be gained only with great difficulty, there the misunderstanding keeps creeping in that the Gospel has to do with a mere amnesty, which can be repeatedly and continuously received without concern on our part.

From this point of view a slightly different light falls on the many forms of self-sanctification which we discussed in the first two chapters and which we there rejected. To use the language of the 21st Thesis of Claus Harms: To desire to gain pardon after the manner of medieval practice by paying for it through indulgences and penances is not as bad as the present custom when "each one ministers it to himself." The external discipline of the Roman Church certainly has an advantage over the utter lack of inner means of instruction that now prevails in large circles of Protestantism. Methodist efforts to promote perfection with all their dangerous exaggerations are infinitely better than the spiritual laziness and desire for indulgence that marks erotic vitalism. "Better to become guilty" in the heated, dangerous work of governmental publicity, "than to have no part in it."[3] Here a word must be said in defense of the honor of German Idealism. As the German Pietism of 125 years ago prepared the way for a reawakening of the confessional Reformation faith among the people, so the German Idealism in its day was a *praecursor Christi* for countless numbers in academic circles,[4] a schoolmaster to lead them to Christ, and it is well known how it keeps on repeating that service, time and again, in our own day. Particularly in times of laxity and decadence

---

[3] E. Hirsch, *Deutschlands Schicksal*, p. 141, Göttingen, 1920.
[4] For example, K. von Raumer, Niethammer, Heinr. Thiersch, G. H. von Schubert, Friedr. von Roth, Claus Harms, von Hofmann, Löhe, Harless. *Cf.* W. Lütgert, *Die Religion des deutschen Idealismus und ihr Ende*, III, 173 *seq.*, Gütersloh, 1926.

the Church has no grounds to find fault with moral zeal, even if it appear in a Roman Catholic or a pietistic dress. Above all we have to guard against talking prematurely in the presence of youth about a crisis of ethics before we have first deeply impressed on them the holy imperative of the divine Law as well as the exalted and noble ideals of duty in their unqualified obligation, that have been maintained in the lofty moral standards of Kant and Fichte. From such independent champions of strict ethical discipline God has always chosen His preachers of the righteousness of faith and has prepared these Jacob-like men, who have praised God's grace most loudly when they had "thighs lamed by wrestling."

If the faith of justification is endangered when the gift of sanctification is not exercised, so the sanctification will still more surely enter into false paths if it is not based on justification and guided by it. We might sum it up in two statements: (1) Without the continual return to justification, sanctification falls into Pharisaism and the wildest exaggeration. (2) When, however, we hold fast to the condemning and pardoning word of forgiveness, sanctification receives its true modesty and its true vitality.

1. If men like Luther have declared that we need a whole lifetime to learn to believe rightly in our Baptism, if many Christians have had to contend bitterly with the "offense" of the Cross till late in life, it shows how deeply the desire for self-righteousness is rooted in man's nature. We may perhaps admit that for the tearing out of the old nature and the first beginnings of the new work a divine act of grace is necessary, because we cannot do so of our own powers, but when the fruit comes the root of the energy is forgotten and men become proud and self-satisfied. In the process of sanctification they would like to spare themselves the daily *reditus ad baptismum*, and the humility and thankfulness it requires, they would like to hurry on to ever higher perfection, they trust that because of their renewal they are able to unfold themselves continuously without a continuous dependence on the miracle of a divine promise. But as they want to rise without passing through the depths of forgiveness they plunge into the depths of error. Sanctification becomes a Pharisaism in its double aspect of meritoriousness and legalism. Men become unwilling

to live alone by the grace of God that levels all things. They want to have "a special crown" (Beck), to bring "accomplishments" of prayer, asceticism and almsgiving that excel those of their brethren and so by the stringing together of sacrifices that would be well pleasing to God in themselves, if offered in the right spirit, they are turned into gross egotists. If the word of forgiveness be no longer heard, the Spirit that leads into all truth is also lost. Nature produces "side shoots and wild growths that want to grow up with the rest and rob the true branches of their sap and strength, so that they cannot develop" (Luther).[5] Sanctification that has lost the Holy Ghost falls into literalism and becomes anxious, casuistic, greedy, violent. The life that men have wanted to gain for themselves dies.

When God would cast a man down He makes him blind to his own failings. This oft-quoted statement is particularly true of the fate of every work of sanctification that is no more controlled by or permeated with the critical sternness of justification. The language of Christian experience becomes all too loud, all too confident. When it is reported in connection with the activities of the Christian work among young men that "The Savior leads us from one victory to another; there is an advance all along the line"; when the youth of the Anthroposophists laud their convention as "as visible bestowal of the spiritual world to us"; when the Pentecostals proclaim the fortune of "complete sanctification" that has befallen them, evangelical temperance can only admonish those who issue such bombastic proclamations to consider what they are saying and warn them: Be not proud but afraid! If there is not a continual return to the humbling word of the Cross there will inevitably be a shallow, precipitate, optimistic confusion of spirits and the Holy Spirit, of cosmos and Creator, of emotion and faith, of self-control and self-denial, of *eros* and *agape*, of the occult world and the eternal world. Men confuse the spiritual individual with one "full of the Spirit," a new conduct with "renewal from above," an evolutionistic philosophy of culture with eschatology, peace between nations with "peace on earth." Without justification, Christian ethics will become neo-Protestant or "American," sanctifica-

[5] Er. Ed. 49, 274. *Exposition of the 14th and 15th Chapters of St. John, of the year 1538.*

tion of the emotions will turn into romanticism, the "renewal of thought" result in a monistic philosophy of immanence. The Kingdom of God will be secularized into the idea of an "alcohol-free, world republic, a communistic realm of peace, or a League of Nations on a republican basis."

For this reason we will always have to desire some sort of a "Theology of Crisis" for the Church. As long as the earth remains it will be necessary to protest sharply against all heathen and Christian dreams of anticipating the consummation. Only by the constant pressure of such an opposing force will the individual as well as the congregation be kept within the proper bounds of modesty in the process of sanctification. Only in this way are we prevented from exalting religious feelings over sound doctrine, from placing moral growth above the gift and promise of God, from esteeming one's own conversion above the Sacrament or deeming one's own separatistic notions greater than the Confessions of the Church. Without a life *in nuda fiducia misericordiae* foreign missions becomes propaganda or the colonization of some brand of culture instead of remaining what it ought to be, the message of the mighty deeds of God which He wrought for the salvation of the nations. Only with this background can the ever-present danger be avoided of turning inner missions into organized social service and so externalizing it, of making the liturgy a mummery, of turning evangelization into an arousing of mass hysteria and education into psychological artifices.

2. Sanctification without the grace of justification first makes men self-satisfied, then self-tormenting; first brings false security, and then false anxiety. But where any undertaking is supported by the purifying promise of forgiveness the false feeling of power that comes from self-esteem will be missing as well as the false despair of the hour of despondency. Bengel's motto, *nec temere nec timide,* here becomes a reality. Because our service and prayer is not good in itself but only becomes so through its acceptance by God, the great fact to which faith holds fast, all arrogant self-praise is excluded. Because God's faithfulness triumphs over our unfaithfulness the faithless steward, when he bows before his Lord in true penitence, may still hope to be restored to his office and to receive new treasures that he may ad-

minister. Because justification excludes all thought of our establishing our own righteousness or assisting in its attainment, the way is left open for God. As it destroys self-love it opens the way for the love of our neighbor. As it gives us a bitter knowledge of ourselves it bestows a blessed knowledge of God. As the Gospel takes away from man all the goodness and faithfulness of his actions and places both in God's hands, faith is liberated from the anxious self-examination of its own fitness and fidelity because it receives from God a glad certainty and a tireless ardour in its labors.

We have tried briefly to describe all the relations that bind justification and sanctification together with so many threads. The connection between the two is actually so intimate that if one were to perish the other would be taken away and "where one remains and is rightly used, it also brings the other with it." It is true on the negative side, that faith dies through the failure to use the sanctification that has been made possible by God's assurance, and that sanctification dies through the lack of a penitent faith in forgiveness. It is also true on the positive side that where there is faith there likewise is sanctification. The more truly we hold fast to the "God-for-us," the more "our-being-for-God" grows and is strengthened. Again, where there is exercise in sanctification through faith, there will be a growing knowledge of sin and with it an increased desire for the gracious pardon of God for the sinner. But when one thus flows from the other, life from faith and faith again from life, disobedience from unbelief and unbelief from disobedience, when each thus requires and furthers the other and the lack of one hinders and destroys the other, then it is clear that in this part of theology we always need a twofold statement if we want to present the truth fully and completely. It is sure that since justification is the mother of sanctification the chief stress will always be laid on the word of forgiveness. But since the daughter "sanctification" though she cannot beget the mother "forgiveness" can destroy her, the significance of sanctification must be presented with all emphasis in evangelical preaching. So there are always *two* statements essential, only the antithesis of *sanctificatio* and *justificatio* will not be a mere *et - et*, but a *cum - tum*, not a simple "both-and" but as the Latin can give it more exactly, "both-and also in particular." The immediate superiority of justification over sanctification requires such a clear statement of pre-eminence, but the terrible influence that disobedience exerts on faith also requires the addition of the second antithetical statement.

The Gospel must be protected as carefully against legalism as against antinomianism. An active pride is as dangerous for faith as the laziness that shirks every task. The merit-seeking efforts of a penitential suppression of the desires of the flesh can harden the heart as effectively as the desires of the flesh that are unrestrained. The battle against dead works is just as important as that against dead faith. If justification is continually exposed to the misunderstandings and dangers of quietism, so sanctification is endangered by the abyss of self-righteousness. A super-ethical, predestinarian monergism is as questionable as the moralizing of the Christian religion by Kant and Ritschl. A transformation of the world through sanctification, that would become a boundless union with general culture, is just as much to be avoided as a separation through justification that would lead to a world flight. Daily renewal of the baptismal covenant is indispensable for a life of faith, but the following devotion to the performance of God's will is no less necessary. Justification robs all conduct of its appearance of holiness, sanctification guards men against sinning against grace. The promise of forgiveness gives the basis of action, direction and power to all conduct; the Christianity of action prevents "pure doctrine" from becoming mere talk. Each statement is only true in its antithesis, in the answer given by the other.

The attacks that are made on Pharisaical piety dare never come to such one-sidedness that any one through them falls into moral indifference because he lacks the opposing corrective. In the same way the opposition to the present libertinism dare not be carried on in such a naive fashion that each good deed appears as a *direct* result of the relation sustained to God. This second danger is especially present in moral reform and social-religious movements, but even the work of Inner Missions is continually threatened with it. The theology of Karl Barth on the other hand seems to us to be very inadequately protected against an antinomistic misunderstanding of faith. Here there is such a reckless polemic against even a devoted exercise in sanctification

that from a purely theological point of view it becomes most questionable and on its practical side can become actually dangerous. Here
we gain the impression, all too easily, that there is only one kind of
booty for Satan, namely the pious sinner, and that the great multitudes of the ungodly who are enumerated in the catalogs of vices are
a small number in comparison. It is true Karl Barth, in his vigorous
apology for the dialectic theology, has explained that to "take God
seriously," to speak correctly as a man of grace, means to speak of
"justification *and* sanctification, of faith *and* obedience." But practically these double statements are not adequately carried out (we have
only to recall the scanty references to the exercise of prayer and asceticism) but, with an exceedingly undialectic persistency, even the statements concerning a Biblically grounded renewal are opposed as if our
message were limited to one word and consisted of one single warning. In fact, however, here as everywhere else, it consists of *two* words.
Our effort therefore has been to carry the statements of the dialectic
theology to their logical conclusion where its advocates up to this time
have not done so themselves.

Apparently there is a fear that when this is done, when sanctification and justification are carried together to their logical conclusion
at the professor's desk, in the pulpit, in books and in instruction, the
mighty emphasis and impulse of this one-sidedness, which is the secret
of its influence, will be lost. Of course, any one who continually keeps
both sides in view will deal with a phenomenon like Pietism, for
example, in a somewhat more cautious and kindlier manner that is
common in the "Theology of the Crisis," especially as "the continual
attacks on Pietism are in themselves the most abominable Pharisaism."
We see that the Church in the past and the present alike has needed
allies not only against pious over-zealousness but also against the
undevout inactivity and profligacy of the masses, even if such an
ethics has not always been able to keep clear of legalistic narrowness.
Fundamentally it is simply not possible to see why a theology that is
logical in its antithetical statements concerning justification and sanctification should have to cut its strength in two and so exert only a
feeble influence in either direction, but it should be possible to use the
same strength that has been used successfully in warring against one

extreme with equal effect against its opposite. To attempt to do so has been the aim of all our efforts. Of course we are conscious of the fact that in so doing we have not produced anything new, but have simply once more reworked, in connection with older and newer forms of theology, what the Scriptures, and following them Luther and his spiritual posterity, have witnessed with great clearness.

The very preaching of Jesus is full of "a peculiar antithesis between two statements." "With unconditional graciousness" Christ calls to Himself those oppressed by the Law and brings them the full pardoning love of the Father. Alongside it, however, is the unqualified requirement, "only those who do the will of God and have a pure heart" shall share in the reign of the King. The same double note of acceptance and responsibility runs through the preaching of St. Paul. For this reason he was hated by legalistic Jews and fanatics alike. And as if it were to prevent the last bit of possible misunderstanding of Pauline preaching the Epistle of St. James found a place in the New Testament canon. Any one whose ears have been opened will detect throughout Scripture the paradoxical antithesis of justification and sanctification, of God's free redemptive acceptance on the one hand and of the holiest obligation on the other. "Ye have not chosen me but I have chosen you, and ordained you that ye should go and bring forth fruit, and that your fruit should remain." As ἅγιοι, that is as those who belong to God, Christians are also to hallow themselves, to strive after purity; as "bought with a price" they are to praise God in body and soul. Whoever has died with Christ is to mortify his members. Whoever has risen with Him, is to walk in newness of life. Whoever has apprehended Him must strive for the goal that has been set before him. Whoever has the treasure must still so run that he grasps it.[6] All these statements of the Gospel are so familiar that we are hardly conscious of the tremendous paradox that is actually concealed in them. Here we have to do not with any causal, conditional or synergistic relationships, as though our activity produced or supplemented the act of God, but with those unbreakable limits of

[6] Cf. Phil. 3:13 seq.; I Cor. 9; Titus 2:11-14; Heb. 9:13 seq.; St. James 1:25; St. Luke 1:74 seq.; St. John 15:16.

God's sole activity in effecting our salvation and of the judgment we cannot escape if we receive His grace in vain.

If Christ in His humiliation in human form needs a double statement; if Scripture, that witnesses concerning Him, in its servant's form needs the double note of faith *and* life, then for the messengers of Jesus there can be no liberation from this twofold message: reconciliation and salvation, justification and sanctification, faith and obedience, thanksgiving and service, consolation and admonition. For this reason all the attempts of systematic or practical theology, from the most ancient times to the present, to describe the nature of faith, its origin and preservation with a single statement must be regarded as inadequate. "Christianity is life," "Christianity is doctrine"—each statement in its one-sidedness is equally false. We get nowhere with the alternatives of transcendent or immanent, imputed-forensic or effective, quietistic or active. A man like St. Paul cannot be completely described by either of these formulas. As soon as only one side of the matter is stated without being restricted by the other everything will inevitably become confused and distorted. When such methods are used in the interpretation of the New Testament we will land either in a transcendentalism in the sense of Neo-Kantianism or into an immanence in the sense of Spinoza, each of them equally serious errors. In the one case the Gospel is stripped of its character of a religion of salvation, in the other of its character as an historical religion.

While medieval Catholicism distorted the message of the Gospel by a legalistic, meritorious teaching of sanctification, and humanism and fanaticism weakened the moral strictness of the Biblical teachings, Luther, as the preacher and theological leader of his Church, stands very clearly apart from both of these byways that are forever appearing in the course of Church history. Even in the years when he was most actively engaged in the conflict against Rome, against the mass, monasticism and indulgences, he never forgot that his doctrine of justification as the *caput doctrinae christianae* was a *periculosissima praedicatio*, that could be misused in the maddest way. As early as the treatise on *The Freedom of a Christian Man* he says, "We must not simply preach one side but must present both statements of God."[7] When it

[7] Er. Ed. 27,194.

comes to those who are slavishly addicted to works and ceremonies and to those who think themselves righteous because they omit and despise such things, "a Christian shall pass midway between them and shall rightly understand both classes of men." The more Luther in the course of his life had to come into conflict with Agricola and the Antinomians, the more anxious and embittered the Reformer became at the misuse of his doctrine of grace as a "new lip service," combined with an unregenerate moral frivolity. Yet in spite of all that, the antithetical statements of the great teacher of the *sola fide* concerning justification and sanctification become still more intense.[8]

The climax of his expositions of the subject is probably the short controversial treatise *Against the Antinomians*, of 1593.[9] Here Luther expresses the opinion that any one who understands the accounts of the beginnings of the Church will see "that it has always been so that when the Word of God has begun to take root and a little band has been gathered together, the devil has perceived the light and has blown, stormed and blustered against it from every direction with strong and mighty winds, trying to extinguish the divine light. And when one or two blasts have been restrained or diverted he has again and again blown into some other opening, and stormed against the light, and there has been no cessation nor ending, neither will there be till the last day." Then the antagonists of every sort are enumerated; the papacy, Münzer, Carlstadt, the Anabaptists, Servetus and Campanus, and Luther complains that when in conflict with one of them, "I have almost ceased to fear the sputtings of the devil," and Christ has hardly closed one opening, before the evil one breaks in through another, "tears out several panes from the window," breaks open doors and windows, so that we "have always to await new and fresh storm winds of the devil, as has been the case from the very beginning." Because the Gospel is attacked not only by the work-righteous, but also by the self-sufficient, unbridled spirits "we have to take heed

---

[8] *Cf.* Buchwald, *M.L. Predigten.* To St. Matt. 9:1-8 (1528): The forgiveness of sins "is the chief part of Christian teaching, and yet it is a very dangerous teaching . . . men at once conclude we will not do any works, will idle, be secure and sleep, if the forgiveness of sins by itself can give us a joyful heart! So this teaching is dangerous . . . no matter how it is presented it involves danger to souls." Further I, 19 *seq.*

[9] Er. Ed. 32,1 *seq.*, 10 *seq.*

and guard ourselves against the papal teaching of penance as against hell and the devil himself, much more, however, must we guard against those who leave no sort of penance in the Church."[10] One of the finest passages in which Luther expresses himself concerning this twofold character is found in his annotations to the 11th chapter of Deuteronomy, of 1525.[11] We quote according to the German translation: When the rain does not cease it ruins everything as badly as when heat and drought do not cease. Therefore we must deal with the people not only by teaching, but after the teaching must also engage in the works of faith. But when strength has become exhausted through labor and suffering we must again resort to teaching to raise up, to strengthen and to encourage the heart. Thus man grows in the knowledge of God."

Luther on occasion compared the world with a drunken peasant who when he was shoved into the saddle on the one side toppled out of it on the other, so that it was impossible to help him, do what one would. The history of theology tempts one to use the same comparison. What venturesome statements have men permitted themselves to make, statements that ultimately had to lead to disaster because the attempt was made to present a truth that was correct enough in itself but which was taught in a one-sided, undialectic form, with complete contempt and disapproval of its antithesis. We recall that Swedish tendency of the first half of the nineteenth century which has its parallels in the present day. The Bornholmerians who in contending against a new life found special gratification in seeking out the sins and weaknesses of the saints that are related in Scripture; the Hedbergians and the followers of Rosenius, who taught "the justification of the whole world" and regarded every admonition to amendment as a "hindrance to salvation," as "an outgrowth of an evil doctrine of works" because God is "just as gracious when men go a-whoring, are drunken and steal, as when they pour out their prayers on their knees in fervent devotion."[12] So here the balance of the moral side of the preaching of Jesus was lost in the interests of an exaggerated

[10] *Cf.* Th. Harnack, I, 386.
[11] Er. Ed. *Op. lat.* XIII, 189 *seq.*
[12] *Cf. Realencyklopädie f. prot. Theol. u. Kirche,* III, 326 *seq.*

teaching of amnesty, so the same mistakes were made in the other direction, for example in the Pentecostal movement, where the sanctifying fanaticism of these enthusiasts derided the deadly seriousness of the teaching of the atonement as a "traditional conviction that daily sinning is inevitable" (Jellinghaus). Such a "falling off the horse" is only possible where the reverence for and the obedience to the *totum verbum* of Scripture has been relinquished. Scripture knows nothing of such solutions of the paradox as this, that sanctification as a work of God, as the answer of the thankfully obedient man, should be suppressed in the interests of a purely other-worldly, forensic transaction, nor that faith in the forgiveness of sins is transformed into an actual vision of the glory of perfection and an actual participation in it, even in this world.

Our investigations have shown at many points how the Confessions of the Lutheran Church reject and avoid every such evasion. We can truly say that here the harmony of divine spiritual endowment and the effective appropriation of yielding faith have found a classic expression. The danger of pious pride is recognized for what it actually is, the greater danger, because it is the less evident temptation of the Christian life. Therefore the warnings and the polemic against it occupy the first place. But the other danger that threatens from the other side is not forgotten on that account, and consequently there is express admonition to confession and the avoidance of all epicurean serving of the flesh. Above all the hymn books of the Lutheran Church are inexhaustible storehouses of the *full* truth, not by a mere joining together of two separate parts, each of which deals with one side of the problem, but by a real combination of antithesis that runs continuously through single hymns, (as for example, those of Paul Gerhardt). A special investigation of these sources would prove exceedingly fruitful. In the writings of the great leaders of Lutheranism in the nineteenth century, in Hofmann, Frank, Zezschwitz, Harless, Löhe, Delitsch and Vilmar, we find a mutual interaction of dogma and ethics that was vigorously and fully developed. Here the high value placed on the doctrine of justification did not lead to an undervaluation of sanctification, and the emphasis on sanctification did not lead to a disregard of free grace. Each was stated with equal clearness.

There is no redemption from the power of sin without a preceding cleansing from the guilt of sin, but there is likewise no liberation from guilt that does not also break the domination of evil and bestow strength for a new life. For this reason we find here besides the highest evaluation of Baptism, Holy Communion and the Scriptures the highest regard for prayer, discipline, labor and churchly customs, not as an artificial, unbalanced combination but as a living expression of the total Biblical view of justification and sanctification.

The theological and ecclesiastical situation of the present displays extreme divergencies in the discussion of this question both to the right and to the left. Whoever deals with it discreetly will do well to hear and consider carefully the calls from both quarters. We believe it is just as dangerous to accept Barth's corrective theology without qualification as it is to ignore its admonitions. The dispute with Pietism must not be taken too lightly by the Church. It seems to us that it would be most profitable to begin with the ideas of men like Bezzel, Schlatter, Ihmels and Heim, and then to carry them on to a further development. When we read the published sermons of these men, as they deal with this problem, we find there an understanding of the whole matter that is really a model treatment of the subject.

The progress of their thought is not simply determined by a polemic against Romanism or other beliefs in the attainment of moral progress. They attack just as decidedly that "slothful piety" that does not want to think, love, act or pray, but "wants to be blessed only in its faith, and consequently loses it." Bezzel could preach the fear of judgment and could call men to holiness, not like some tabernacle preacher but more like a medieval preacher of repentance, because in our lawless and godless times "our nation has been spoiled through the misuse of the compassion of Christ and has become lazy through the continual preaching of grace." Bezzel was able to talk about "the superficial intoxication of grace" by which "our nation has drunk death" and yet at the same time could unconditionally extol the "joyous stream" of grace that at Christmastide was poured out over the world of sin. *Sola gratia, sola fide* and "holy self-discipline in dealing with God's Word and in the life of prayer" (Ihmels); the Church as a fellowship of love and action (Althaus) do not exclude each other for Lutheran theologians, but essentially belong together. We must particularly call attention to the sermons of Karl Heim in this connection. We might call them a great commentary on the antithetical relation of justification and sanctification. Here the interplay of repose and exertion, of the greatest consolation and the greatest zeal, of the inescapableness of sin and the duty that nevertheless exists of avoiding it, never ceases. What Heim has formulated more systematically elsewhere is applied to his homiletics and is resolutely carried to its conclusions. "Our Christian faith is manifestly only sound when a complete balance exists between the quiescent element of our inmost attitude of faith, which is completely independent of any external exertions, and the active element that presses forward, changes the world, and transforms the relationships of life. As soon, however, as this balance is disturbed we go astray."

To keep one's balance on a narrow mountain path or on a tight rope is apparently a static act, in fact it is possible only as a ceaseless progress. So the unsolved paradox of the grace of forgiveness and renewal, the effort to attain a unity of faith and action immediately reminds us that we have not yet come home, that we are still on our way, as "pilgrims and strangers." If justification were a mere promise "without consequences in our life history" (Schlatter, *op. cit.,* 468), if sanctification were a transformation to seraphic purity, in both cases the pilgrim's journey would not be so difficult as it is when light and darkness are in continual conflict within the believer; when "on the first stages of the uneven way of freedom we are still so hard pressed by the serving of vanities." Because Christian faith does not know a transcendence that is without its Pentecost, nor an ecstatic mysticism or clairvoyant visions; because the crucified and risen Lord is not silent to faith but still does not triumph visibly before it; because faith hears the deep secret "Yea" under and above the "No" (Er. Ed. 11, 120), therefore and just therefore the waiting for the revelation of the Kingdom of God is so restless, so yearning. The one who has already received the pledge of the Spirit yearns more anxiously for the final understanding than the one who has never known it, just as certainly as it is first in the face of Jesus Christ that we really gain the knowledge that we are beggars. Whoever holds fast in confident desperation to the promises of the complete removal of the guilt of sin will await more eagerly the beginning of the new era, which will bring with it the complete overcoming of the power of sin, than the one who dreams of a present life of victory and of complete sanctification. As soon as we speak only of justification or of sanctification the diabolical ease begins that imagines it possesses all things, whether present or future and that, as a result, forget either prayer and labor, or faith and hope, and consequently, in either case, suffers spiritual shipwreck. We find a true Christian eschatology only where the decree of justification and sanctification, possessing and not possessing, perfection and imperfection are ever experienced together. Whoever tries to speak without paradoxes and would consider each one of these realms alone, who tries to find a solution of the paradox now, betrays either Good Friday or Easter and fails to understand our present status between Pentecost and the Parousia, in which it is equally sin and disobedience against God if we do not "grow in grace" or if we seek to anticipate the glory of the final perfection.

Gogarten has well said that to speak of a "dialectic" theology is like talking about an "albino white horse," but theological thinking has always and will always be so constituted. According to Barth as long as we are here on earth our conversation can never lose its form of a dialogue, of question and answer; there can be no "fundamental last word," unless we fall into the mistake of confusing our conversation with God, while we are yet sinners, "with the dogmatics of the saints in heaven." We are in fundamental agreement with such statements, only in the question as to what it really means "to speak dialectically concerning justification and sanctification" we are of another opinion. The obedience required in our particular situation in the world is first fulfilled when we really unite our discussions of justification *and* prayer, of the Word *and* our service, of faith *and* asceticism, of the Kingdom of God *and* our activity. Only as this contradiction is constantly carried to its conclusion do we fully realize the promise of the returning Lord, Who was crucified by the world and Who is unseen, but Who is nevertheless clearly present to faith, love and obedience. It is only through this paradox of future hope and present possession that it is possible to establish practically and theologically an eschatological attitude in the life of a Christian.

When the double note of justification and sanctification is regarded not simply as a theological speculation of more or less paradoxical character but is realized by men in the practical affairs of work-day life, all their judgments and attitudes towards the questions of religious and secular life will receive a new slant. In many specific cases that has already been indicated. To carry it out in all particulars would require a special volume. So in conclusion we can only indicate a few possibilities. If we want to hold fast to our previous results then the task of preaching is, *Christus pro nobis et in nobis*, quietness and restlessness, the choice between life and death, eternal salvation through pure mercy or destruction through the wickedness of our own will. Prayer then becomes a gift and an obligation, an impulse from above and compulsion against the forces beneath, a holy privilege and a faithfully exercised duty. Pastoral care will then mean consolation for those who are heartily sorry for their sins and hard reproof for those who regard them lightly—a recognition of the fundamental needs of all men and a recognition of the special needs and dangers of the individual—Christ as the One Who removes all guilt and as the Helper against the power of sin. In the education of the coming ministry, in actual pastoral care, and in the relations with other brethren in the ministry, both must have a place; both "sound doctrine" (I Tim. 1:10) and sound ethics, attention to the Word and a care in the choice of his own words, humility and a holy self-discipline, *orare et laborare*. The Church must fear an exaggerated activity as well as a growing inaction. She must be eager to serve but must guard against a striving after power. She must sit in judgment on the world, but first she must judge herself. She will not confuse herself with the future Kingdom of God, with the new Jerusalem that comes down from above, but neither will she be a synagogue that still awaits the coming of the Messiah out of Zion. She will remember that Christ has already come, and will wait expectantly till He returns.

But our dialectic reaches much further than theological and ecclesiastical thought and action in its moulding influence. It will influence our attitude towards all living, towards our bodies and nature, towards the nation and culture. Justification prevents the canonization of the natural basis of life. It reminds us of our guilt by which all things have been involved in transitoriness and imperfection. It tells us that even our testimony and our efforts need forgiveness. Sanctification, however, prevents us from regarding the world as being utterly without relation to the Triune God and from settling down to a mere state of resignation. Justification teaches the need of redemption by all things, sanctification the possibility of their redemption. The one warns us, "It doth not yet appear what we shall be," the other admonishes us, "The night is far spent, the day is at hand, let us therefore cast off the works of darkness, and let us put on the armour of light." If the antithesis of the two cease we run into the danger of either despising the body or else deifying the body instead of remembering its mortality and hallowing it in the expectation of the resurrection day. A mere religious refining and deepening of national character must count for as little as a senseless disregard of nationality. The message of the Cross forbids us to transform the First Article of the Creed into the Third Article by omitting the Second. It requires a break with the past, repentance, a lasting submission to the judgment of God that has been passed on all flesh. But faith in the Spirit that quickeneth also permits us to understand the place of the nations in God's plan of salvation and turns the service of the nation into a holy duty. From this standpoint a naive approval of the human spirit and its creations is as impossible as a withdrawal from the vocational duties of the world. To be able to work in the world and for the world, without despairing we need a complete certainty concerning the Triune God, Who is gracious, Who still holds a fallen creation in His hand and Who has given to faith the strength and guidance necessary for sanctification.

The Personal Decision

ANY one who has once understood that here on earth we can never rightly express the truth of God with the one statement, but require both, comes into a curiously difficult situation as soon as in his personal contacts or in the study of history he meets with some one who with great force and clearness exemplifies only the one side of the matter. He will not be able to refrain from admitting the energy, zeal and acumen with which he perhaps speaks of justification in the Biblical sense. He will be aided, confirmed and strengthened in the fundamental knowledge of the Christian faith. But he will have the same experience when somewhere in the historic past or in the present he meets with some one who exemplifies sanctification in a similar way. Even in the face of the consuming zeal of revival circles we feel the kinship to the primitive Christian congregations in their readiness to make sacrifices, their discipline and feeling of brotherhood and are reminded of the unqualified nature of the New Testament requirements. The deeper we have ventured into the truths of the entire Scripture the more full of understanding we will become and the more restrained in criticism; the easier it will become to judge each phenomenon quietly and so much the more difficult will it be to take our stand in all the burning, dividing ecclesiastical questions of our day. But that is only one side of our impressions.

On the other side we have to struggle continually with the temptation not to become unjust, annoyed and sarcastic when we find one of the great truths of Scripture, whether justification or sanctification, exalted at the expense of the other. The more thoroughly this is done in any one case the further the resulting separation from the *totum verbum* of Scripture, the more antagonistic our attitude towards such a movement is bound to become. We can understand the violence of the controversies because each antagonist, with a certain justification, sees in his opponent a manifestation of that evil spirit that lies in a partial truth, and yet we cannot favor either party because both are fundamentally in the same condemnation. If we turn aside from both and try to express the two statements that are made by the words justification and sanctification, in their proper order and in correct relation to each other, we must be ready to assume the cross of the misunderstanding of this paradox that will come from either side and the attacks that are bound to follow. Any one who is unable to perceive these consequences will probably class him as a "spokesman of mediation," as "a man of compromise," a "virtuoso in bridge building." He will have to make up his mind to encounter opposition on every hand, to satisfy nobody, even though in fact he has done nothing and proposes to do nothing except to carry the Pauline paradox of Phil. 2:12 *seq.* to its ultimate logical, theological and practical conclusions.[1]

What in our days we may encounter as an isolated happening is in fact only a participation and fellow-suffering in the universal experience of Lutheranism now and at all times. For some Luther was too free, for others not free enough. Here his doctrine of justification was accused of endangering morality and there men censured him for his moralism. Luther's faith was too autonomous for the cardinals, too heteronomous for the mystics; he was too holy for the knights, too revolutionary for the learned and "too lacking in piety, too luxurious" for the fanatics. So today Lutheranism is again attacked on every side. It is too energetic for the orient and too passive for the occident. For

[1] H. Bezzel. "I might say that it is a most thankless undertaking but still the true Lutheran principle always to follow the middle course, not because it is the most convenient but because it is the most difficult. The middle course involves such a degree of self-restraint and self-denial, such readiness to carry the reproach of Jesus that only the Church that in all her existence has not hesitated to bear the reproach of her Savior has been in a position to do so. Extreme views have the advantage of remarkable consistency. People who carry out any idea even to the point where it becomes impossible are called firm characters, when in fact they are obstinate. Men think they have discovered a peculiar characteristic of Lutheranism, a special strength of its Confessions, in all their parts, when they can take any correct idea out of its proper relations, from which and for which it came into existence, generalize it, universalize it and simply reject all the practical consequences that might be drawn from it. That is very bold and also very cheap but it is not Christian nor apostolic." *Berufung und Beruf,* p. 64 *seq.*, Neuendettelsau, 1926.

one it is too forensic and eschatological, for another too real and immanent. Now it does not speak loudly enough, now "too triumphantly." All these reproaches it is well to accept calmly, yea, with a certain glad superiority, and to go on cheerfully in our historic way of destiny, in that third position that holds fast to *both sides completely*; that maintains justification *and* sanctification, not as a weak mediating synthetic fusing of two halves, but as a unity existing above both. From this "standpoint" which is not a mere standpoint but an eager pilgrim's step towards the consummation, it is possible to understand and consider many other objections without yielding to them or through them losing the full truth of Scripture or the heritage of the fathers.

It is true that the antithetical consideration of justification and sanctification can become an intellectual, paradoxical diversion, that it can become the catch phrase of a theological party without becoming a part of prayer, penitence or faith. But it is the tacit supposition in all theological study that our thinking and speaking will be moved by our conscience, and ever and again moved by it anew, if everything is not to degenerate into a "vain repetition of the heathen." If true anywhere at all, it is particularly true of the inseparable connection of these two statements, that it is "not a geometrical science, where it is enough if we have grasped it once, but we must always be learning it, and through tribulations we must be schooled in acquiring it" (Luther).

If "God's name is to be hallowed also among us" then thought, life, preaching, instruction and pastoral care, every effort in the nation and the Church must be equally permeated by that double aspect of prayer, beyond which there cannot be any further solution, so long as we are still "only guests in a strange tabernacle" (Paul Gerhardt): "When the Word of God is taught in its truth and purity and we, as God's children, lead holy lives in accordance with it, this grant us, dear Father in heaven! But whoever teaches and lives otherwise than as God's Word teaches, profanes the Name of God among us, from this preserve us, heavenly Father!"

Classified Index

BIBLICAL

Isaiah, 36, 51, 74
James, St., 20, 40, 120, 188, 212, 223, 232
Jeremiah, 25
Job, 20
John the Baptist, 25, 85, 147, 232
John, St., 16, 40, 59, 155, 195, 222
Mechthild, 10

Paul, St., 16, 20, 23, 25, 36, 38, 39, 50, 56, 57, 59, 63, 65, 66, 69, 70, 75, 76, 80, 86, 89, 103, 124, 136, 137, 147, 149-151, 159-161, 165, 169, 173, 180, 187, 192, 194, 200, 203, 223, 228, 232, 239, 245, 249, 257
Peter, St., 20, 80, 158, 160, 165

JEWISH

Cabalists, 29
Chokma Literature, 19
Essenes, 29
Gamaliel, 54

Hillel, 54
Schammai, 54
Talmud, The, 50

COMPARATIVE RELIGION

Aurelius, Marcus, 50
Baal Mysticism, 19, 28
Brahma, 8, 171
Buddha, 29, 33, 37, 74
Buddhism, 73, 74
Confucianism, 69
Confucius, 3
Dionysian Mysteries, 8, 17
Encratites, 29
Gnostics, 29
Hellenistic Cults, 10, 86
Laotse, 17, 50, 129
Mani, 29
Marcion, 85

Mithra, Cult of, 55
Mohammedanism, 73
Neo-Pythagoreans, 29, 54
Nicolaitans, 29
Nirvana, 35
Orpheus, 50
Philo, 29, 190
Proclus, 29
Severus, Alexander, 50
Sufism, 8, 10
Taoism, 8, 129
Upanishads, The, 8
Yogis, The, 29, 177
Zarathustra, 29, 50

EARLY CHURCH FATHERS

Alexandrine School, 55
Ambrose, 29
Augustine, St., 13, 24, 59, 66, 69, 93, 132, 136, 138, 153, 155, 167, 173, 225, 249
Donatists, 65

Ignatius, 66
Jerome, 4, 29
Justin Martyr, 66
Nestorianism, 130
Origen, 29, 66, 173
Tertullian, 29, 173

CATHOLIC

d'Ailly, 25
Anselm, 20, 24, 93
Apollonius of Tyana, 29, 50
Aquinas, Thomas, 14, 24
Bernhard, 9, 10, 107, 110, 173

Biel, Gabriel, 25
Böhme, Jakob, 29, 208
Bonaventura, 13, 37, 105
Brothers of the Common Life, 9
Catherine of Siena, 105

269

LUTHERAN

REFORMED

PHILOSOPHERS

MODERN THOUGHT

Bible References